Thomas D. Jordan Jr.

A Handbook of
Gravity-Flow Water Systems
for small communities

INTERMEDIATE TECHNOLOGY PUBLICATIONS

Intermediate Technology Publications Ltd
Schumacher Centre for Technology and Development
Bourton Hall, Bourton on Dunsmore, Rugby,
Warwickshire CV23 9QZ, UK

Reprinted 1992, 1996, 2000, 2004, 2006

This work was originally published by UNICEF, Kathmandu, with special
reference to gravity-flow water systems in Nepal. This international edition
is published by arrangement with UNICEF. The publishers gratefully
acknowledge the financial assistance of Oxfam and ITIS in the publication
of this international edition.

ISBN 0 946688 50 8
ISBN 978 0 946688 50 0

Intermediate Technology Publications Ltd, is the publishing arm of Intermediate
Technology Development Group Ltd. Our mission is to build the skills and
capacity of people in developing countries through the dissemination of
information in all forms, enabling them to improve the quality of their lives
and that of future generations.

Printed and bound in India by Replika Press Pvt. Ltd.

TABLE OF CONTENTS

ABBREVIATIONS AND SYMBOLS

cm = centimeters

cm^2 = square centimeters

cm^3 = cubic centimeters

kg = kilogram

kg/cm^2 = kilograms per square centimeter

LPS = liters per second (flow)

m/sec = meters per second (velocity)

LPCPD = liters per capita per day

GI = galvanised iron (pipe)

HDP = high-density polyethylene (pipe)

Q = flow

ID = inner diameter

OD = outer diameter

CGS = corrugated galvanised steel

RCC = reinforced concrete

RF = reinforcement

m = meters

m^2 = square meters

m^3 = cubic meters

H = head

@ = at

Ø = diamter

" = inches

$\sqrt{}$ = square-root

$\underset{\overline{\underline{}}}{\triangledown}$ = water surface of tank (@ atmospheric pressure)

HGL = Hydraulic Grade Line

IMPORTANT NOTICE

The pipeline problems worked out as examples in the text and figures of this handbook were made using a frictional headloss table for HDP pipe according to DIN (German) specifications. Since the examples were worked out, a new frictional headloss table was obtained for HDP pipe manufacture to ISI (Indian) specifications, which are the specifications adopted by UNICEF for Nepal. The new headloss tables have been included in the reference tables at the end of this handbook, but the original examples have not been re-worked. The principles described wherever possible should be applied in the light of manufacturers' specifications, or local standards.

PREFACE

This handbook is written with the intention of collecting together all the knowledge, theory, and practices necessary for the surveying, designing, and construction of gravity-flow drinking water systems for rural communities. Although the book is written specifically for the construction of such systems in Nepal, most of the principles presented herein are equally applicable in most locations around the world. Efforts have been made to organize the material for quick reference, and to present it in a manner that allows overseers of both engineering and non-engineering backgrounds to readily understand.

The stress of this handbook has been in presenting the fundamental principles of design, illustrated with several general examples of sucessfully constructed structures, rather than to present strict and unenlightened "standardized designs". This is because the author feels that, due to the typical ruggedness of the Nepali countryside, such standardized designs may not always be perfectly feasible. However, the overseer who understands the principles of the design can easily modify them to fit the locations.

This handbook will now replace the "Village Water Systems Technical Manual" written by Carl R. Johnson in 1975. In the years since that time, there have been several changes in design policies, new available materials, and much valuable field experience gained. New ideas, and better understanding of the principles and problems inherent in projects of this type have hopefully made their way into these pages. Johnson's original efforts paved the way, and this handbook is built upon the good foundations that he created.

Additionally, the author wishes to acknowledge those members of the Local Development Department, the American Peace Corps, the German Volunteer Service, the British Voluntary Service Overseas, the World Health Organization (WHO), and UNICEF who supported, encouraged, criticized, advised, and in many other ways helped in the making of this book.

However, this volume is by no means the final tome on this subject. Creative and inventive overseers will be constantly evolving new ideas, new uses for old materials, and new solutions for old problems. It is hoped that such resourceful persons will pass along their ideas to UNICEF, where they can be preserved and disseminated.

--Thomas D. Jordan, Jr.

Kathmandu, Nepal
March 1980

1. INTRODUCTION

1.1 DESCRIPTION OF SYSTEMS

This handbook concerns itself with all the knowledge, theory, and material necessary to survey, design, and construct a community water supply (CWS) system to meet the drinking water requirements for rural villages of small-to-moderate populations. The systems described herein are of the gravity-flow type; that is, the action of gravity is used to move the water downhill from a source to the village. This type of system is shown schematically in Figure 1-1: a suitable source is located at an elevation higher than the village. An intake structure is built to collect the water, which is then piped down to the village through a buried pipeline of High-Density Polyethylene (HDP) pipe. If needed, a reservoir tank is built above the village. From there, the water is distributed to several public tapstands that are scattered throughout the village, via the mainline, branchlines, and taplines. Where multiple sources are used, a collection tank may be built, and due to the topography of the land, at certain points break-pressure tanks may be required to prevent excessive pressures from bursting the HDP pipe. If the source water is carrying a lot of suspended particles, a sedimentation tank may be required to clean the flow of these.

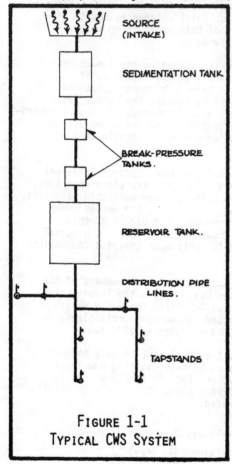

SOURCE (INTAKE)

SEDIMENTATION TANK

BREAK-PRESSURE TANKS.

RESERVOIR TANK.

DISTRIBUTION PIPE LINES.

TAPSTANDS

FIGURE 1-1
TYPICAL CWS SYSTEM

Each of these system components (intake works, pipeline, various tanks, tapstands, etc.) are discussed in this handbook.

1.2 FUNDAMENTAL PROBLEMS

The construction of a CWS system in rural villages is often beset by many problems which prolong, frustrate, or even cancel the project. And even when these initial problems are successfully circumvented and the project is completed, the system may soon be broken down due to misuse or unforeseen circumstances.

The technical problems encountered during construction may be such things as difficult terrain for pipelaying landslides or erosions which threaten to sweep away tanks, or water sources which unexpectedly yield less water than counted upon (or even dry up completely).

These are problems which are often clear and easily comprehended by the overseer in charge of construction, who can usually plan a strategy to overcome them.

Less obvious problems, however, arise from the "human factor." Because such projects are community efforts, often they become unavoidably embroiled in local disputes, arguments, politics, and economics. Here, the problems that arise are rarely clearly defined or easily solved. Water rights of the sources, locations of the tapstands, and division of labor are most often major problems, and until they are solved (if ever!) the future of the system, even if it is eventually completed, is dim.

Human problems that plague water systems are things such as neglect (inadequate or zero maintenance), abuse (from children and curious adults), or deliberate sabotage (by discontented villagers determined to punish the rest, or by selfish ones who cut open the pipeline to irrigate their fields). These are all very real problems that have effectively destroyed many water systems.

The technical problems can be grasped and dealt with by the overseer and consultant engineers, who are trained to recognize and solve these problems. The human problems, however, must be recognized and solved by the entire community, which is often the far more difficult task.

This hand book tries to address both types of problems: technical as well as human. Technical theory and construction practices alone will not build a successful water system. Many times, if the overseer underestimates the innocent destructiveness of children, or fails to

understand some special needs of the villagers, there will be much
lost time, damaged materials, repetition of labor, and general
feelings of anger and frustration. Wherever possible, this handbook
tries to mention these potential problems, and suggest possible means
to minimize them.

1.3 ORGANIZATION OF THIS HANDBOOK

The material herein is roughly arranged in the order of the three
phases of a CWS project: surveying, designing, and construction of
the system. All dimensions and calculations are in the metric system
of units, except for the GI pipe sizes which are given in inches
(since this is how they are supplied in Nepal). The designs presented
are carefully calculated to yield necessary structural strength and
utility without using an excess of materials. Each system component
is discussed in terms of function and good design characteristics,
and several drawings are given of such structures that have been
sucessfully built. The last pages of this handbook are a series of
reference tables for fast reference and general information.

2. VILLAGE EVALUATION AND FEASIBILITY STUDY

2.1 INTRODUCTION

The first phase in creation of a CWS system is a visit to the village by a surveyor, for the purposes of determining the feasibility of the proposed project. Should he determine that the project is feasible, the surveyor must then conduct a topographic survey.

Evaluation of a village is both an objective and subjective process. Objectively, the surveyor determines facts: village population, locally-available materials, supply of skilled labor, logistical information, etc. Subjectively, the surveyor determines feelings: who are the influential people of the village, what are villager reactions and attitudes towards the project, do they realize the amount of work that they will be required to do, and will they do it? How real are the needs of the village, and who stands to benefit?

A project should be considered feasible only if both the technical factors and the human factors indicate success. To get accurate and reliable answers to the above questions, the surveyor must involve himself in discussion with as many villagers as possible. Relying only upon two or three persons for information is quite wrong. The surveyor must get out and walk around the village, meet the people in public places (such as in teashops, around temples, etc).

Once the surveyor is satisfied that the villagers are enthusiastic about the project, he should proceed with the technical aspects of surveying the system.

The entire village evaluation and topographic survey can rarely be done in less than two days. Time must be taken to ensure that a complete investigation has been made, and accurate results obtained. When the surveyor finally leaves the village, he should have resolved in his mind whether or not the project should be undertaken. If he feels that it should, then he must have all the necessary data for himself, or another person, to draw up the complete designs and estimates for the system.

This chapter will set forth guidelines for the surveyor to use when visiting a village on a feasibility study. The next chapter will present specific details on how to conduct the topographic survey.

2.2 POPULATION SURVEY

An accurate population survey of the village is absolutely necessary, since population determines water requirements. A village population, for the purposes of a water system, includes all persons who will depend upon it for their drinking water. Thus are included patients in health posts, students living in dormitories, employees in government offices, etc. Although most rural mountain villages will not usually have these special populations, they must be taken into account where they are found.

Field experience has shown that villagers usually have a very poor idea of their own population, and tend to grossly overestimate their real numbers. They also sometimes will slant their answers to suit their purposes. Care must be taken to obtain an accurate count. Three techniques have proven successful :

1) Making a written list of every household and the number of people living in it.

2) Walking around the village and counting houses, determining the number of people living in each one.

3) For very large villages, counting every single person in the village is not really feasible. Instead:

- At each tapstand site, determine the number of houses to be served;

- Personally survey about a dozen of those houses, and determine the average number of persons in each;

- Apply that average to determine the number of persons to be served by that tapstand;

- Total up the total population served by the tapstands.

In any case, discuss with as many villagers as possible these numbers, especially with those who live in that part of the village. To rely upon two or three persons alone is easier, but not as accurate.

2.3 VILLAGE ENTHUSIASM AND MOTIVATION

The ability of the villagers to work together and carry out a drinking water construction project is something that is difficult to judge in advance. Better estimates of the "motivation factor" will come with experience. Never-the-less, it is necessary to get some idea of the motivation, cooperative ability, and potential social and political conflicts while visiting the village. Talking to people; examining past community construction efforts (such as schools, temples, etc); inspecting the conditions of paths, buildings, temples, and public areas (how well are they maintained?); and talking with local government officials, will all yield helpful clues as to the possible success or failure of the construction effort. The surveyor should strive to explain to the villagers, as clearly as possible, the role that they and the government will be expected to fill.

No matter how technically feasible the project may be, it can only succeed if the villagers are truly interested in it, and concerned enough to provide the long-term maintainence necessary to keep the system in working condition.

2.4 CURRENT WATER SOURCES

One of the best ways of determining the likely motivation of the villagers is to examine their current sources of water, and deduce how helpful a CWS project would truly be. Those villagers living close to an adequate source of water will be less inclined to work on the project than those who are not so conveniently located. This reasoning can be applied to the whole village as well, and the surveyor can form a good idea how essential a new system will be.

2.5 SOURCE INVESTIGATION

Investigating a source for a water system should not be confined to only the most convenient source. At this time, water treatment techniques are not generally practical in Nepal, thus it is necessary to locate the cleanest source possible, even if it is not the closest one to the village. Rather than relying upon villager descriptions alone, the surveyor should personally visit all possible sources. Quantity and quality of the flows must be determined, means to develop the intake works must be studied, and water rights must be investigated.

Before beginning his examination of the sources, the surveyor should have completed his population survey. From the information presented in Chapter 4, he can calculate the daily water requirements of the village. No source is feasible if, in 24 hours, it cannot provide that much water.

Springs and small streams are the most common sources for water systems. Whenever possible, a spring should be the first considered, since springs are generally of better water quality, and easier to protect against further contamination.

Springs: Springs are points where water from an underground source is able to seep to the surface. Flows are typically less than 2 LPS, but some can be quite substantial. The flow of a spring is governed by several factors: watershed collection area, percolation rate of water through the ground, thickness of ground above the aquifer (ie- overburden), and the storage capacity of the soil. Springs are seasonally variable, tending to lag behind the seasonal rainfall patterns (ie- springs can give normal flows well into the dry season before tapering off, and may not resume full flow until after the rainy season is well under way). Due to ground percolation and filtration, most springs are quite free of the pathonogenic organisms that cause many health problems; however, some springs flow through limestone or geologic cracks and fissures in the rocks. In such cases, filtration effects are minimal, and the flow may still be contaminated. Also, it is possible that the source is not a true spring at all, but rather a stream that has gone underground for a short distance and is re-emerging. Investigation around the source will reveal the type of spring it is. Figure 2-1 shows the typical geology of a spring, showing the different levels of ground water during the dry - and rainy seasons.

Small streams: These are not as desirable sources, especially when there is human habitation and/or animal grazing areas further upstream. However, sometimes the water demand of the village cannot be met by other sources. Streams are very much seasonally variable, and also can react strongly (and quickly) to daily rainfall as well. When investigating a stream source, study the proposed intake site carefully, with an eye towards future erosion. Question the villagers closely about flood levels of the stream during heavy rainfall.

Big streams and rivers: These are the least-desirable sources, as they are sure to be grossly contaminated from points further upstream. They do offer, however, the best sources for hydraulic ram pumps (hydrams) which can supply villages at a higher elevation and for which there is absolutely no other feasible source. Refer to Chapter 18 for technical information on hydrams.

2.6 FLOW-MEASURING TECHNIQUES

In most investigations, accurate flow measurements of a source will require some earthwork, usually just a simple type of earth bank, dam, or drainage channel. Thus it is advisable to bring along one or more villagers with digging tools and a machete-type knife (for clearing away underbrush, etc). After the channels or dams have been constructed, wait a few minutes for the water to achieve steady, constant flow, before attempting any measurements.

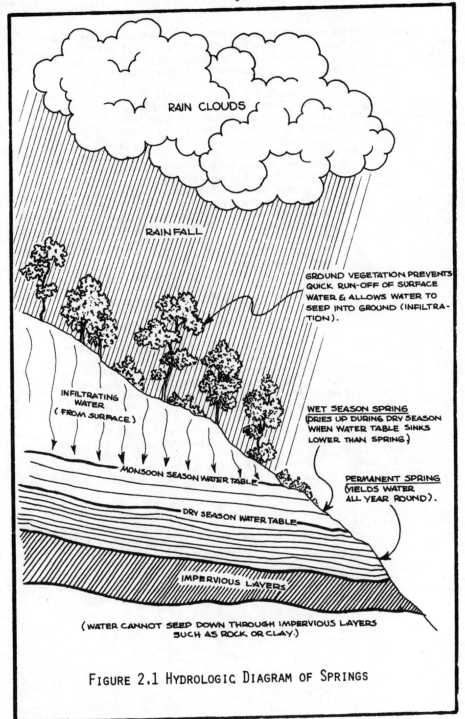

FIGURE 2.1 HYDROLOGIC DIAGRAM OF SPRINGS

Discussed below are three simple methods for measuring the flows of springs and streams. <u>Always</u> measure the flow several times, and calculate an average reading. Any measurements which are obviously deviant should be repeated. Question the villagers closely about seasonal variations in the flow.

<u>Bucket and stopwatch</u>: Spring flows are most conveniently measured by using a wide-mouthed container (of known capacity) and timing how long it takes to fill up. A large-size biscuit or kerosene container (capacities of about 18-20 liters), or a bucket, is usually available in the village. For the most accurate results, the capacity of the container should be such that it requires at least 15 seconds to fill (smaller containers, such as one-liter drinking canteens, should only be used if nothing larger is available). An ordinary wristwatch (that has a sweep-second hand) can be used for timings, but it is best in this case if two persons work together: one concentrating on the wristwatch, the other filling the container. The flow is calculated:

$$Q = \frac{C}{t}$$ <u>where:</u>   Q = flow (liters/second)

C = capacity of container (liters)

t = time to fill (seconds)

<u>V-Notch weir</u>: The V-notch weir can be used to measure the flow of large springs and small streams. This weir has a notch angle of 60°, and is recommended for the normal range of flows encountered in typical village sources. The surveyor may carry his own weir, or one can be easily made in the village from a wooden board or a sheet of tin. The weir is placed as a dam, perpendicular to the flow, with all the water overflowing in the notch. The stream or drainage channel above the weir should be straight and unobstructed for a distance of at least 2 meters. Flow is determined by using a ruler to measure the depth of water overflowing the notch (measured in centimeters), which is then read off of the calibration curve shown in Figure 2-2. The dimensions of a 60° V-notch weir are also shown in the figure.

<u>Velocity-area method</u>: This method requires more work and is not as accurate at the V-notch weir, yet for particularly wide streams it can be easier to use. Measure the surface water velocity of the stream by timing how long it takes a drifting surface float (such as a block of wood) to move down a measured length of the stream (this measured section must be fairly straight and free of obstacles, for a length of 6-10 times the average water depth). Measure the cross-sectional area of the stream. The measurements

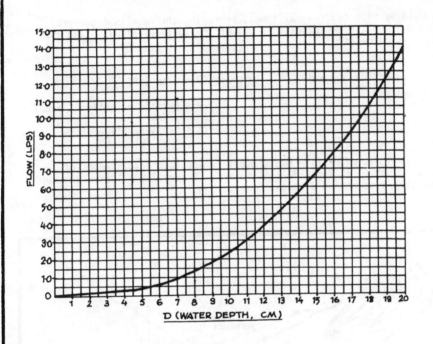

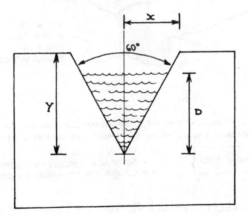

$$\frac{X}{Y} = \frac{1}{1 \cdot 73}$$

FIGURE 2.2 V-NOTCH (60°) WEIR & FLOW GRAPH

should be repeated several times, averaging the results together. The average stream velocity is 85% of the surface velocity, and the flow is calculated:

$$Q = 850 \times V \times A$$

where: Q = flow (LPS)

V = surface velocity (m/sec)

A = cross-sect'l area (m^2)

This method of flow measurement is applicable to streams of water depth of at least 30 centimeters. Figure 2-3 illustrates the velocity-area method of measurement.

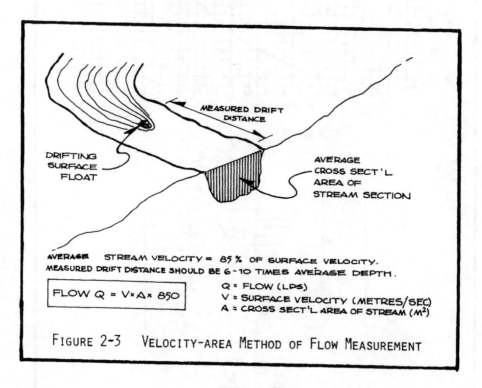

AVERAGE STREAM VELOCITY = 85% OF SURFACE VELOCITY.
MEASURED DRIFT DISTANCE SHOULD BE 6-10 TIMES AVERAGE DEPTH.

FLOW Q = V×A× 850

Q = FLOW (LPS)
V = SURFACE VELOCITY (METRES/SEC)
A = CROSS SECT'L AREA OF STREAM (M^2)

FIGURE 2-3 VELOCITY-AREA METHOD OF FLOW MEASUREMENT

2.7 SAFE YIELD

The safe yield of the source is typically the minimum flow of the source during the dry season. The safe yield is the flow of water that the source can be counted upon to deliver all year round, and it is this flow that is used in designing water systems. Unless the source is measured in April or May (the driest season) the villagers must be consulted to determine as accurately as possible what the safe yield of the source is. Should the water flow be critical, measurements should be repeated during the dry season, or stand-by sources also selected.

The maximum flows should also be determined by questioning the villagers. As the safe yield is important for pipeline and reservoir design, the maximum flow is also necessary for estimating structural protection of the intake and overflow requirements.

2.8 WATER QUALITY

At this time, practical water treatment schemes are not widely available, especially for remote project sites. However, if a source has turbidity (cloudiness),taste, and/or odor problems, these might be easily remedied by the simple treatment schemes discussed in Chapter 17.

In any case, the surveyor will have to use his own judgement about the suitability of a source. Villagers will know through experience if the water of a source is drinkable, therefore they should be consulted.

2.9 SOURCE DEVELOPMENT

When investigating a possible source, the surveyor must be developing an idea about how the intake works will be built. He should be thinking about methods of protecting the structure against erosion, floods, and contamination by surface run-off of rain. What amount of excavation will be called for, and will a dam or drainage channel be required? What further protection can be included to keep animals and curious villagers from tampering with the works? All these aspects should be carefully thought about, and measurements and sketches made in his field book, along with notes about topography, surrounding areas, etc. To depend upon memory alone when trying to design the intake works (which could be several weeks after having last seen the source) is unprofessional and unreliable   Figure 2-4 is a sample page of field notes relating to a source.

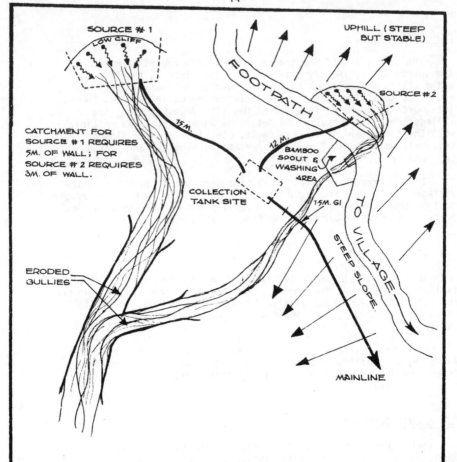

SOURCE #1

LOW CLIFF

UPHILL (STEEP BUT STABLE)

FOOT PATH

SOURCE #2

CATCHMENT FOR SOURCE #1 REQUIRES 5M. OF WALL; FOR SOURCE #2 REQUIRES 3M. OF WALL.

15M.

12 M.

BAMBOO SPOUT & WASHING AREA

COLLECTION TANK SITE

1·5M. GI

TO VILLAGE

STEEP SLOPE.

ERODED GULLIES

MAINLINE

NOTES:
1. SOURCE #1 = SPRING @ 0·35 LPS. ELEV = 1000M.
2. SOURCE #2 = SPRING @ 0·22 LPS. ELEV = 998 M.
3. COLLECTION TANK @ ELEV = 993 M.
4. SOURCE AREA JUNGLE W/LITTLE UPHILL CULTI-
   VATION OR GRAZING.
5. MAINLINE NEEDS 1·5M. GI PIPE CROSSING GULLY.
6. SURVEY BEGUN @ SOURCE #2.

FIGURE 2.4   EXAMPLE SOURCE NOTES & SKETCH

2.10 WATER RIGHTS

The final aspect of source investigation must include resolving the water rights of those people currently depending upon that source for their water. Although it is not the surveyor's responsibility to become involved in settling this question, it is his responsibility to make sure all disputes are resolved satisfactorily. If such problems cannot be solved, he should consider alternative sources. In the past, some projects have been deliberately sabotaged by disgruntled villagers who felt they were not being considered fairly. At such times, there have been unhappy consequences, and much wasted time, labor, and materials.

2.11 LOCAL MATERIALS, LABOR, AND LOGISTICS

Before leaving the village, the surveyor should sit down and obtain all the information relevant to the following aspects:

- the full proper name of the village, ward number(s), panchayat, district, and zone;

- name of nearest roadhead, and distance;

- name of nearest airfield, and distance;

- portering time and fees between roadhead, airfield and village;

- supply of local skilled labor (masons, carpenters, etc) and wages;

- supply of local materials (slate, wood, bricks, etc) and costs;

- sources of sand and stone;

- schools (number of students) and health posts (number of beds);

- names of those villagers who were helpful and familiar with the surveyed route;

- accurate population count;

- other necessary information about special needs of the village.

The answers to these above queries should be carefully recorded in the surveyor's field book.

3. TOPOGRAPHIC SURVEYING

3.1 INTRODUCTION

This chapter shall present methods of conducting a topographic survey along a proposed pipeline route. Such a survey can be done using a theodolite, barometric altimeters, or an Abney hand level. Each of these methods will be discussed, although the main emphasis of the chapter shall be on surveying with the Abney level, since that is the easiest and most-widely used technique.

3.2 THEODOLITE SURVEYING

The theodolite is a high-precision instrument, and requires special training in its use. A two-man team is required, one for sighting through the instrument at an assistant, who is holding a vertical scale "rod" several meters tall. Although surveying with the theodolite will yield measurements accurate to within a few centimeters, it is a relatively slow method. The accuracy of this instrument is not usually needed for the entire length of a pipeline survey, though it is sometimes useful to use it to measure the depth of U-profiles, or for accurate positioning of break-pressure tanks.

3.3 BAROMETRIC ALTIMETER SURVEYING

As altitude increases, the barometric pressure (ie- air pressure) of the atmosphere decreases. A barometric altimeter measures the atmospheric pressure, and the corresponding elevation is read directly off of the instrument.

Normal weather patterns cause the air pressure at any altitude to fluctuate slightly throughout the day. Thus, even if an altimeter is at a point, the elevation reading may increase and decrease by several meters throughout the day. Such pressure variations must be measured and accounted for when conducting a barometric altimeter survey.

Properly done, such a survey requires three persons, each with his own altimeter. The three altimeters are brought together and calibrated (for the same altitude reading) at the same time. One assistant then takes his altimeter to the highest point along the survey, while the other assistant takes his altimeter to the lowest point. They remain at those points during the entire time of the survey, and at regular intervals (such as every 15 or 30 minutes) they record the elevation readings of the altimeters, and the time. The surveyor takes the third altimeter along the route of the pipeline. Ground distances are measured with a tape measure, and at each station the surveyor records altitude and time. Later, the true elevations can be made by adjusting the surveyor's reading with the pressure changes recorded by the stationary altimeters.

Although not necessarily as accurate, this type of surveying can be done with two altimeters: one stationary at the mid-elevation of the route, while the surveyor carries the other.

This type of survey is the fastest to conduct, and accuracy limited only by the accuracy of the altimeters themselves. This method can be best used for feasibility surveying of a system, with a more careful survey conducted later.

3.4 ABNEY LEVEL SURVEYING

The standard method of conducting surveys for water system pipelines is using the Abney hand level (technically of the type known as a clinometer level). It is faster to use than the theodolite, and although not as accurate, it still yields results that are within acceptable limits needed for this type of survey. It is a lightweight instrument, easy to use, and of simple construction to make it rugged and easy to adjust. The remainder of this chapter shall deal with various aspects of using the Abney, adjusting it, and proper recording of survey field notes.

3.5 DESCRIPTION

The Abney level is basically a square tube (dimensions of about 16 x 1.5 x 1.5 cm) with an eyepiece at the observer's end and horizontal cross-hair at the objective end. Figure 3-1 shows a typical Abney level. Near the center of the tube is a 45° mirror, which reflects half of the line-of-sight upwards through an aperture in the tube. Mounted above the aperture is a bubble level with an index mark etched at its center. The bubble level is affixed to a movable index arm, which adjusts against scale graduations on a nickel-silver arc. Some types of Abney levels have interchangable arcs, offering different types of scales (such as degrees, percent, etc). For the purpose of this handbook, the degree arc is used.

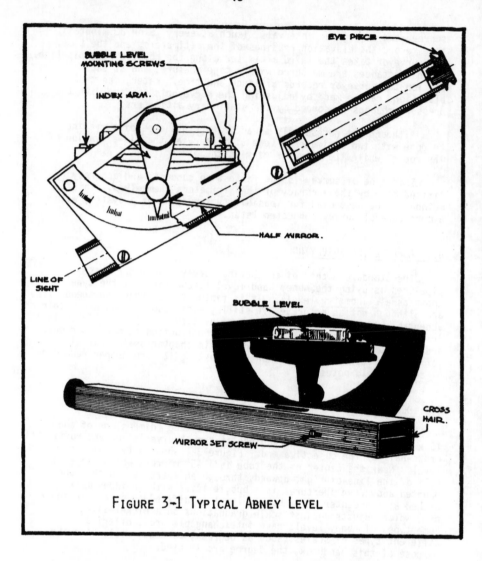

FIGURE 3-1 TYPICAL ABNEY LEVEL

3.6 SIGHTING WITH THE ABNEY

To use the Abney, the instrument is held to the eye and sighted on
a target, centering the cross-hair against the target. The index arm
is then adjusted until the bubble (visible in the right half of the
field-of-view) is centered against the target and the cross-hair.
When correctly adjusted, the target, the cross-hair, and the bubble are

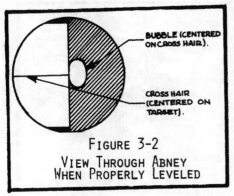

BUBBLE (CENTERED ON CROSS HAIR).

CROSS HAIR (CENTERED ON TARGET).

FIGURE 3-2
VIEW THROUGH ABNEY
WHEN PROPERLY LEVELED

all aligned horizontally, as shown in Figure 3-2. The angle of view (technically known as the <u>vertical angle</u>) is then read on the arc in degrees.

If the index is pre-set at exactly 0°, then the level may be used as a rough carpenter's level for construction of walls, beams etc.

3.7 ADJUSTMENT OF THE ABNEY

Like any precision instrument, the Abney level is liable to creep out of adjustment from time to time. When used in the field, it should be checked for levelness each day. No surveyor should ever begin a survey with an unfamiliar Abney, or one that has not been used for a long time, without first checking the adjustment. If the instrument is ever dropped, the adjustment should be checked before proceeding.

Adjusting the Abney is a quick and simple task. The various methods of adjustment are discussed below :

Two-post method: When checking the adjustment for levelness in the field, select two trees, posts, or building corners that are about 7-10 meters apart (refer to Figure 3-3). At Station A, the surveyor holds the Abney against a mark (located at approximately eye-level), and with the index of the Abney preset at 0°, he sights over to a Station B. An assistant, standing at Station B, moves a target (such as a pencil, his finger, stick, etc) up or down until it lies on the line-of-sight. At that point, he makes a mark. Then he and the surveyor exchange places, and the surveyor sights from the mark on Station B back towards Station A. The assistant sets a new mark on Station A that lies on this line of sight. If the two marks on Station A coincide, then the Abney is truly level, and no adjustments must be made. If they do not coincide, the assistant sets a third mark exactly halfway between the two other marks. Sighting on this mark, the surveyor then adjusts the bubble level until the bubble comes into alignment with the cross-hair and target mark.

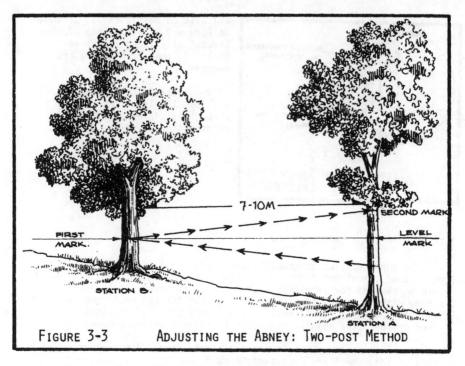

FIGURE 3-3   ADJUSTING THE ABNEY: TWO-POST METHOD

Many surveyors set up permanent level sight lines
in their offices or on convenient outbuildings, so that
it is only the work of a moment to check the Abney and
adjust it themselves (not needing an assistant at all).

Flat surface method: In addition to adjusting for
levelness, this method is also needed to make the further
adjustments of the bubble level and mirror, described later.

A smooth, level surface is required. If nothing
better is available, place a smooth board on a firm support,
arranged so that it is possible to sight lengthwise along
its surface. Place the Abney lengthwise on the board and
outline its position with a pencil. Center the bubble
against the etched index mark of the bubble level. Reverse
the instrument end for end and place it within the penciled
outline. The bubble should center. If it does not, move
it half-way toward the etched mark (adjusting with the
index arm), then wedge up the board until the bubble
centers. Reverse the instrument end for end, repeating
the whole procedure until the bubble centers when the
instrument is in both positions. The penciled position on
the board now provides the level surface required for
making adjustments:

     <u>Setting the bubble</u>: Set the index arm at 0° . Center the bubble against the etched mark on the bubble level by adjusting the mounting screws (turn the screws equal amounts in <u>opposite</u> directions).

     <u>Setting the mirror</u>: With the instrument still in position, place a white surface a few centimeters in front of the tube so that the horizontal cross-hair can be clearly seen when sighting through the instrument. The bubble should center on the cross-hair when sighting through the instrument. If it does not, loosen the screw on the right-hand side of the tube and slide it backward or forward until the bubble centers properly against the cross-hair. Tighten the screw and check the setting.

     <u>Setting the height of the bubble level</u>: Fix the instrument firmly to the edge of the board, angled downward about 30° (refer to Figure 3-4). Center the bubble against the etched index mark.

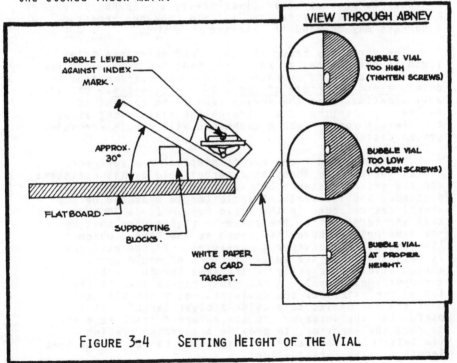

VIEW THROUGH ABNEY

BUBBLE LEVELED AGAINST INDEX MARK.

APPROX. 30°

FLATBOARD.

SUPPORTING BLOCKS.

WHITE PAPER OR CARD TARGET.

BUBBLE VIAL TOO HIGH (TIGHTEN SCREWS)

BUBBLE VIAL TOO LOW (LOOSEN SCREWS)

BUBBLE VIAL AT PROPER HEIGHT.

FIGURE 3-4   SETTING HEIGHT OF THE VIAL

Hold a white card in front of the tube and sight through
the instrument. The bubble should be centered on the
cross-hair. If it is not, adjust the height of the bubble
level by tightening or loosening the mounting screws
equal amounts in the same direction. If the bubble appears
too low, then lower the level by tightening the screws,
and vice versa.

The above information is taken from the Keuffel & Esser
Co. manual no. 80 0204, "Topographic Abney Levels". Refer
to this manual for further information concerning Abney
levels.

3.8 SURVEYING WITH THE ABNEY

Conducting a survey with the Abney requires minimally
two persons, but additional ones are helpful, especially
when surveying through terrain where underbrush must be
cut away to provide clear lines-of-sight. An Abney level,
a 30-meter tape measure, and a field book are necessary;
a compass may be used if bearings are desired.

The survey is begun at some fixed reference point
(such as the source, or some prominant landmark along the
pipeline route) and proceeds upstream/downstream from that
point, along the route of the proposed pipeline. Villagers
will sometimes lead the survey team along convenient
footpaths, when the actual trenchline will be dug along
a different route; such a technique will create erroneous
ground distances.

The surveying technique is simple: the surveyor
sights through the Abney at a target held by his assistant,
and the ground distance between them is measured. This
distance, and the vertical angle (angle measured by the
Abney) are recorded in the field book. It is important
that the target which the surveyor sights upon must be
the same height above the ground as the Abney, which is
the same as the surveyor's eye-level. If the assistant
is not as tall as the surveyor, then he sould carry a
target stick cut exactly to the same length as the
surveyor's eye-level. A red cloth can be tied to the
top of the stick, or the assistant can place his hand
over the end of it, to provide a clear target. It is also
useful for the surveyor to use a forked stick as a stand
to rest the Abney on, to provide a steadier reading
(in this case, the target stick should be cut to the same
length as this forked stick).

Figure 3-5 shows the basic arrangement and calculation
used in trigonometric leveling with the Abney: the
surveyor and his assistant are 28 meters apart (ground
distance), and the vertical angle is $-16°$ (the negative

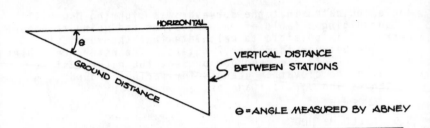

HORIZONTAL

θ

GROUND DISTANCE

VERTICAL DISTANCE
BETWEEN STATIONS

θ = ANGLE MEASURED BY ABNEY

VERTICAL DISTANCE = GROUND DISTANCE × SIN θ

EXAMPLE ILLUSTRATED BELOW :
θ = -16° (NEGATIVE SIGN INDICATES SIGHTING DOWNHILL)
SIN θ = 0.276 (FROM TRIGONOMETRIC TABLE)
GROUND DISTANCE = 28 METERS
VERTICAL DISTANCE = 28 × 0.276 = 7.73 METERS.

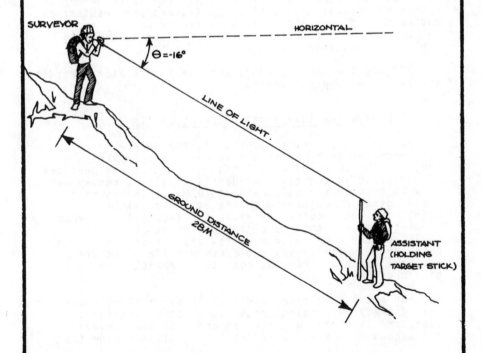

SURVEYOR

HORIZONTAL

θ = -16°

LINE OF LIGHT.

GROUND DISTANCE
28M

ASSISTANT
(HOLDING
TARGET STICK)

FIGURE 3-5 TRIGONOMETRIC SURVEYING WITH AN ABNEY LEVEL

angle indicates that the surveyor was sighting downhill).
By consulting a table of natural sines and using trigono-
metry, it is possible to calculate that the vertical
distance between them is 7.7 meters. The reference tables
at the back of this handbook present the natural sines,
and also the elevation changes for various ground
distances and vertical angles.

3.9 FIELD METHODS

At the same time he is conducting the survey, the
surveyor must also be observing the ground over which he
walks. As he proceeds, he must constantly keep in mind
that, at some later time, he or another person will actually
have to dig a trenchline along that route. Thus, notes
must be made about the type of terrain being traversed,
such as stretches of jungle, cultivated fields, footpaths,
gullies, soil conditions (ie- gravel, soft dirt, bare rock,
etc). It is easy to survey across terrain which might
be exceedingly difficult or impossible to lay a pipeline!
The surveyor should make use of as many reference points
as possible, so that if a section of the pipeline needs
to be resurveyed at a later time, a convenient starting
point can be found. Reference points should be permanent
or semi-permanent; suitable examples are prominent trees,
rock outcroppings, etc. If the surveyor carries one or
two bottles of nailpolish, he can paint an identifying
lable onto his landmarks.

Figure 3-6 shows a good, precise format for recording
accurate and complete notes.

3.10 CLOSING THE SURVEY AND ACCURACY LIMITS

Closing the survey means tying the survey into two
reference points of known elevations, thus providing a
check on the surveyed elevations. For practical purposes
of surveying in the hills of Nepal, closing a survey can
only be done by repeating it entirely, beginning from
the original endpoint and ending at the original starting
point, but not necessarily along the same original route.
Needless to say, this is a time-consuming process; however
it is advisable to resurvey a few short sections of the
pipeline, especially where elevation differences are
critical (such as crossing over tops of ridges or bottoms
of U-profiles).

An acceptable technique that allows a close check on
the accuracy of readings requires a second assistant. One
assistant is at the new station ahead of the surveyor,
and second assistant is at the last station behind the

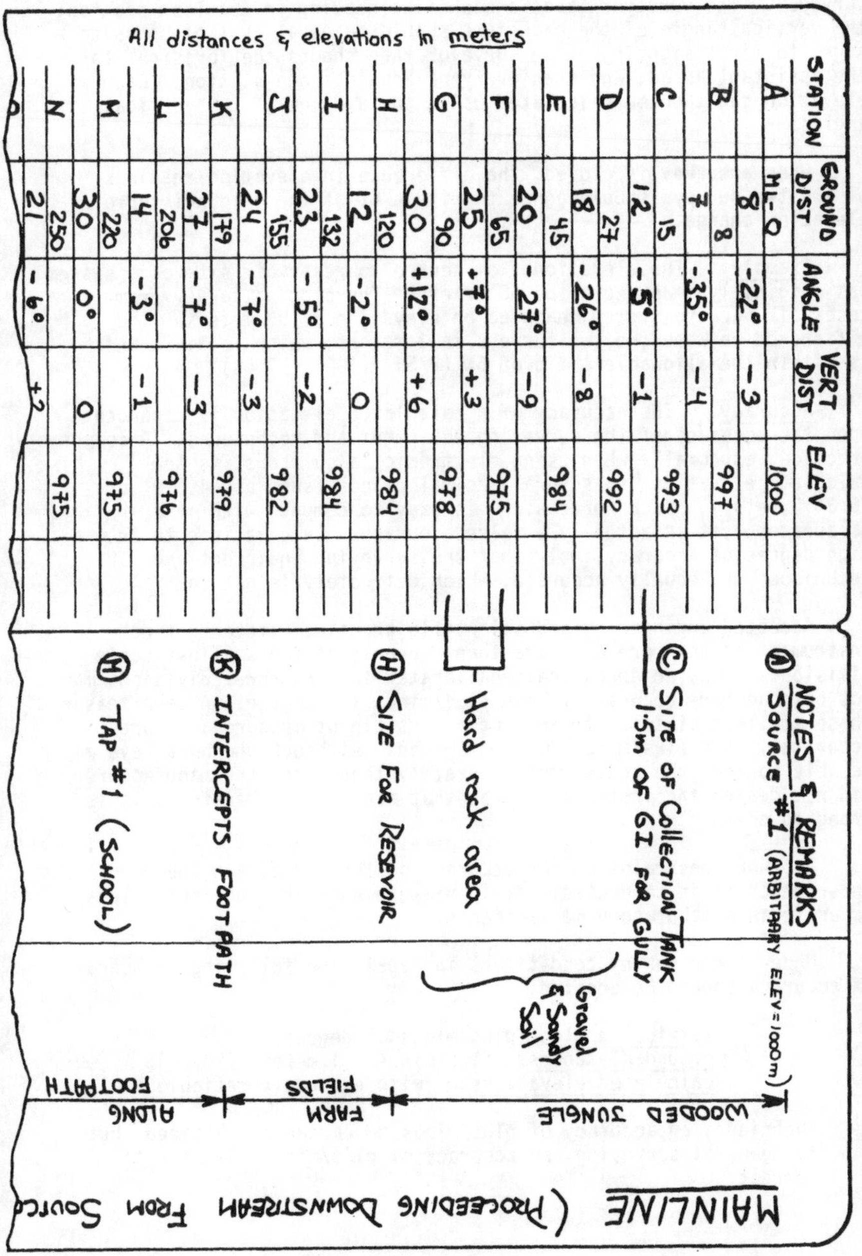

All distances & elevations in <u>meters</u>

STATION	GROUND DIST	VERT ANGLE	VERT DIST	ELEV
A	Mi-0 / 8	-22°	-3	1000
B	7 / 8	-35°	-4	997
C	12 / 15	-5°	-1	993
D	18 / 27	-26°	-8	992
E	20 / 45	-27°	-9	984
F	25 / 65	+7°	+3	975
G	30 / 90	+12°	+6	978
H	120	-2°	0	984
I	12 / 132	-5°	-2	984
J	23 / 155	-7°	-3	982
K	24 / 179	-7°	-3	979
L	27 / 206	-7°	-3	976
M	14 / 220	-3°	-1	975
N	30 / 250	0°	0	975
O	21	-6°	+2	

NOTES & REMARKS

(A) SOURCE #1 (ARBITRARY ELEV=1000m)

(C) SITE OF COLLECTION TANK 1·5m OF GI FOR GULLY

Gravel & Sandy Soil

Hard rock area

(H) SITE FOR RESERVOIR

(K) INTERCEPTS FOOTPATH

(M) TAP #1 (SCHOOL)

MAINLINE (Proceeding Downstream From Source)

WOODED JUNGLE | FARM FIELDS | ALONG FOOTPATH

FIGURE 3-6
EXAMPLE FIELD BOOK NOTES

surveyor. The surveyor makes a backsight reading on the last station; the vertical angle of the backsight should be equal (but of opposite sign) to first sighting. The surveyor then shoots the foresight to the assistant ahead, and then everyone advances one station. Each elevation can then be calculated using the average of two vertical angles.

When a survey is closed, the difference in elevation readings of the two surveys should agree to within 6% of the original surveyed elevation change.

Example: The elevation from source to reservoir site of a system was originally measured to be 55 meters. The closing survey from reservoir back to source measured an elevation of 53 meters. The difference between the two surveys is 2 meters, which is 3.6%, which is within the allowable limit of 6% (2/55 x 100% = 3.6%).

Accuracy: The accuracy of a calculated elevation is dependent upon the accuracy of the surveying equipment and techniques. A common practice, especially when using electronic calculators, is to calculate elevations to several decimal places (such as "4.679" or "6.341", etc.). Such "precision" is easy to compute with the calculator, yet is actually a false accuracy. Calculations to such a high degree of accuracy imply that the surveying equipment and techniques are equally accurate, which definately is not so.

Accepted engineering and scientific practices state that no instrument is any more accurate than one-half of the smallest scale division. Thus, an Abney scale calibrated in one-degree divisions may not be read more accurately than plus/minus 0.5-degree. A tape measure whose smallest division is in centimeters cannot measure any more accurately than plus/minus 0.5-centimeter. Although the human eye may be able to read the scale more accurately than this, the manufacturer did not design the instrument to be that accurate. Therefore, it is wrong to do so.

Another constraint on the accuracy of the survey are the conditions under which it is conducted: field measurements are inherently less accurate than laboratory measurements.

Under field survey condititons in Nepal, the following standards of accuracy should be adopted:

> vertical angle: plus/minus 0.5-degree
> ground distances: plus/minus 0.1 meters (10 cm)
> calculated elevations: with extremely meticulous

technique, an accuracy of plus/minus 30 cm can be obtained, but for general surveying, an accuracy of plus/minus 0.5-meter is correct.

4. DESIGN PERIOD, POPULATION, AND WATER DEMANDS

4.1 INTRODUCTION

This chapter will present the manner of calculating the daily water demand of a village. The population growth rate for that regional area of Nepal is used to project the village's current population to the future population after 15-25 years. The water demands of the village are then calculated, based upon the future population.

4.2 DESIGN PERIOD

Community water supply systems should be designed and constructed for a 15-25 year lifespan. The choice of either a 15, 20, or 25-year design period is made by the surveyor, based upon the amount of potential change that he can foresee for the village. A remote area, far from future development efforts, might well be designed with a 25-year water demand projection. However, in an area where a new highway or airfield is slated for construction, a shorter design period should be considered, because the long-range water demands cannot be accurately forecasted.

4.3 POPULATION FORECAST

Selection of the design period leads directly to an estimate of the village population for the last year of that period. This design population is calculated using the current village population and the population growth factor for the design period, given in Figure 4-1.

Example: A village in the Far Western hills of Nepal has a current population of 436 people. The design period was selected to be 20 years. What is the design population?

Future population = current population + 34%

= 436 x 1.34

= 584 people

Within the design report, the design period and population forecast should be carefully indicated, as should any special criteria for their selection.

GEOGRAPHIC AREA	1961-1971 average annual growth rate	PERCENTAGE INCREASE			
		10-yrs	15-yrs	20-yrs	25-yrs
FAR WESTERN DEVELOPMENT REGION					
Mountains	1.4	14	22	30	39
Hills	1.5	16	25	34	45
Indian border districts	2.3	25	40	56	75
Surkhet Valley	2.3	25	40	56	75
Plains	3.4	40	66	96	130
WESTERN DEVELOPMENT REGION					
Mountains	1.1	12	18	25	33
Hills (northern)	1.6	17	27	38	48
Hills (southern)	2.1	23	36	51	68
Plains	3.7	44	73	110	150
CENTRAL DEVELOPMENT REGION					
Mountains	1.0	11	17	23	30
Hills	1.6	18	27	38	48
Kathmandu Valley	1.3	13	20	28	36
Plains	3.8	45	74	110	150
EASTERN DEVELOPMENT REGION					
Mountains	1.1	12	18	25	33
Hills	1.5	16	25	34	45
Plains	4.1	50	84	120	170

Note: All figures derive from the 1952-54, 1961, and 1971 census data. The 10-25 year growth figures are based upon 1961-1971 average annual growth rates, computed by C. Johnson.

FIGURE 4-1
POPULATION FORECAST TABLE

4.4 WATER DEMANDS

The total water demands for the village at the end of the design period is the sum of the per capita demand plus special need demands.

Per capita demand is the water required per person of the projected village population. A per capita demand of 45 litres per person per day is the present design standard. This figure derives from World Health Organization (WHO) studies, and includes allowances for personal washing, drinking, cooking, and a portion of domestic animal needs.

When a marginal water source is encountered, and the target figure of 45 LPCPD (liters per capita per day) cannot be met, then one may go as low as 230 liters per household per day. This figure is based upon minimal needs, and assumes 8-10 persons per household.

Special need demands are those required by additional facilities in the village, such as schools, health posts, government offices, etc. The amount of water needed daily by these facilities is given below, based upon WHO ideal target usages:

Facility	Daily Demand (liters)	
	Ideally	Minimally*
Schools -day students	10 liters/student	6.5
-boarding students	65 liters/boarder	42
Hospitals & Health Posts	500 liters/bed	325
Health clinics (no beds)	2500 liters/day	1625
Government Offices	500-1000 liters/day (depending upon size)	325-560

*Minimal figures are 65% of ideal

The village's total daily water requirements will be the sum of the per capita demand plus the special needs demand, as projected for the end of the design period.

5. TYPES OF SYSTEMS

5.1 INTRODUCTION

There are several types of gravity-flow water systems, each type being determined by certain design characteristics. These systems fall into two general catagories: open systems, and closed ones.

An open system derives from the concept that the taps can be left open and flowing continuously all day long, and still provide constant and steady flow. This means that the safe yield of the source(s) is sufficient enough to supply all tapstands directly, without requiring a reservoir tank.

A closed system is one where the safe yield of the source cannot provide continuous flow to all taps, or where the safe yield is such that a reservoir tank is necessary to store water for peak demand periods which the source alone could not meet. All tapstands on the system must have a faucet, either of the self-closing or manually-operated type.

Both catagories of systems may require break-pressure tanks, but an open system will never require a reservoir tank. At all tapstands, regardless of the type of system, a control valve must be installed to proportion and regulate the flow between taps.

From these two catagories, there are five different types of systems which can be built, as discussed below.

5.2 OPEN SYSTEMS WITHOUT FAUCETS

This type of system has continual, 24-hour flow from the taps, with no faucets to shut off the water. The primary advantage to this system is that there are no faucets that can be abused, worn out, broken, stolen, etc. The primary disadvantage arises out of the copious amounts of wastewater issuing forth all day and night. Strategic location of taps to make efficient use of wastewater (such as irrigation of nearby fields, etc) and construction of non-erodible drainage channels to carry these flows away will minimize the problems of large wastewater quantities.

5.3 OPEN SYSTEM WITH FAUCETS

The problems of copious wastewater flows from an open tapstand can be eliminated by installing faucets on some of the tapstands. Provisions must be made for handling overflow water from the lowest break-pressure point (i.e. reservoir tank, break-pressure tank, etc.), since excess water will overflow at that point.

This type of system is one of the more desirable types, since it requires no reservoir tank, provides more than sufficient water for the villagers, and has minimal wastewater problems.

5.4 CLOSED SYSTEM WITH RESERVOIR

A reservoir tank is required when the peak water demands of the village cannot be met by the source alone. The reservoir stores wate from low-demand periods(such as overnight) to supplement the source flow during peak demand periods (such as early morning). A reservoir system is able to provide water at any time demanded, but depends upon faucets and pipeline being well maintained (a broken faucet or a leaky pipeline will not allow the reservoir to fill).

A reservoir system may actually be less expensive to build than an open system, since usually a smaller pipe size can be used between the source and reservoir. The savings in pipe cost can offset the cost of the tank (refer to Section 5.7).

5.5 CLOSED SYSTEM WITH INTERMITTENT SERVICE

There are some topographic situations where the yield of the source and geography of the terrain act in such a way that the system must be designed with one (or more) break-pressure tanks located downstream from the reservoir tank. This arrangement has required an intermittent supply system: except for a few hours each day (ie- in the mornings and evenings), the water is shut off at the reservoir tank to allow it to refill. Without doing this, the tank would never refill, since it would be constantly draining out through the lower break-pressure tanks.

This intermittent system is the least-desirable type to build. Hydraulic problems, such as air entrapment, can complicate the draining and refilling of the pipeline each day; there will be increased wear on the control valves at the reservoir; support of the system caretaker requires considerable village organization; negative pressures in the pipeline during system shut-down can suck in polluted groundwater via small leaks; and since the entire water demand period is compressed into just a few hours (rather than spread out over the full day), the taps must be designed to deliver greater flows, which in turn requires larger pipe sizes and substantially increases the cost of the system.

Fortunately, it is possible to avoid intermittent systems by installing float-valves (also known in Nepal as "ball-cocks") in the downstream break-pressure tanks.

5.6 CLOSED SYSTEM WITH FLOAT-VALVES

As mentioned above, there are some situations where it is inescapably necessary to install break-pressure tanks downstream from the reservoir.

Float-valves are installed in these break-pressure tanks, and act on the same principle as those commonly used in household toilets. These valves automatically adjust the flow in the pipeline to exactly match the amount demanded by any open taps. When all taps are closed, the break-pressure tank fills with water, lifting the float and gradually closing the valve until the flow is cut off. This allows the upstream reservoir tank to refill.

Sturdy-quality float-valves are now becoming part of the standard supplies provided by UNICEF for water supply projects in Nepal. Locally available float-valves (usually manufactured in India), although not of high quality, can also be used and offer the advantage that, if broken, they can be easily and inexpensively replaced by the villagers themselves.

5.7 OPEN SYSTEM VS CLOSED SYSTEM

The decision to build a system as either open or closed is governed by several factors: pipeline profile, safe yield of the source, design population, and availability of construction materials. In some instances, the decision is an obvious one, and in other cases the designer must evaluate the economics of both types before making a decision.

As mentioned above in Section 5.4, a reservoir system may be a more economical system than an open system. An open system will usually require a large-size pipe between the source and the village, whereas if a reservoir tank was constructed, then a lot of that pipe could be replaced with a smaller-size. The designer should always investigate both of these alternatives if it is possible that a system may be built as an open one. However, sometimes the specific pipe sizes, or enough cement,may not be quickly available, in which case the alternate system may have to be built if delays in construction are to be avoided.

5.8 LIMITED EXPANSION

One aspect with which planning and designing a water project is concerned is the extendibility of the system. Although the population is projected through the end of the design period, the physical growth of the village may expand in such directions that the villagers may wish to add one or two more tapstands to the system at some future date. It is also possible that the village's population growth may in fact be much greater than initially assumed, resulting in the design water demands long before the end of the design period. This section discusses possible means of limited expansion of the system to resolve these problems, provided that preparations are made during the initial survey, design, and construction of the system. These expansion possibilities are only aimed at meeting these unexpected needs for the duration of the initial design period. It is presumed that by the end of the original design period, the condition of the system and the new village water needs will require a major overhaul of the system, or even construction of an entire new one.

Additional taps: The need for additional taps can be minimized by trying to predict in which directions the village is likely to expand in the future, and locate tapstands accordingly. Although this anticipation of the future will rarely be easy to make, the geography of the land around the village will sometimes set limits on expansion (such as rivers, cliffs, direction of ridges and hills, etc.).

If additional tapstands are needed, no changes in the pipeline will be necessary if the villagers are willing to slightly reduce the flow from the other taps to make water for the new taps. Decreasing the flow of four tapstands by 20% will allow the addition of a fifth one to the line. The system designer should indicate in the design report just where additional tapstands may be added, and what flow re-adjustments would be necessary. This information should be in the project file at the LDD office, and also should be discussed with the village leaders.

Increased water demands: This problem can only be solved if there is another water source located above the intake or reservoir level, so that the flow from the new source can be added to the existing one. In the future, water purification schemes may become available to many projects, thus a near-by water source which is currently unacceptable may some day be able to be added to the system. Despite such increased flows, additional water storage capacity may be required. This can be accomplished by either of two methods: select the original reservoir site so that a second tank may be constructed next to it and cross-connected;   or alternatively, design the first tank such that its walls can be raised enough to add another 30-50 centimeters of water depth to the tank.

Again, the design report should indicate just how future expansion of storage capacity has been planned for.

5.9 PHASED EXPANSION

Expansion of a system does not necessarily have to remain within the domain of the original system. There may be a small ward or village close at hand which, currently, has its own adequate water supply and does not have to be included in the system initially. After a number of years, however, that small population may have outgrown its water source, and then consideration should be given as to how the original system may be extended to incorporate it.

The best way to accomplish this is to plan for it when initially preparing the system design. Certain pipelines of the system would have to be of a larger size than otherwise necessary, and the reservoir should be designed so that it can be expanded as discussed above.

Branchpoint tees and/or control valves for the future extension may
be installed at the time of initial construction. The design report
should indicate after how many years it is intended to extend the
system, and the matter discussed with the LDD regional engineer and
village leaders.

6. HYDRAULIC THEORY

6.1 INTRODUCTION

In this chapter, the basic hydraulic principles that govern the behavior of gravity-flow water systems will be presented. It will not be possible to understand this material in a single, cursory reading, yet full understanding of these concepts is necessary before any person can properly design such a system. The designer should read, study, and repeatedly refer back to this chapter until he is satisfied with his knowledge of these principles.

The next chapter shall discuss special strategies in designing a pipeline section where there are potential air-blocks.

6.2 ENERGY

To move water, whether moving it uphill, downhill, or horizontally, requires energy. As its name implies, in a gravity-flow water system the source of energy is the action of gravity upon water.

A gravity-flow water system is "powered" by gravitational energy. The amount of such energy in the system is determined by the relative elevations of all points in the system. Once it has been constructed, all points in the system are immovably fixed (ie- buried into the ground) and their relative elevations cannot change. *Thus, for any system, there is a fixed, specific quantity of gravitational energy available to move water.*

As water flows through pipes, fittings, tanks, etc, some energy is lost forever, dissipated by friction. Due to the changing topographic profile of the system, at some points there may be a minimal amount of energy (ie- low pressure), while at other points there may be an excessive amount of energy (ie- high pressure). A poorly designed or constructed system will not conserve energy properly enough to move the desired quantities of water through the pipeline.

The purpose of pipeline design, therefore, is to properly manipulate frictional energy losses so as to move the desired flows through the system, by conserving energy at some points and burning it off (by friction) at other points. This is accomplished by careful selection of pipe sizes and strategic location of control valves, break-pressure tanks, reservoirs, tapstands, etc.

6.3 HEAD: The Measure of Energy

On the Earth's surface, fresh water weighs 1 gram per cubic centimeter (1 g/cm^3). A column of water one centimeter square and

100 centimeters high (1 x 1 x 100 cm) would therefore weigh 100 grams.
The same column 1000 cm high would weigh 1000 grams (1 kilogram). The
area at the base of this column is one square centimeter (cm^2) and supports
the entire weight of the column. Therefore, the pressure at the base of
this column is 1 kg/cm^2. The same column 20 meters high (2000 cm) would
weigh 2 kgs, and exert a pressure of 2 kg/cm^2; a column 30 m high exerts
a pressure of 3 kg/cm^2; a column 43 meters high exerts a pressure of
4.3 kg/cm^2, and so on.

In hydraulic work, rather than repeatedly calculate water pressures,
it is an easier practice to simply report the equivalent height of the
water column. Technically, this is called the head, and represents the
amount of gravitational energy contained in the water. In the metric
system of units, head is always measured in meters.

By this practice, a water pressure of 1.4 kg/cm^2 is reported as
14 meters of head; a pressure of 4 kg/cm^2 is 40 meters of head;
5 kg/cm^2 is 50 meters of head, etc.*

6.4 FLUID STATICS: Water at Rest

Any person who has ever dived to the bottom of a lake or swimming
pool quickly learned that the water pressure increased as he descended
but that swimming horizontally at a constant depth produced no change
in pressure. This common experience serves to illustrate a major
principle in hydraulics:

> Water pressure at some depth is directly related
> to the vertical distance from that depth to the
> level of the surface, and is not affected by
> any horizontal distances.

Consider the system shown in Figure 6-1. The water pressure at
point A is determined by the depth of water at that point. The pressures
at points B and C are likewise determined by the height of the vertical
distance from those points to the level of the water surface:

Point	Water Pressure	Head
A	1 kg/cm^2	10 meters
B	.2 kg/cm^2	20 meters
C	3.5 kg/cm^2	35 meters

---

* the pressure exerted by other fluids, such as mercury, oil, etc, can
also be reported as equivalent heads of that fluid. Barometric
pressure, for example, is often measured as "millimeters of mercury".

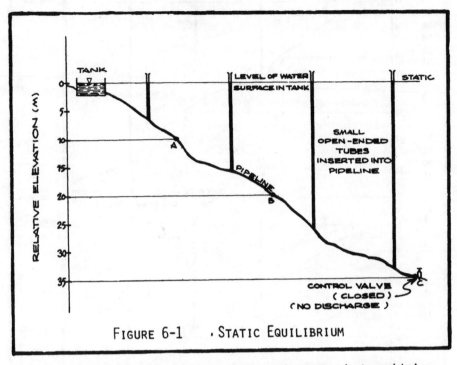

FIGURE 6-1 , STATIC EQUILIBRIUM

In a pipeline where no water is flowing, the system is termed being in static equilibrium. In such systems, the level of the water surface is called the static level, and the pressures are reported as static heads.

If small tubes were inserted into the pipeline, as shown in Figure 6-1, the water level in each tube would rise exactly to the static water level. The height of water in each tube is the pressure head exerted on the pipeline at that point.

Since no water is flowing, there is no energy lost to friction and the static level is perfectly horizontal.

6.5 FLUID DYNAMICS: Water in Motion

Now suppose that the control valve at point C in Figure 6-1 is partially opened, allowing a small flow of water through the pipeline (and also assume that the tank refills as fast as it drains, so that the surface level remains constant). The water levels in each glass tube decrease a bit. As the valve is opened further and further to allow greater flows through the pipeline, the water levels in the tubes drop even lower, as shown in Figure 6-2.

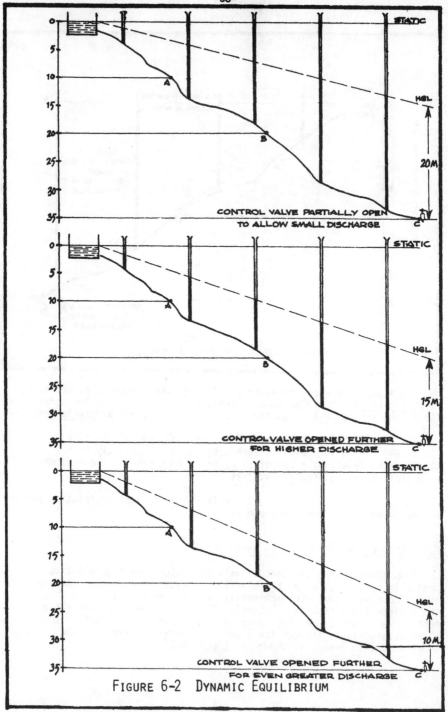

FIGURE 6-2 DYNAMIC EQUILIBRIUM

It can be seen that the water heights in these tubes form a new line for each new flow through the system. For a constant flow, the line formed by the water heights will remain steady. The system is now said to be in __dynamic equilibrium__. The line formed by the water levels in the tubes is called the __hydraulic grade line__, commonly abbreviated as HGL. A different flow establishes a different dynamic equilibrium, and a new HGL.

6.6 HYDRAULIC GRADE LINE (HGL)

The HGL represents the new energy levels at each point along the pipeline. For any constant flow through the pipe there is a specific, constant HGL. The vertical distance from the pipeline to the HGL is the measure of pressure head (ie- energy), and the difference between the HGL and the static level is the amount of head lost by the friction of the flow.

The water pressure at air/water interfaces (such as the surfaces in tanks or discharges at tapstands) is zero. Thus, the HGL must always come to zero wherever the water comes into contact with the atmosphere.

Since frictional losses are never recovered, the HGL always slopes down along the direction of flow. The steepness of the slope is determined by the rate at which energy is lost to friction. Only under static conditions is the HGL perfectly horizontal, although for practical purposes the HGL may be plotted as horizontal for extremely low flows in large pipes (where the headloss is less than 1/2-meter per 100 meters of pipelength). For practical purposes, the HGL will never slope upwards.

Appendix A gives a more mathematical discussion on the HGL, with relevant examples of how it applies to a gravity-flow water system.

6.7 FRICTION: Lost Energy

As mentioned at the beginning of this chapter, a system has a specific amount of gravitational energy, determined by the relative elevations of points in the system. As water flows through the pipeline, energy is lost by the friction of the flow against pipe walls, or through fittings (such as reducers, elbows, control valves, etc), or as it enters/discharges from pipes and tanks. Any obstruction to the flow, partial or otherwise, causes frictional losses of energy.

The magnitude of energy lost due to friction against some obstacle is determined by several factors. The major factors would be the roughness of the obstacle, and the velocity of the flow. Minor factors would include water temperature, suspended particles, dissolved gases   etc.

-40-

The diameter of the pipe, and the amount of flow through it, determine the velocity of the flow*. The greater the flow, the faster the velocity, and the greater the frictional losses. Likewise, the rougher the surface of the obstacle, the greater the frictional losses.

Frictional losses are not linear: doubling the flow does not necessarily double the losses: usually, losses are trebled, quadrupled, or even greater.

6.8 VALVES: Variable Friction Devices

An excessive amount of energy (ie- high pressure) can cause the pipe to burst. One method of controlling excessive amounts of energy is to install control valves at strategic points throughout the system. A valve is a device which can be adjusted to create greater frictional losses as the water flows through it. There are two types of control valve : gate valves, and globe valves. Both are shown below in Figure 6-3:

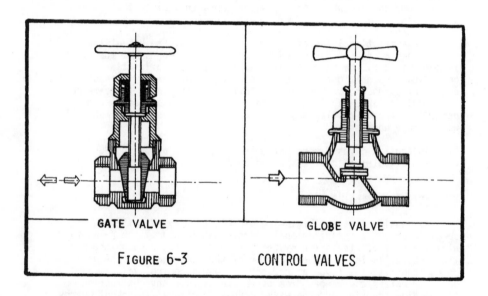

GATE VALVE   GLOBE VALVE

FIGURE 6-3   CONTROL VALVES

Gate valves: Gate valves serve as on/off control valves, for the purpose of completely cutting off the flow. Generally, they are located at the outlets of intakes, reservoirs, strategic break-pressure tanks, and at major branchpoints. They are not recommended for use in regulating flow (ie- partially open or closed) since the water will erode the bottom edge of the gate and result in a leaky valve whenever it is meant to be closed. Direction of flow through the valve is unimportant.

---

*flow, velocity, and pipe size are all related by the Equation of Continuity presented in Technical Appendix A.

Globe valves: These valves are designed for regulating flow through
the system. They are best located near discharge points, so that it is
easier to measure the flow through the valve. They are generally located
at discharge points in reservoirs, strategic break-pressure tanks, and
at every tapstand*. Direction of flow through a globe valve is important:
there is an arrow stamped on the valve that indicates the proper direction
of flow, and care must be taken to see that the valve is installed correctly.

6.9 FRICTIONAL HEADLOSS FACTORS

It is obvious that to properly design a system, the designer must be
able to determine how much energy will be lost to friction by the time the
flow reaches various critical points in the system. Frictional headloss
tables are used for this purpose. The common method is to report the
amount of frictional headloss per unit length of pipe, for a specific
flow. Typically this would be expressed as "meters of headloss per
100 meters of pipelength", or as "m/100m" or "%".

The frictional headloss tables for both HDP and GI pipe are given
at the end of this book. These headloss factors are never perfectly
accurate since frictional losses are affected by many different factors
which may vary from system to system. For this reason, it is necessary
to always include a margin of safety when plotting the HGL (see Section
6.13).

Example: What are the frictional headlosses in the pipeline
section below?

a)   1350m of 32mm HDP @ 0.45 LPS:

Frict'l headloss factor = 2.56m/100m

1350 x 2.56/100 = <u>34.6 meters headloss</u>

b)   730m of 2" GI pipe @ 1.30 LPS:

Frict'l headloss factor = 1.84%

730 x 1.84/100 = <u>13.4 meters headloss</u>

c)   2075m of Class IV 50mm HDP @ 1.40 LPS:

Frict'l factor = 3.22%

2075 x 3.22/100 = <u>67 meters headloss</u>

Frictional headlosses can be rounded off to the nearest 1/2-meter,
or even to the nearest meter.

Frictional headlosses of flows through fittings such as elbows,
reducers, tees, valves, etc, are given as equivalent pipelengths.

---

* the 1/2" globe valve used on tapstands is known in Nepal as a
<u>corporation cock</u>.

6.10 EQUIVALENT PIPELENTHS OF FITTINGS

A pipeline fitting (such as an elbow, tee, valve, etc) acts as a concentrated point of frictional losses. The amount of headloss in the fitting depends upon the shape of the fitting, and the flow through it. The headlosses are computed by determing the equivalent length of pipe necessary to create the same amount of headloss. For fittings, this is commonly given as the L/D Ratio (length/diameter). The L/D ratios for various fittings are given below:

Fitting	L/D Ratio
Tee (run-side)	68
Tee (run-run)	27
Elbow (90°, short-radius)	33
Union	7
Gate valve (fully open)	7
Free entrance	29
Screened entrance	150

Example: What is the equivalent pipelength of a 1-1/2" GI elbow?

1-1/2" x 33 = 50" = 126 cm = 1.26 meters

Where fittings are located at isolated points along a long pipe-length, the amount of headloss they generate is considered minor compared to the normal headloss through the pipe. Such headlosses do not have to be shown on the plotted HGL when the pipelength is more than 1000 diameters. For the common pipe sizes used in CWS projects, these losses can be ignored if the pipe section is longer than:

20mm HDP:	20 meters
32mm HDP:	32 meters
50mm HDP:	50 meters
63mm HDP:	63 meters
90mm HDP:	90 meters

When several fittings are located close together, however, the total headloss is actually greater than the sum of individual head-losses through each fitting. Thus, special concern must be given to selecting the proper pipe sizes for the GI plumbing of a tank outlet. This is explained in Technical Appendix G.

Since a valve is adjustable, it can be set for any equivalent pipelength. This is discussed further in Section 6.13 and Figure 6-7.

6.11 PLOTTING THE HGL

To illustrate the basic principles of plotting the HGL, the simple system of Figure 6.4 will be used. In this example, the pipe sizes have already been selected. The desired flows out of each tap are 0.225 LPS, the safe yield of the source is 0.50 LPS. The elevations and pipelengths are given for the source, Tap # 1 and Tap # 2.

The HGL is plotted in sections (technically called <u>reaches</u>) between strategic points in the system.

<u>First reach</u>:   In this example, the first reach is from the intake to the end of the 50mm HDP pipe section. The desired flow through this reach is 0.45 LPS (ie- the sum of the tap flows), and since the safe yield of the source is greater than 0.45 LPS, no reservoir tank is required (ie- the system can be built as an open system, with or without faucets).

> 340m of 50mm HDP @ 0.45 LPS
>
> Frict'l factor = 0.30%
>
> 340 x 0.30/100 = <u>1 meter headloss</u>

This is plotted on the profile.

The <u>second reach</u> ends at the first tap, 480 meters of 32mm HDP pipe. The desired flow is still 0.45 LPS.

> 480m of 32mm HDP @ 0.45 LPS
>
> Frict'l factor = 2.56%
>
> 480 x 2.56/100 = <u>12 meters headloss</u>

The residual head at Tap # 1 is therefore 13 meters (refer to Chapter 15.4 for standards on acceptable residual heads for tapstands).

The <u>third reach</u> is from Tap # 1 to the end of the 32mm HDP pipe section: 500 meters of pipe. The desired flow in this section is now only 0.225 LPS (ie- flow for just the remaining single tap).

> 500m of 32mm HDP @ 0.225 LPS
>
> frict'l factor = 0.78%
>
> 500 x 0.78/100 = <u>4 meters headloss</u>

The HGL at this point is now 17 meters below the static level, meaning that a total of 17 meters of head has been lost to friction by the flow between the source and end of this reach.

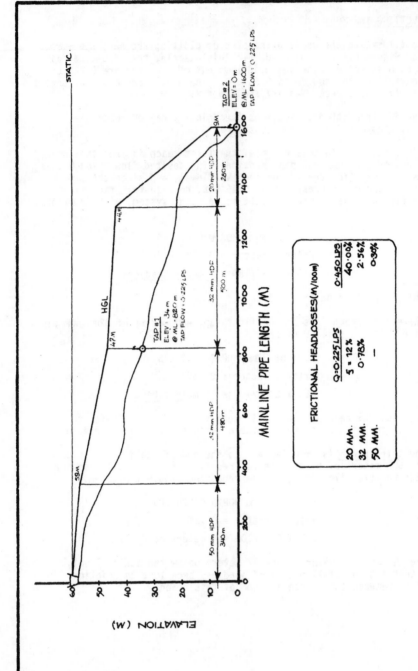

FIGURE 6-4 PLOTTING THE HGL (EXAMPLE SYSTEM)

The final reach is 280 meters of 20mm HDP pipe, carrying a flow of 0.225 LPS.

280m of 20mm HDP @ 0.225 LPS

frict'l factor = 12.0%

280 x 12/100 = 34 meters headloss

The residual head at Tap # 2 is 9 meters.

Observe that the HGL only changed slope at points of-new pipe sizes and/or new flows. To allow only the desired 0.225 LPS out of each tap, globe valves must be installed in the tap pipeline (tapline) and adjusted so that precisely the 0.225 LPS comes out of the faucets. When adjusted like that, the valve for Tap # 1 will be burning off 13 meters of head, and the valve for Tap # 2 will be burning off 9 meters of head. The effects of residual heads are discussed in Section 6.13.

6.12 REQUIRED HGL PROFILES

The plotted HGL of Figure 6-4 represents the hydraulic profile of the system specifically when both taps are open. Naturally, there will be a different profile if just Tap # 1 is open, or just Tap # 2 is open, or if both taps are closed (ie- the static profile). Normally, it is not necessary to calculate the HGL profiles for the various combinations of open/closed taps in a system. The HGL should only be plotted for the two extremes: all taps open, and 'all taps closed. As can be seen in Figure 6-4, both of these cases have been plotted on the single profile. This allows the designer to easily determine points of high and low pressure in the system, to ensure that they are within allowable limits (as will be discussed in Sections 6.14 - 6.16).

6.13 RESIDUAL HEAD: Excess Energy

The significance of residual heads at tapstands, reservoirs, and break-pressure tanks must be understood by the designer before a proper system can be planned.

Residual head is the amount of energy remaining in the system by the time that the desired flow has reached the discharge point. It represents excess gravitational energy.

Installing a control valve at the discharge point will burn off residual head. (For this purpose a globe valve, not a gate valve, should be used).

Whilst this will reduce the quantity of flow, it may produce more desirable pressure characteristics within the pipeline.

A more specific discussion on design residual heads follows:

When plotting the HGL for a flow which discharges freely into the atmosphere (such as into a tank or out of a tap), the residual head at the discharge point may turn out to be either positive or negative, as shown in Figure 6-5:

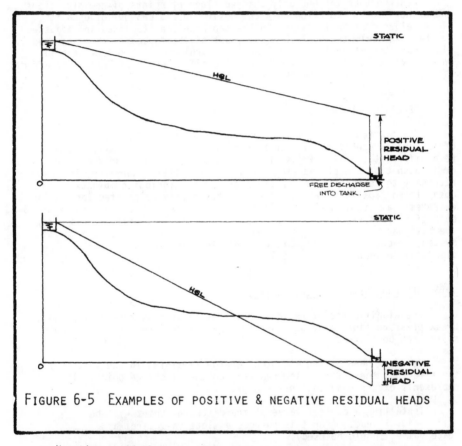

FIGURE 6-5 EXAMPLES OF POSITIVE & NEGATIVE RESIDUAL HEADS

Negative residual head: This indicates that there is not enough gravitational energy to move the deisred quantity of water, hence this quantity of water will not flow. The HGL must be replotted using a smaller flow and/or larger pipe size.

Positive residual head: This indicates that there is an excess of gravitational energy; that is, there is enough energy to move an even greater flow through the pipeline. If allowed to discharge freely, a positive residual head means that gravity will try to increase tne flow through the pipe; as flow increases, the frictional headlosses will decrease the residual head. The flow will increase until the residual head is reduced to zero.

Natural flow: When the residual head of a pipeline discharging freely into the atmosphere is zero, then the maximum amount of flow is moving through the pipe. This is the natural flow of the pipe, and is the absolute maximum flow that can be moved by gravity. The natural flow of the pipe can be controlled by selective pipe sizing.

Figure 6-6 shows the calculation of the natural flow of an example pipeline.

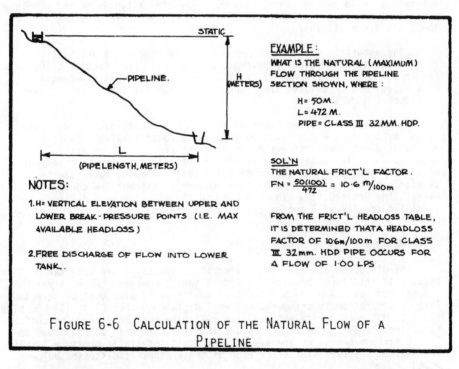

FIGURE 6-6 CALCULATION OF THE NATURAL FLOW OF A PIPELINE

If the natural flow of a pipeline is greater than the safe yield, then the pipe will drain faster than it can be filled, and the result will be that the pipe will not flow full. In such a case, the HGL will lie on the surface of the water inside the pipe. A non-full flowing pipe is not under any pressure (except where the pipe flows full in U-profiles). If there are no tapstands located along a pipeline section that is not flowing full, then this is of no consequence.

However, if there is a tapstand, then it is very important that the pipeline be kept flowing full (ie- under pressure) to ensure the proper functioning of the tap.

Pipelines that otherwise will not flow full must have a control valve at the discharge point. This control valve will burn off the residual head, rather than allowing the flow to increase too much. The control valve is adjusted until the desired flow is discharged; at that setting, it is burning off exactly the correct amount of head.

In practice, control valves are adjusted under the hydraulic conditions where all taps are opened. As mentioned earlier, different HGL profiles will occur when different combinations of taps are opened and closed. For each possible combination, new residual heads will occur at the discharge points. Since it is not desirable to have the villagers constantly re-adjusting control valves every time a tap is opened or closed, the actual discharges will fluctuate. However, such fluctuations will be small and are negligible.

The amount of frictional headloss of flow through a valve is reported as the equivalent pipelength of the valve (see Section 6.10). Figure 6-7 given an example of calculating the equivalent pipelength of a valve, and calculates the fluctuating flows for the example system of Figure 6-4.

Since every tapstand requires some amount of residual head, then it is obvious that every tapstand requires a control valve. Control valves at discharges into reservoir or break-pressure tanks are only required where it is necessary to keep a specific flow in the pipeline, or to keep the upstream section of the pipeline flowing full (due to tapstands or branchpoints along that section). Without the control valves, the desired flow cannot happen in the pipeline, and the real hydraulic profile will not match the plotted HGL.

6.14 MAXIMUM PRESSURE LIMITS

As discussed already, it is seen that pipe sizes are selected because of frictional headloss considerations. However, there is yet another consideration which determines what type of pipe must be selected. This consideration is pressure, and will dictate whether Class III HDP pipe, Class IV HDP pipe, or galvanized iron (GI) pipe must be used. The choice is determined by the maximum pressure that the pipe will be subjected to (these maximum pressures are always the result of static pressure levels). The maximum pressure limits for each of these pipes is discussed below:

85 psi   Class III HDP pipe: Maximum pressure rating = 6 kg/cm^2 (60 meters of head). This is the standard pipe used in Nepal where pressures do not exceed 60 meters of head. Since the other classes of pipe are much more expensive, the system should be designed to use as much Class III as possible.

140 psi   Class IV HDP pipe: Maximum pressure rating = 10 kg/cm^2 (100 meters of head). This class is used where pressure exceed 60 meters of head but not 100 meters. Its wall thicknesses are greater, which allow it to

10 meters head = 1 kg/cm^2 = 14.15 psi

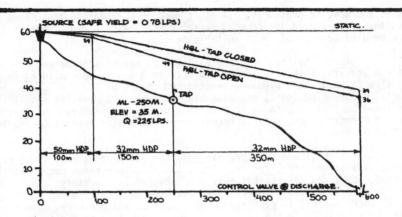

TAP OPEN

First Reach (Source--Tap)
Q= 0.78 LPS
L= 100m of 50mm HDP + 150m of 32mm HDP
Headlosses= 1m (50mm HDP section) + 10m (32mm HDP section)
Residual head @ Tap= 14m;   Tap flow= 0.225 LPS

Second Reach (Tap--Tank)
Q= 0.55 LPS
L= 350m of 32mm HDP
Headloss= 13m
Residual head @ Tank discharge= 36m

This residual head at the tank discharge will be exactly burned off when the control valve at the discharge is adjusted to allow precisely 0.55 LPS into the tank. At this setting, the equivalent pipelength of the valve is 974m (ie- the length of 32mm HDP pipe required to burn off exactly 36m of head at 0.55 LPS flow).

TAP CLOSED

The equivalent pipeline of the system is:

    100m of 50mm HDP
    500m of 32mm HDP
    974m of 32mm HDP (the equivalent pipelength of the valve)

To learn the new discharge flow into the tank, it is necessary to calculate the natural flow of the equivalent pipeline (ie- the flow at which 60m of head will be burned off by 100m of 50mm HDP + 1474m of 32mm HDP). By trial-and-error calculations and interpolations from the Frictional Headloss Table, the flow is found to be about 0.575 LPS. At this flow, the headlosses are:

100m of 50mm HDP @ 0.46 m/100m =	0.46m
500m of 32mm HDP @ 4.05 m/100m =	20.25m
974m of 32mm HDP equivalent pipelength @ 4.05 m/100m =	39.44m
TOTAL HEADLOSS =	60.15m

Thus, when the tap is open, the discharge into the tank will be 0.55 LPS, and when the tap is closed, the discharge will be slightly less than 0.575 LPS.

FIGURE 6-7 EQUIVALENT PIPELENGTH

withstand greater pressures, but it is much more expensive than Class III and therefore should not be used except where pressure requires it (it should **not** be used because of more suitable headloss factors).

350 p^{cl}

GI pipe: Maximum pressure rating = 25 kg/cm^2 (250 meters of head). Galvanized iron pipe used in CWS projects in Nepal is manufactured in India. GI pipe is used where pressures exceed 100 meters of head, or where proper burial of the pipeline is not possible. Current LDD policies set limits on the amount of GI pipe to be used in a project, therefore consultation with the regional engineer is necessary when a system appears to require a lot of GI pipe.

In all the above pressure ratings, for HDP pipe as well as GI pipe, there is a large safety factor. Thus, the above pressures can be safely exceeded by a few meters, but only when absolutely necessary. In the case of HDP pipe, the manufacturers state that the working lifetime of the pipe is 50 years when it is properly joined, buried, and pressures do not exceed the class rating. In the case of GI pipe, the safety factor is even larger, but it must be kept in mind that the pipe corrodes over the years, reducing wall thicknesses and therefore reducing its strength.

6.15 U-PROFILES & MULTIPLE PIPELINES

A special pressure problem to many systems in mountainous regions is the U-shaped profile, similar to the example below:

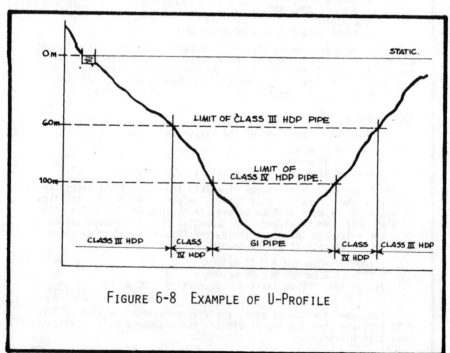

FIGURE 6-8 EXAMPLE OF U-PROFILE

It is apparent from the figure above that, under static conditions, the pressures in U-profiles can be quite high. Sections where the pressures exceed 60 meters of head will require Class IV HDP pipe, and where there is more than 100 meters of head GI pipe will be required.

Although Class IV is usually available in all sizes, there may be times when a particular Class IV size cannot be had. In such cases, it is possible to select a combination of smaller pipe sizes to be put down in parallel that will provide suitable headlosses (such a combination may be even less expensive than a single larger pipe size). Figure 6.9 gives the procedure for determining how the flow will divide itself between two pipes of unequal diameters.

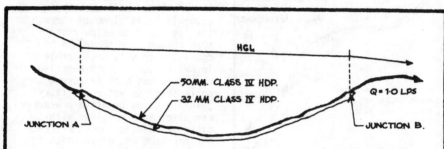

The pressure at <u>Junction A</u> must be equal for all three pipes, since they are all joined at a common point, and likewise the pressure at <u>Junction B</u> must also be the same for all pipes. This implies that both pipes in the multi-pipe section must lose equal amounts of head. As these pipes are equally long, then there must be an equal rate of frictional headloss in both pipes. Thus, the flow will automatically divide itself between the two pipes such that each pipe has a frictional headloss factor equal to the other.

In the example drawn above, a flow of 1.0 LPS will flow through a multi-pipeline of 32mm and 50mm

HDP (both of Class IV series). Consulting the frictional headloss table for these two pipe sizes, it can soon be determined that the only way that the flow can divide itself is approximately as follows:

| Class IV 32mm HDP @ 0.225 LPS |
| " " 50mm HDP @ 0.75 LPS |

It can be seen that for the above flows, the frictional headloss factor for both pipes would be approximately 1.1 m/100m.

This same principle applies also to multi-pipeline section of three or more pipe sizes.

FIGURE 6-9 DIVISION OF FLOW BETWEEN PIPES OF UNEQUAL SIZES

6.16 MINIMUM PRESSURE LIMITS

It is possible when plotting a HGL to discover that, due to the topo-graphical profile of the pipeline, the HGL will actually "go underground;" that is, it will cross below the goundlevel profile and pass some distance underground before emerging again. An example is shown in Figure 6-10:

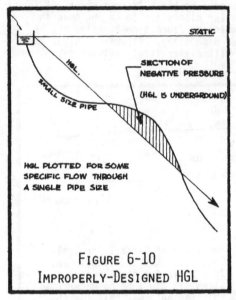

FIGURE 6-10
IMPROPERLY-DESIGNED HGL

The pressure in the pipe along the section where the HGL is underground is a negative pressure (measured as "negative head"). Negative pressure in the pipeline means that the water is being siphoned through (ie- sucked from below rather than pushed from above), a condition that is undesirable in CWS systems. Such negative pressures can suck in surrounding, polluted groundwater via leaky joints. Large negative pressures can also cause problems with dissolved air in the water (such air can come out of solution in the water and form trapped pockets of air at high points in the pipeline; more on air-blocks in the next chapter).

Therefore, as a general standard design, do not design any system where the HGL will fall less than 10 meters above the ground, except when unavoidable. Never allow the HGL to go under-ground at all.

Figure 6-11 shows the same profile, with pipe sizes selected to keep the HGL at least 10 meters above the ground.

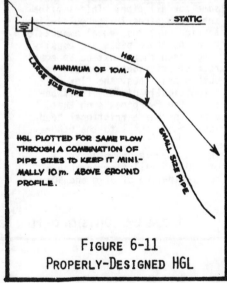

FIGURE 6-11
PROPERLY-DESIGNED HGL

6.17 VELOCITY LIMITS

The velocity of flow through the pipeline is also another matter of consideration. If the velocity is too great, suspended particles in the flow can cause excessive erosion of the pipe; and if the velocity is too low, then these same suspended particles may settle out of the flow and collect at low points in the pipeline, eventually clogging it if left unattended. The recommended velocity limits are :

maximum: 3.0 meters/second

minimum: 0.7 meters/second

The corresponding flows for the various sizes and classes of HDP pipe are (in LPS):

	20mm	32mm (III) (IV)		50mm (III) (IV)		63mm (III) (IV)		90mm (III) (IV)	
Maximum:	0.60	1.85	1.62	4.64	3.96	7.33	6.27	15.00	12.76
Minimum:	0.14	0.43	0.38	1.08	0.92	1.71	1.46	3.50	2.98

The frictional headloss tables indicate low flows with an asterisk (*), and do not give headloss factors for flows greater than the recomended ones.

When a pipeline carries a low flow, provisions must be made for sedimentation problems: a sedimentation tank should be built at the intake site, and washouts located at strategic low points to allow flushing out of settled matter. Refer to Chapter 12 for information on sedimentation tanks, and to Chapter 7.6 for information on locating washouts.

6.18 SUMMATION

This chapter has presented the design methods needed to select pipe sizes and classes, and how to arrange the pipe to keep the HGL within acceptable limits above the ground profile. One more final consideration, that of air-blocks, must be discussed. This will be done in Chapter 7; and then Chapter 8 will present the specific procedures for turning a topographic survey into a properly designed system.

7. AIR-BLOCKS & WASHOUTS

7.1 INTRODUCTION

This chapter considers the details of determining whether or not a pipeline is likely to be affected by trapped pockets of air which could interfere with the flow. If the designer determines that his system is a likely victim of air-blocks, he can then refer to Technical Appendix B for the analysis and procedures needed to deal with these air-blocks.

The chapter also discusses washouts, which allow settled sediments to be periodically flushed out of the pipeline.

7.2 AIR-BLOCKS,   Introduction

An air-block is a bubble of air trapped in the pipeline, whose size is such that it interferes with the flow of water through the section.

When the pipeline is first constructed, or subsequently drained for maintenance purposes, it is "dry", that is, all points within are filled with air at atmospheric pressure. When water is allowed to refill the pipeline, air cannot escape from certain sections and is trapped. As pressure builds up, these air pockets are compressed to smaller volumes. In the process, some of the hydrostatic pressure of the system is absorbed by compressing these air pockets, reducing the amount of energy available to move water. If too much energy is absorbed by compressing air, then no flow will reach the desired discharge point until something is done about the air-blocks.

Generally, there will be no problems of air-blocks in a system where a tank is located at an elevation lower than the air-blocks, as long as the air-blocks are at least 10 meters below the static level. This is shown in Figure 7-1 below:

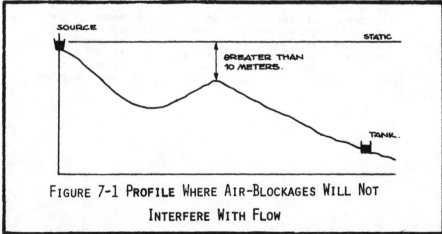

FIGURE 7-1 PROFILE WHERE AIR-BLOCKAGES WILL NOT
INTERFERE WITH FLOW

Air-blocks analysis should be done in U-profile systems similar to that shown in Figure 7-2 below:

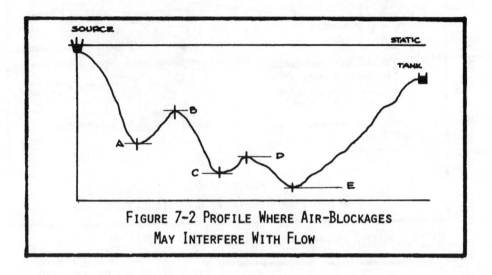

FIGURE 7-2 PROFILE WHERE AIR-BLOCKAGES
MAY INTERFERE WITH FLOW

7.3 AIR-BLOCKS: Pipeline Design Practices

These are guidelines for arranging pipe sizes in such a way so as to minimize trapped air and potential air-blocks. Only after such an arrangement has been analysed and found inadequate should air-valves be installed.

1) Arrange the pipe sizes to minimize the frictional headloss between the source and first air-block.

2) Use larger-sized pipe at the top, and smaller-sized pipe at the bottom of the critical sections where air is going to be trapped (sections BC and DE in Figure 7-2). Pipe sizes elsewhere do not affect the air-blocks.

3) The "higher" air-blocks (ie- closer to the static level) are the more critical ones. Eliminate or minimize them first.

7.4 AIR-VALVES

Airvalves provided by UNICEF are sturdy devices, and operate automatically. Maximum pressure rating is 60 meters of head. Details of installation are shown in Figure 7-3.

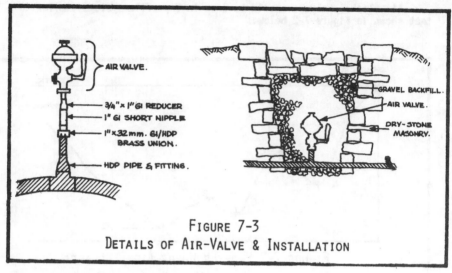

FIGURE 7-3
DETAILS OF AIR-VALVE & INSTALLATION

7.5 ALTERNATIVE AIR-RELEASES

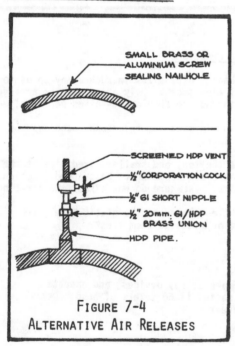

FIGURE 7-4
ALTERNATIVE AIR RELEASES

At times when the above air-valves are not available, there are two alternative methods for allowing trapped air to be released from the pipeline: install a normal control valve, or puncture the pipe with a nail and seal it off with a brass or aluminum screw. Although these alternative methods are not as expensive as an air-valve, they are not automatic, and require manual operation by the villagers. At times when the pipeline is being refilled with water, the valve is opened (or the screw is removed), allowing trapped air to escape. To discourage tempering with these air-release devices, they should be well buried (removing the handle from the valve will also keep unauthorized persons from opening it).

7.6 WASHOUTS

Over a period of time, suspended particles carried in the flow will tend to settle out, particularly at low points in the pipeline or where the flows are low enough so that the flow velocity drops below 0.7 meters/ second. Reservoirs usually allow most of these particles to settle, but pipeline sections upstream from the reservoir do not benefit from this. Break-pressure tanks do not allow any sedimentation to occur, since flows through these are extremely turbulent.

Washouts should be located at the bottom points of major U-profiles, especially those upstream from the reservoir tank. The number of washouts in a system depends upon the type of source (a stream yields more suspended materials than a spring), whether or not there is a sedimentation tank and/or reservoir, and the velocity of flow through the pipeline.

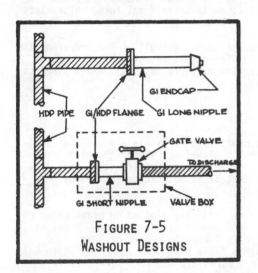

FIGURE 7-5
WASHOUT DESIGNS

The washout pipes should be of the same size as the pipeline at that point. Endcap-type washouts will require that the pipeline will be completely drained before the end-cap can be replaced (since it is impossible to put it back on while there is water gushing out of it), which is not so with a washout that has a gate valve (a globe valve is definately not suited for this type of work). Handles should be removed and valves well buried to discourage tampering. Endcaps should be torqued lightly with a wrench (so that they cannot be removed by hand) but not extremely tightly, since they will tend to rust onto the pipe and be very difficult to remove at a later time. Figure 7-5 shows some washout designs.

8. PIPELINE DESIGN

8.1 INTRODUCTION

The concepts of hydraulic theory, descriptions of various factors which influence flow, techniques for determining pressures and the HGL, have all been presented so far. In this chapter, all of it will be brought together to show how it is practically applied in the design of a real system.

The pipeline design phase begins with the graphic plotting of the topographic survey (from the initial survey of the system) and ends when all sections of the pipeline (ie- mainline, sourcelines, branchlines, and taplines) have been designed in their final form. Blueprints are then made of the design.

This chapter will present standards and guidelines for preparing the pipeline drawings, example designs for mainlines, branchlines, source collection lines (ie- for systems with multiple sources), and a pipeline section of combination pipe sizes.

8.2 PIPELINE DRAWINGS

The purpose in plotting the profile is to create a visual, easy-to-understand picture of the topographic elevations along the pipeline. Because the profile contains so much information on it, it is necessary that it be carefully laid out so that it is not cluttered, sloppy, difficult to read, or incomplete.

Graph profile: The profile is initially plotted on graph paper of centimeter divisions. Vertical scale should be either 1 cm = 5 meters or 1 cm = 10 meters; horizontal scale 1 cm = 50 meters or 1 cm = 100 meters. Each sheet should contain a title block (as shown in Figure 8-1) and the axes laid out as shown in Figures 8.2 and 8.4. The profile, title block, axes, and tapstand sites are done in ink, but tank locations and HGLs are worked in pencil until properly designed, and then inked. The designs must be approved by the LDD regional engineer.

Tracing profile: When the pipeline design is finished and approved, it is traced onto tracing paper. Dark-color ball-point pens, soft-tip markers, or drafting pens should be used. Lettering must be neatly printed. All tanks, taps, washouts, air-valves, branch points, strategic points, etc, should be labeled with distance and elevation. Tapstand flows must be indicated if they are not the standard 0.225 LPS. Pipe sizes and lengths must be indicated.

Blueprinting: When the final tracing is completed, it is ready for blueprinting. A sheet of ammonia-sensitized paper, slightly larger than the tracing paper, is laid out on the tracing paper and then both are rolled through a fluorescent-tube light box. The ammonia paper is then slipped into another air-tight box, where it is exposed to ammonia

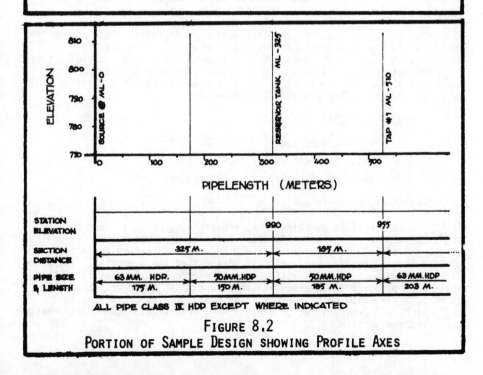

FIGURE 8-1 TITLE BLOCK

FIGURE 8.2
PORTION OF SAMPLE DESIGN SHOWING PROFILE AXES

vapors for a few minutes to "develop" the blueprint. Size of a blueprint page should be about the same as the graph paper size (larger-sized sheets are awkward to handle). The total number of copies of each blueprint is determined by LDD, so consult the regional engineer.

General plan view & key plan: In addition to the profile design, blueprints should be made of the general plan of the system, which shows the rough layout of the system, with village landmarks indicated. A key plan of the system is also made, showing the relative arrangements of tanks, control valves, branchlines, tapstands, etc. An example is shown in Figure 8-3.

NOTE: Since these design examples were worked out, new frictional headloss tables for HDP pipe were obtained. The new tables are now in the back of this book, and are not the ones referred to in the following examples.

8.3 DESIGN EXAMPLE: Mainline

Figure 8-4 will be used as the design example of a mainline. The basic procedure for designing a pipeline is to divide it at strategic points (usually tanks and tapstands). The pipeline section between each of these points is called a reach. For each reach, determine the desired amount of head to be burned off, and the length of pipeline, and with these determine the desired frictional headloss factor. From the Headloss Table, select the pipe size which is closest to that desired frictional factor. If no size is suitable, then using two different pipes in the reach can be done. The method for determining the length of these combination pipes is given in Section 8-6.

When designing the pipeline, the designer can begin at the source and plot his way downstream, or begin at the end and plot his way upstream, or begin at the ends and plot towards the middle, depending upon his intuitive feelings. With experience, he will develop more intuition at where to best begin. In this example, however, plotting will begin at the source and proceed downstream.

Reservoir calculations:

Safe yield of source = 1.40 LPS

Demand by 6 taps @ 0.225 LPS = 1.35 LPS

Therefore reservoir tank not required

Preliminary pressure analysis:

This profile contains a major U-profile, so it is best to begin by examining it there. If Class III pipe were used along the bottom of the U-profile, the pressure in the pipeline would exceed 60 meters of head before the flow could make it back out of the U-profile. Therefore, Class IV pipe must be used, with a break-pressure tank located 100 meters above the bottom of the U-profile. This tank would therefore be located at ML-600, elevation of 900 meters. The Class IV pipe would have to begin at ML-870 (which is at an elevation 60 meters below the break-pressure tank) and run until ML-1720.

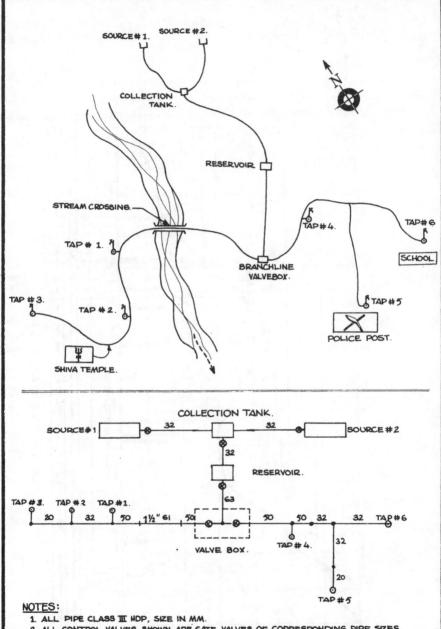

FIGURE 8-3 PLAN VIEW & KEY PLAN OF EXAMPLE SYSTEM

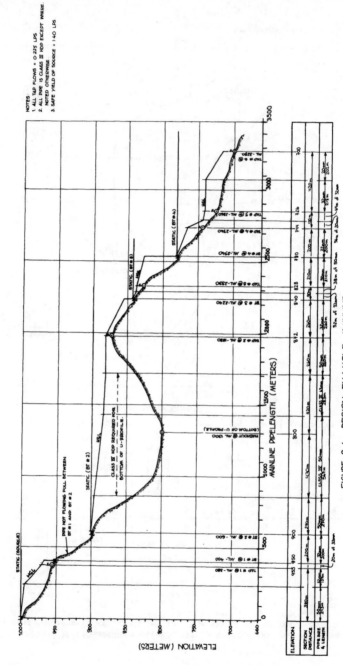

FIGURE 8.4 DESIGN EXAMPLE: MAINLINE

From the break-pressure tank to the source is 100 meters of elevation. It would be possible to use Class IV in this section, but it actually is less expensive to install another break-pressure tank and use Class III pipe. Thus, another break-pressure tank will be required 60 meters lower than the source. This would put it just downstream from Tap #1 (for the sake of convenience, let's locate the break-pressure tank 5 meters lower than the tap, which would place it at ML-400). This will be break-pressure tank #1 (BT #1), and the next one downstream will be break-pressure tank #2 (BT #2).

A third break-pressure tank must be 60 meters lower than BT #2, which puts it at an elevation of 840m, between Taps #2 and #3.

The next break-pressure tank (BT #4) must be 60 meters lower than BT #3, which puts it at an elevation of 780m, between Taps #3 and #4.

From BT #4, there is 80 meters of vertical distance to the last tap, which would require either another break-pressure tank or Class IV pipe. In this case, it is rather likely that 20mm HDP pipe will be used to reach the last tap, and such pipe is provided only in Class IV. So for the time being, the design will proceed assuming that no break-pressure tank will be required (this will have to be specially checked once the total design is completed, however).

So the four break-pressure tanks have been tentatively located as follows:

> BT #1: ML-400, elev 950m
>
> BT #2: ML-600, elev 900m
>
> BT #3: ML-2240, elev 840m
>
> BT #4: ML-2540, elev 780m

and Class IV pipe: ML-870 (elev 840m) - ML-1720 (elev 840m)

Now, the pipeline will be designed, reach-by-reach, beginning at the source.

First Reach (Source - Tap #1)

Design flow = 1.35 LPS (flow for 6 taps)
Pipelength: 380 - 0 = 380 meters

1000m (elev of HGL @ source)
-955m (elev of Tap #1)
-15m (desired residual head @ Tap #1)
30m DESIRED FRICTIONAL HEADLOSS

$$\frac{\text{desired headloss}}{\text{pipelength}} = 30/380 \times 100\% = 7.89\% \text{ (desired frictional headloss factor)}$$

Consulting the HDP Frictional Headloss Table (at the back of this Handbook) for a flow of 1.35 LPS, it is seen that the headloss factor of 32mm HDP pipe is too high (18.15%) while that of 50mm HDP pipe is too low (2.08%). Thus, a combination of both of these pipe sizes is needed to produce exactly the desired headloss. Calculations* indicate the following lengths are needed:

243m of 50mm HDP @ 2.08% creates 5m of headloss

137m of 32mm HDP @ 18.15% creates 25m of headloss

30m TOTAL HEADLOSS

Elev of HGL @ Tap #1 = 970m

Second Reach (Tap #1 - BT #1)

Design flow = 1.125 LPS (flow for 5 taps)
Pipelength: 400 - 380 = <u>20m</u>

970m   (elev of HGL @ Tap #1)
-950m   (elev of BT #1)
<u>-10m</u>   (desired residual head @ BT #1)
10m   DESIRED FRICTIONAL HEADLOSS

10/20 x 100% = 50% desired frict'l factor

Consulting the Headloss Table, it is seen that no factor is given for this flow for 20mm HDP pipe (because the flow velocity would be too high), therefore there is no choice but to use 32mm HDP pipe:

20m of 32mm HDP @ 12.6% creates 3m of headloss

actual residual head = 17m (acceptable)

BT #1 must be constructed with a globe valve at its discharge, adjusted to allow exactly 1.125 LPS flow. For convenience sake, a gate valve can be installed on the outlet of the tank, permitting the downstream pipeline to be shut down without cutting off the flow for Tap #1.

The HGL is now at the surface level of the water in the tank, at 950m elevation.

Third Reach (BT #1 - BT #2)

Design flow = 1.125 LPS
Pipelength: 600 - 400 = <u>200m</u>

Since there are no tapstands along this reach, there is no reason why the pipe must flow full. Select the smallest size that will allow the design flow through:

---

* see Section 8-6 for combined pipe calculation example

```
 950m    (elev of HGL @ BT #1)
-900m    (elev of BT #2)
   0m    (desired RH @ BT #2)
```
```
  50m    MAXIMUM ALLOWABLE HEADLOSS
```

50/200 x 100% = 25% maximum allowable frict'l factor

32mm HDP is the smallest pipe size that has a frictional factor less than 25%, so this is the pipe size to be used. Since there is no need to maintain pressure in the pipeline, the pipe is allowed to discharge freely into BT #2. Gravity will drain the line faster than it will fill, so it won't flow full.

Fourth Reach   (BT #2 - Tap # 2)

Design flow = 1.125 LPS
Pipelength: 1980 - 600 = 1380m (including 850m of Class IV)

```
 900m    (elev of HGL @ BT #2)
-872m    (elev of Tap #2)
  -7m    (minimum desired RH @ Tap #2)
```
```
  21m    MAXIMUM DESIRED HEADLOSS
```

21/1380 x 100% = 1.52% desired frict'l factor

This reach will require 530m of Class III pipe and 850m of Class IV pipe. Once again, combination pipe sizes are required. Class III 50mm HDP pipe will be used for the entire Class III length:

530m of 50mm HDP @ 1.40% creates 7m of headloss

(therefore only 14m of allowable headloss left)

The proper combination of Class IV pipe is:

```
567m of 50mm HDP @ 2.12% creates  12m of headloss
283m of 63mm HDP @ 0.70% creates   2m of headloss
                                   14m of total headloss
```

Thus, the pipe arrangement for the entire reach is:

```
270m of Class III 50mm HDP pipe
567m of Class IV 50mm HDP pipe
283m of Class IV 63mm HDP pipe
260m of Class III 50mm HDP pipe
```

Elev of HGL @ Tap #2 = 879m

A washout is located at the bottom of the U-profile, since it is a major low point in the system, and there is no reservoir tank to allow sedimentation to occur. The presence of a washout does not affect the hydraulic profile of the system (except when the washout is opened.).

Fifth Reach   (Tap #2 - BT #3)

Design flow = 0.90 LPS   (flow for 4 taps)
Pipelength: 2240 - 1980 = 260m

879m	(elev of HGL @ Tap #2)
-840m	(Elev of BT #3)
-10m	(desired RH at BT #3)
29m	DESIRED HEADLOSS

29/260 x 100% = 11.2% desired frict'l factor

The only pipe size which gives a close frictional factor is 32mm HDP:

260m of 32mm HDP @ 8.9% creates 23m of headloss

actual residual head = 16m (acceptable)

BT #3 must have a globe valve at its discharge so that the exact desired flow of 0.9 LPS comes through. A gate valve may be installed on the outlet to cut off downstream flow without effecting the upstream taps.

elev of HGL @ BT #3 = 840m

Sixth Reach   (Tap #3 - BT #3)

Design flow: 0.90 LPS
Pipelength: 2330 - 2240 = 90m

840m	(elev of HGL @ BT #3)
-828m	(elev of Tap #3)
-7m	(minimum allowable RH @ Tap #3)
5m	MAXIMUM ALLOWABLE HEADLOSS

5/90 x 100% = 5.56% Maximum allowable frict'l factor

For this flow, 50mm HDP pipe must be used:

90m of 50mm HDP @ 0.99% creates 1 meter of headloss

actual residual head = 11m (acceptable)

elev of HGL @ Tap #3 = 839m

Seventh Reach   (Tap #3 - BT #4)

Design flow: 0.675 LPS (flow for 3 taps)
Pipelength: 2540 - 2330 = 210m

839m	(elev of HGL @ Tap #3)
-780m	(elev of BT #4)
-10m	(desired RH @ BT #4)
49m	DESIRED HEADLOSS

49/210 x 100% = 23.33% desired frict'l factor

Again there is no choice but to use 32mm HDP:

210m of 32mm HDP @ 5.3% creates 11m of headloss

actual residual head = 48m (acceptable)

This residual head is getting close to the maximum allowable limit of 56 meters. High residual heads increase wear and tear on control valves, reducing their lifetimes and requiring more frequent replacement.

elev of HGL @ BT #4 = 780m

Eighth Reach (BT #4 - Tap #4)

Design flow: 0.675 LPS
Pipelength: 2740 - 2540 = 200m

780m   (elev of HGL @ BT #4)
-744m   (elev of Tap #4)
-15m   (desired RH @ Tap #4)
21m   DESIRED HEADLOSS

21/200 x 100% = 10.5% desired frictional factor

Again, there is no choice but for 32mm HDP:

200m of 32mm HDP @ 5.3% creates 11m of headloss

actual residual head = 25m (acceptable)

elev of HGL @ Tap #4 = 769m

Ninth Reach   (Tap #4 - Tap #5)

Desired flow: 0.45 LPS
Pipelength: 2860 - 2740 = 120m

769m   (elev of HGL @ Tap #4)
-726m   (elev of Tap #5)
-15m   (desired RH @ Tap #5)
28m   DESIRED HEADLOSS

28/120 x 100% = 23.33% desired frict'l factor

A combination of 32mm HDP and 20mm HDP pipe sizes are used:

67m of 20mm HDP @ 40% creates 27m of headloss
53m of 32mm HDP @ 2.56% creates 1m of headloss

actual residual head - 15m (perfect!)

elev of HGL @ Tap #5 = 741m

<u>Tenth Reach</u>   (Tap #5 - Tap #6)

Design flow: 0.225 LPS
Pipelength: 3280 - 2860 = <u>420m</u>

741m   (elev of HGL @ Tap #5)
-700m   (elev of Tap #5)
 -15m   (desired RH @ Tap #6)

26m   DESIRED HEADLOSS

26/420 x 100% = 6.2% desired frictional factor

A combination of 32mm HDP and 20mm HDP is needed:

218m of 32mm HDP @ 0.78% creates 2m of headloss
202m of 20mm HDP @ 12.0% creates 24m of headloss

actual residual head = 15m (perfect!)

In this last reach, it can be seen on the profile that the final 16m of 32mm HDP pipe will be exposed to a static pressure greater than 60m of head. However, the maximum static pressure on this pipe would only be about 66m of head, which is a tolerable amount. However, the designer may also use Class IV 32mm HDP for some or all of this reach, or install another break-pressure tank. If he is not sure, the designer should consult with the LDD regional engineer.

<u>Final Check</u>

Once the designer has tentatively completed selecting pipe sizes, he must go back over the design, checking that at no point the pressures under static conditions are excessive. When this is done, he inks in the final HGL and tank locations, then gets the design approved by the LDD regional engineer.

8.4 DESIGN EXAMPLE: Branchline

Figure 8-5 is an example profile of a branchline with two taps (not related to the design example of Figure 8-4). In this example, the mainline has already been designed, so that the residual head of the branchpoint is known, as is the static level.

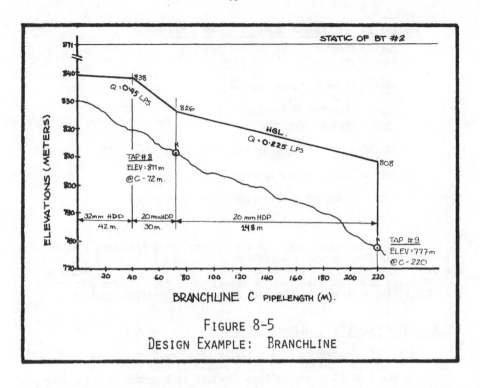

STATIC OF BT #2

BRANCHLINE C PIPELENGTH (M).

FIGURE 8-5
DESIGN EXAMPLE: BRANCHLINE

Branchline "C", First Reach (B'point - Tap #8)

Design flow: 0.45 LPS   (flow for 2 taps)
Pipelength: 72 - 0 = 72 meters

839m   (elev of HGL @ b'point)
-811m   (elev of Tap #8)
-15m   (desired RH @ Tap #8)

13m   DESIRED HEADLOSS

13/72 x 100% = 18.1% desired frict'l factor

A combination of 32mm HDP and 20mm HDP pipes is needed:

42m of 32mm HDP @ 2.56% creates 1m of headloss
30m of 20mm HDP @ 40% creates 12m of headloss

actual residual head = 15m (perfect')

elev of HGL = 826m

Branchline "C", Second Reach (Tap #8 - Tap #9)

Design flow: 0.225 LPS
Pipelength: 220 - 72 = <u>148m</u>

826m   (elev of HGL @ Tap #8)
-777m   (elev of Tap #9)
<u>-15m</u>   (desired Rh @ Tap #9)
34m   DESIRED HEADLOSS

34/148 x 100% = 23.0% desired frict'l factor

The only possible choice is 20mm HDP:

148m of 20mm HDP @ 12% creates 18m of headloss

actual residual head = 31m (acceptable)

The final pressure check for static conditions indicates that no pressures exceed the pressure ratings of the pipes. If there was such a point, then either break-pressure tank #2 (on the mainline) would have to be moved down (and thus require re-designing the mainline once more) or installing a break-pressure tank along the branchline itself

8.5 DESIGN EXAMPLE: Collection Lines

It is not uncommon to have a system which must combine several small sources to obtain a useful safe yield flow. In such cases, it is easiest to bring the individual sourcelines together at a common collection or sedimentation tank. This tank, of course, acts as a break-pressure point and the HGL would have to be plotted as such. If the sources were at different elevations, there would be no problem of hydraulic interference between the sources.

However, it is not always possible to install such a break-pressure point. In such cases, the sourcelines are joined together directly to the mainline, as shown in Figure 8-6 below:

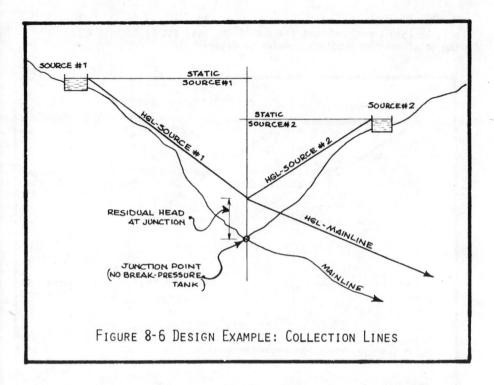

FIGURE 8-6 DESIGN EXAMPLE: COLLECTION LINES

With this type of junction, if the sources are at different elevations then it is possible that the pressure from one will interfere with the flow from the other.

The principle of properly joining the sources at a common point is to realize that the flow from each source will be such that there will be only one possible residual head at the junction. Thus it is necessary to design the sourcelin^s in such a way that they all meet at a common residual head at the junction.

Procedure: Plot the HGL from a single source to the junction. Then select the other pipe sizes of the other sources so that, for the desired flow out of each source, the HGLs all intercept the HGL of the first source; that is, they all have an equal residual head. From that point, continue plotting the HGL for the mainline using the total flows.

8.6 DESIGN EXAMPLE: Combination Pipe Sizes

When designing a pipeline section, there may be no single pipe size available that gives the desired frictional headloss factor. In that case, a combination of pipe sizes is used: one pipe which is "too small" and one which is "too large". The lengths of each pipe must be long enough so that the sum of the headloss of each is equal to the total desired headloss. Refer to Figure 8-7:

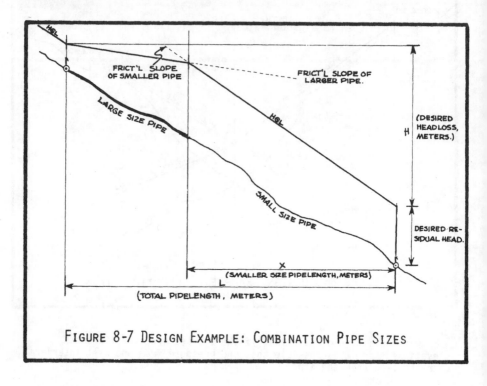

FIGURE 8-7 DESIGN EXAMPLE: COMBINATION PIPE SIZES

Since the total pipelength, design flow, and desired headloss are all known, the lengths of the two pipe sizes can be determined by the following equation:

$$X = \frac{100H - (Fl \times L)}{Fs - Fl}$$

Where: H = desired headloss (m)
L = total pipelength (m)
X = small-size pipelength (m)
Fl = frict'l factor, large pipe (%)
Fs = frict'l factor, small pipe (%)

When the length of the smaller-sized pipe is calculated, it is then subtracted from the total pipelength to determine the length of the larger-sized pipe. See Technical Appendix C for the derivation of the above formula.

8.7 DESIGN EXAMPLE: Excessive Residual Head

There may be points in a system where the residual head at a discharge point is excessively high (ie- greater than 56 meters).   This can particularly happen to tapstands located in positions such as shown in Figure 8-8:

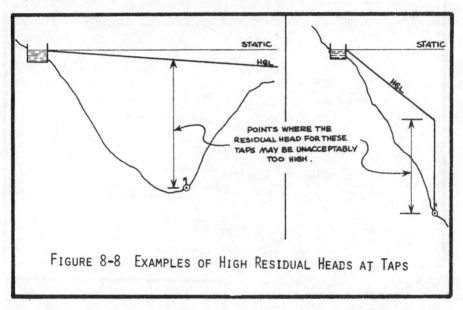

FIGURE 8-8   EXAMPLES OF HIGH RESIDUAL HEADS AT TAPS

For such cases, it is possible to install a device which creates high frictional losses in only a short length of pipeline. This sort of frictional diffuser can be easily manufactured in the field, using HDP pipe and fittings. A design for this is shown on the next page.

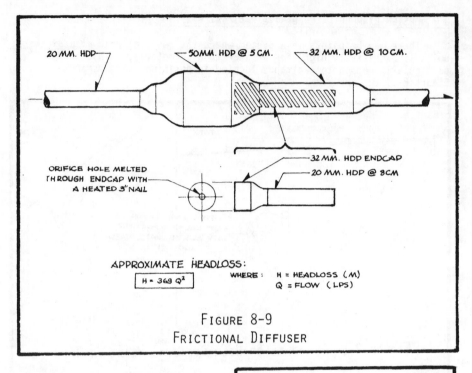

APPROXIMATE HEADLOSS:

$$H = 369 \, Q^2$$

WHERE: H = HEADLOSS (M)
Q = FLOW (LPS)

FIGURE 8-9
FRICTIONAL DIFFUSER

The orifice in the endcap is made using a hot 3" nail to melt a hole. For a flow of 0.225 LPS, this diffuser will create approximately 18 meters of headloss. Adding more holes <u>decreases</u> the headloss; if the headloss of a single diffuser is not enough, add a second one. The pipe section must be of Class IV HDP if the diffuser will be subjected to a static pressure greater than 60 meters of head.

The diffuser is installed just upstream of the tapstand, as shown in Figure 8-10:

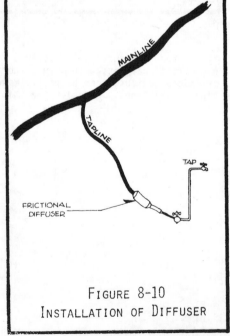

FIGURE 8-10
INSTALLATION OF DIFFUSER

Refer to Technical Appendix D for details on calculating the headlosses through an orifice, for designing similar frictional diffusers.

8.8 TABULATED PROCEDURE

Figure 8-11 shows a tabulated format procedure developed by LDD to organize the design of a pipeline. The format shown helps to keep the different numbers from becoming confused, and allows precise planning of the pipeline in each reach.

However, this procedure is not fool-proof. It is still necessary to plot the resulting HGLs on the graph profile, to determine that pressures and residual heads are within allowable limits at all points in the reach.

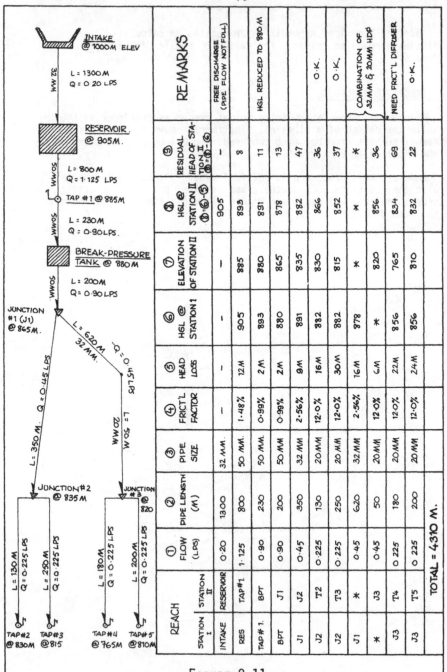

REACH		① FLOW (LPS)	② PIPE LENGTH (M)	③ PIPE SIZE	④ FRICT'L FACTOR	⑤ HEAD LOSS	⑥ HGL @ STATION 1	⑦ ELEVATION OF STATION II	⑧ HGL @ STATION II ⑧=⑥-⑤	⑨ RESIDUAL HEAD OF STATION II ⑨=⑦-⑥	REMARKS
STATION I	STATION II										
INTAKE	RESERVOIR	0.20	1300	32 MM.	-	-	-	-	905	-	FREE DISCHARGE (PIPE FLOW NOT FOLL)
RES	TAP#1	1.125	800	50 MM.	1.48%	12M	905	885	893	8	
TAP#1.	BPT	0.90	230	50 MM.	0.99%	2M	893	880	891	11	HGL REDUCED TO 880 M
BPT	J1	0.90	200	50 MM	0.99%	2M	880	865	878	13	
J1	J2	0.45	350	32 MM	2.56%	9M	891	835	882	47	
J2	T2	0.225	130	20MM	12.0%	16M	882	830	866	36	O.K.
J2	T3	0.225	250	20 MM	12.0%	30M	882	815	852	37	O.K.
J1	*	0.45	620	32 MM	2.56%	16M	878	*	*	*	COMBINATION OF 32 MM & 20MM HDP
*	J3	0.45	50	20MM	12.0%	6M	*	820	856	36	COMBINATION OF 32 MM & 20MM HDP
J3	T4	0.225	180	20MM	12.0%	22M	856	765	834	69	NEED FRICT'L DIFFUSER
J3	T5	0.225	200	20 MM	12.0%	24M	856	810	832	22	O.K.

TOTAL = 4310 M.

FIGURE 8-11
TABULATED DESIGN EXAMPLE

9. SYSTEM DESIGN & ESTIMATES

9.1 INTRODUCTION

Once the profile has been plotted and the final pipeline sizing has been approved, the designer enters the next phase of planning the project: the extensive designing of the system components (such as intakes, reservoir tank, break-pressure tanks, tapstands, etc) and preparing the detailed estimates of material, labor, and money that will be required to implement the project.

In the past, most CWS projects in Nepal have been surveyed, designed, and constructed by the same person. This allowed for a fairly informal manner of designing a system, since the actual construction overseer was intimately familiar with the thoughts of the designer! Detailed plans were not so necessary, as long as he kept the rough design notes and calculations that he had made.

However, there is now an increasing trend in Nepal towards turning over the completed project design to a fresh person who will be the one who oversees its construction. In these cases, the overseer cannot get by with just an estimate sheet and a few cryptic notes in an unfamiliar format. Designers are now required to be more professional, and their designs more detailed, so that a person unfamiliar with the project can take over with minimal loss of information. Unless the designer specifically details just how he intended the system to be constructed, the overseer cannot be expected to build the system according to the designer's materials and cost estimate.

Because of the knowledge and experience that is building up, LDD will soon be able to create standardized designs for most components of a system. Such standardized designs will detail plan specifications, material requirements, labor estimates, etc, and will greatly reduce the task of the designer. However, certain components of the system, such as intakes, will always have to be "custom-designed" for each individual system. Therefore, the designer is still required to develop a clear, professional technique for passing his ideas along to the overseer.

9.2 DESIGN TECHNIQUE

It is the designer's responsibility to prepare a complete record of his designs for the system, which can be given to the overseer. Such a record must include drawings, calculations, and estimates for each individual component of the system. With such records, the overseer is able to compare actual construction requirements against the estimates, and modify accordingly. If some unexpected problems come up during construction, the overseer can judge exactly what new materials he will require to overcome them.

A small exercise book or notebook, of the type commonly used by students, is perhaps the best way of keeping all project notes and calculations contained in one place. The designer should divide the notebook into sections, each section devoted exclusively to a single component of the system. The final section is for totaling up all the materials, labor, and costs.

The contents of each notebook section should contain the information listed in the following discussions.

9.3   PIPELINE SECTION

Sub-divided into mainline, branchlines, taplines, etc. A record of all GI and HDP pipe sizes and lengths; all fittings (tees, elbows, reducers, unions, etc). Washouts and airvalves. Control valves and valveboxes. A rough key plan of the pipeline. Trenchline calculations (volume & labor of excavation). Required tools. See Figure 9-1 for a sample estimate.

9.4   INTAKE SECTION

Sketches of each source area, showing locations of structures. Rough design drawings of each structure (such as intake, collection tank, etc). Construction calculations (volumes of excavation, sand, cement, gravel, stone, brick, slate, etc). Labor (skilled/unskilled). Specific diagram of pipes and valves (with size and lengths). Roofing details. Required tools. Special instructions. If the intake works are particularly complex, a separate blueprint should be prepared. See Figure 9-2.

9.5   SEDIMENTATION TANK SECTION

Only required if there is a sedimentation tank. Design flow, detention time, capacity calculations. Rough design plan. Calculations (excavation, materials, labor). Specific details of pipes and fittings. Roofing details. Required tools. Special instructions. If very big or complex, prepare blueprints.

From	To	Pipe	Fittings
ML-0	ML-540	Class III 63mm HDP (540m)	{63mm tee (Tap 1) {63mm tee (Tap 2)
ML-540	ML-800	Class III 50mm HDP (260m)	63 x 50mm reducer
ML-800	ML-808	1½" GI (8m)	{1½" x 50mm GI/HDP flange set {1½" x 50mm GI/HDP flange set
ML-808	ML-1000	Class III 50mm HDP (192m)	{50mm tee (b'point A) {50mm tee (airvalve #1)
ML-1000	ML-1670	Class III 32mm HDP (670m)	{50 x 32mm reducer {32mm tee (Tap 3) {32mm tee (Tap 4)
A-0 A-200	A-200 A-430	Class III 32mm HDP (200m) Class IV 20mm HDP (230m)	50 x 32mm reducer (b'point A) {32 x 20mm reducer {20mm tee (Tap 5)

FIGURE 9-1
EXAMPLE PIPELINE ESTIMATES

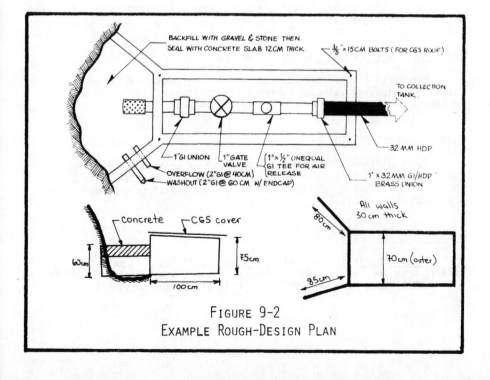

FIGURE 9-2
EXAMPLE ROUGH-DESIGN PLAN

9.6 BREAK-PRESSURE TANK SECTION

Sub-section for each design of break-pressure tank in the system (ie- masonry, HDP, float-valve, etc). Each sub-section should include estimates for the individual design, and for the total number of such designs. Basic drawing of each type. Construction calculations (excavations, materials, labor). Specific arrangements of pipes and fittings. Roofing details. Required tools. Special instructions. See Figure 9-3.

9.7 RESERVOIR TANK SECTION

This is the most important section of the design notebook, since no other single component will consume so much material and labor. Careful drawings of the design are required (wall dimensions, floor construction, pipe arrangements, roofing, etc). Construction calculations (excavation, materials, labor). Required tools. Special instructions. A separate blueprint should be prepared. For an example design and estimate, refer to Chapter 14.8

9.8 TAPSTAND SECTION

As with break-pressure tanks, a sub-section for each different tapstand design. Estimates for each individual design, and for the total number of such designs. Drawings of each type of tapstand. Volumes of cement, sand, gravel, brick, stone, slate. Labor (skilled and unskilled). Pipe sizes, lengths, and fittings. Required tools. Drainage details. See Figure 9-4.

9.9 SPECIAL COMPONENT SECTION

For special components of the system: suspended crossings, gully crossings, pipeline valveboxes, frictional diffusers, etc. For each of these, detailed drawings and estimates are required.

9.10 TOOL LIST SECTION

Every different type of tool that must be supplied (ie- brought out to the field site) for working on the system; quantity of each tool. Refer to the REFERENCE TABLE III at the end of this handbook for a recommended tool list.

9.11 TOTAL ESTIMATES

Total materials: Sub-divided into two lists: all materials locally provided (sand, stone, slate, etc) and all materials brought in (provided by government and UNICEF). Unit price, and total unit cost.

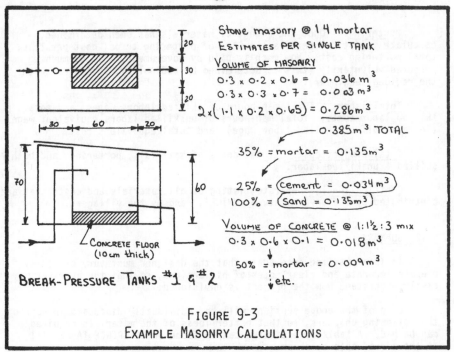

Stone masonry @ 1:4 mortar

ESTIMATES PER SINGLE TANK

VOLUME OF MASONRY

$$0.3 \times 0.2 \times 0.6 = 0.036 \, m^3$$
$$0.3 \times 0.3 \times 0.7 = 0.063 \, m^3$$
$$2 \times (1.1 \times 0.2 \times 0.65) = \underline{0.286 \, m^3}$$

$$0.385 \, m^3 \text{ TOTAL}$$

$$35\% = \text{mortar} = 0.135 \, m^3$$

$$25\% = \boxed{\text{Cement} = 0.034 \, m^3}$$
$$100\% = \boxed{\text{Sand} = 0.135 \, m^3}$$

VOLUME OF CONCRETE @ $1 : 1\frac{1}{2} : 3$ mix

$$0.3 \times 0.6 \times 0.1 = 0.018 \, m^3$$

$$50\% = \text{mortar} = 0.009 \, m^3$$

etc.

CONCRETE FLOOR (10 cm thick)

BREAK-PRESSURE TANKS #1 & #2

FIGURE 9-3
EXAMPLE MASONRY CALCULATIONS

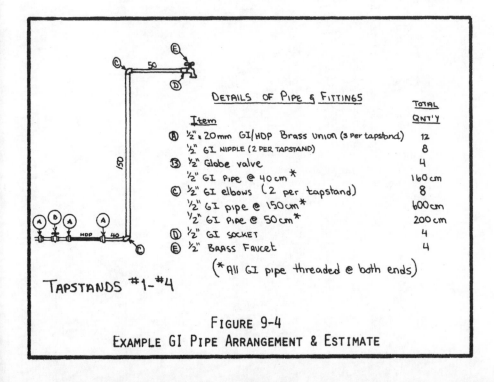

DETAILS OF PIPE & FITTINGS

Item	TOTAL QNT'Y
Ⓐ ½" × 20mm GI/HDP Brass Union (3 per tapstand)	12
½" GI NIPPLE (2 PER TAPSTAND)	8
Ⓑ ½" Globe valve	4
½" GI PIPE @ 40cm *	160 cm
Ⓒ ½" GI elbows (2 per tapstand)	8
½" GI pipe @ 150cm*	600 cm
½" GI PIPE @ 50cm*	200 cm
Ⓓ ½" GI SOCKET	4
Ⓔ ½" BRASS FAUCET	4

(* All GI pipe threaded @ both ends)

TAPSTANDS #1-#4

FIGURE 9-4
EXAMPLE GI PIPE ARRANGEMENT & ESTIMATE

Portering: Once the amount of materials has been determined, calculate logistical details: number of portering trips, cost per trip, total portering cost. How much is paid by government, and how much portered voluntarily (this is determined by LDD policy, so discuss with the regional engineer).

Total labor: Total man-hours of skilled labor, wages, and total skilled labor costs; total man-hours of unskilled labor, equivalent wages (ie- one-half of skilled labor wage), and total equivalent cost.

Total project cost: Total costs of materials, portering, and both skilled & unskilled labor.

Contributions: Separate listing of all materials and costs that are contributed by the government, by UNICEF, and by the villagers.

9.12 SUMMARY

It is emphasized once again that the designer must very carefully prepare accurate and clear notes of his designs, so that the overseer may easily understand how the project is envisioned.

Each of the above sections will be individually discussed in some of the following chapters, so that better ideas of the materials required can be had. A table of estimates can be found in REFERENCE TABLE VIII at the end of this handbook.

10. PIPELINE CONSTRUCTION

10.1 INTRODUCTION

No other phase of a CWS project is likely to consume so much of the labor, or run into more difficulties, than the construction of the pipeline. Difficult terrain, all too common in the rugged countryside of Nepal, can prolong this phase far beyond what would resonably be expected which drains away village enthusiasm, which in turn prolongs the work even more. Motivating the villagers is a major aspect of the overseer's job.

It is important, therefore, that the pipeline work be done properly the first time. To have to locate some internal blockage that is the result of carelessness, or to have to rejoin pipe already buried, or to have to redig the trenchline because of erosion problems which could have been foreseen, are all discouraging tasks.

Although the above problems are not completely avoidable, they can be minimized. This chapter shall deal with the proper technical procedures for constructing the pipeline, and will also discuss some typical problems that experienced CWS overseers in Nepal have been confronted with, and how they overcame such difficulties.

10.2 PROJECT ORGANIZATION

In most projects, especially where the water system is keenly needed, the villagers are quick to organize themselves into a work force, and to divide up responsibility and work among themselves. It is not necessary for the overseer to involve himself with the bookkeeping/ timekeeping records (except for skilled labor), for the villagers can do this better themselves. The division of responsibility and work likewise is best decided by them, for they will do it according to their own established social customs and procedures. The results may not necessarily appear to be equitable to the overseer (especially if he is a non-Nepali), but the important matter is that all the villagers are content and in agreement with the decisions.

The point where the overseer should exert his influence is in planning the overall construction schedule: which sections of the project will be started first, or saved until later.

Experienced overseers in Nepal have made certain observations and recommendations:

The role of the overseer should be that of a technical consultant, assisting the villagers in the system construction. During the first few days of work, one or more village individuals will emerge as natural foremen, quick to understand the needs of the overseer and able to influence and direct the village laborers as required Within a few days, these foremen will be fully capable of directing the routine trench digging, allowing the overseer to initiate construction of masonry works, etc.

There will be high <u>initial enthusiasm</u> of the workers for the first few days or weeks of digging. The work force during this time will never be bigger, nor will the villagers ever work so hard. It is a good time to tackle the most difficult portions of the trenchline. Try to avoid anything which will slow down the work rate (such as lack of materials, or scheduling work just before major holidays, etc).

<u>Laying the pipe</u> as continuously as possible is best. With time and rainfall, open trenches will fill in, requiring them to be cleaned out again before laying the pipe. Digging the trenchline one coil-length at a time is good, laying the pipe down and then immediately burying it. A steady rate of completing the pipeline keeps the enthusiasm high.

The <u>division of work</u> will usually mandate that each villager, or household, or ward, is responsible for digging a certain length of mainline, as well as all of their own particular branchline or taplines. If possible, get the entire village to dig the mainline first, before having the individual sections of pipeline dug.

From the very beginning, <u>establish standards and procedures</u> that must be followed. Getting the trenchline consistantly dug to the proper depth is easiest if the overseer insists on it being so before putting down any pipe in it. Once this routine is established, and firmly maintained, there will be less problems later on.

<u>Communicating with the villagers</u> is very important. The overseer must explain not only <u>what</u> needs to be done, but also <u>why</u> it must be so. Once the villagers see the reasons, they are far more motivated to do the job properly, since it is in their best interests to do so It is not enough that a few village leaders alone know, or even that the foremen know; the typical, average worker on the system must also know. For a non-Nepali overseer, there is a considerable language and cultural barrier which must be overcome, but the effort is worthwhile. As an aid to this, refer to Figure 10-1, presented in both English and Nepali.

10.3 TRENCH WORK

The proper depth of the trenchline should be one meter (100 cm) deep. There is no specific width of trench necessary (in practice, the width of the trench will be determined by the size of the digger, approximately 40 cm). The manufacturers of HDP pipe claim that the lifetime of the pipe, when properly joined, buried, and if not subjected to pressures greater than the pressure rating, is 50 years.

When the pipe is buried one meter deep, it is adequately protected against the weight (and sharp hooves) of heavy animals walking over it; it is well below the depth reached by Nepali farm plows (about 10 cm); it is insulated against freezing temperatures; and there is plenty of overburden (cover of dirt) to allow for erosion over the lifetime of the system. This is all discussed in Figure 10-1.

The reason that we must bury the pipe underground is to protect it against the heavy animals which may walk on it, and to prevent the pipe from being damaged or broken. If the pipe is buried properly 1 meter (3 feet) underground, it will stay protected for the next 25 years. If it is not properly buried, then it will soon be broken and no water will reach the tapstands. It is better to bury the pipe properly now, then to have to build a whole new system after just 5 or 10 years.

We will dig and bury the pipeline in lengths of 200 meters at a time. Each worker will be assigned to dig a length of 3 meters (10 feet), which he must dig to the proper depth. There must be no sharp rocks in the trench which can cut the plastic pipe.

When the full length of trench is ready, we will join the new pipe to the old, then put it in the trench and bury it. When burying the pipe, only dirt should be used to completely cover it. No bushes, leaves, or tree branches should be used. Large stones should be put on top of the trench.

The shovels, hammers, and rock-picks provided by the government are not the personal property of any man, but belong to the project. These tools must be brought to work every day. When digging the trenchline, if a large rock is encountered then these tools must be shared. The workers will take turns hammering at the rock until it is removed, and then the tools should be passed along to where another rock must be removed.

कुली खनेर पाइप गाड्नु पर्ने मुख्य कारणहरू यि हुन कि गाइ-वस्तुहरू हिंड्दा पाइप कुल्चिने, बिग्रिने वा भाँचिने सम्भावना हुन्छ । यदि १ मीटर (३ फीट) कुली खनेर पाइप जमीन मुनि गाड्न सकियो भने त्यस पाइपलाई २५ वर्ष सम्म जोगाएर राख्न सकिन्छ । यदि पाइप राम्रोसँग गाडिएको छैन भने चाँडै ने बिग्रिन सक्छ, जस्ले गर्दा धारामा पानी आउँदैन । त्यसकारण ५ वा १० वर्ष पछि पुरै खाने पानी योजना फेरि बनाउनु भन्दा पाइपलाई पहिले ने उचित तरीकाले गाड्नु राम्रो हुन्छ ।

हामीहरू एक पटकमा २०० मीटर लामो पाइप गाड्छौं । प्रत्येक व्यक्तिले ३ मीटर (१० फीट) लामो कुली खन्नु पर्छ, अनि कुली चाहिनेजति गहिरो हुन पर्छ । कुली भन्दा चुच्ची परेको ढुङ्गा त्यसे भाड्नु हुँदैन किनभने पाइप (प्लास्टिकको) काटिने सम्भावना हुन्छ ।

जहिले कुली पूरा खनेर तयार हुन्छ, अनि हामीहरू न्यौ पाइप पुरानो पाइपमा जोडेर कुलीमा गाडि दिन्छौं । पाइप पुर्दा पहिले माटोले मात्र पुर्नु पर्छ । फ्रारपात वा रुखको हाँगाहरू हालेर पाइप कहिल्यै पनि पुर्नु हुँदैन । पाइप माटोले पुरिसकेपछि मात्र ठुला ठुला ढुङ्गाहरू माथिबाट राख्न सकिन्छ ।

सरकारले दिएको साबेल, घन र ढुङ्गा खन्ने पिक, योजनाका सामानहरू हुन्, कुनै पनि मानिसले आफ्नै सम्पत्ति हो भनेर भन्ठान्नु हुँदैन । यि खन्ने सामानहरू दिन दिन कामगर्न आउँदा लिएर आउनु पर्छ । कुली भन्दा ठुलो ढुङ्गा फिक्नु प-यो भने त्यसबेला खन्ने सामान जस्लेमनि माँग्न सक्छ । ठुलो ढुङ्गा न फिकेसम्म खन्ने मानिसहरूले आली पाली गरी ढुङ्गामा घन खन्नु पर्छ, अनि त्यस पछि अरु ठुलो ढुङ्गाहरू फिक्नु पर्ने ठाउँमा यि औजारहरू पठाइदिनु पर्छ ।

FIGURE 10-1

The pipeline should ideally follow the same route that the original survey was conducted along. However, it is not unusual to have to make detours due to impassable rock areas, land erosions, or because of an original survey along an impractical route. When such re-routing is necessary, the overseer must re-survey the new section to determine how it will affect the HGL of the system, and to see whether additional pipe is necessary.

The pipeline should be kept as far away from erodible points as possible: landslide areas, gullies, streams or riverbanks, etc. When passing through a terrace, keep the trenchline "inside" (as close to the back of the terrace as possible), and when cutting down the faces of terraces, run the trenchline diagonally across the face (refer to Figure 10-2). Motor roads should be crossed perpendicularly and the trench dug as deep as possible up to 150 cm.

Due to hard, rocky ground along some sections, it will not be possible to always get the trench 100 cm deep. The overseer should try to learn what sort of traffic can be expected to walk over the pipeline (human, animal, farming, etc), how vulnerable the section will be to erosion, and from this information he should decide if the soil cover will be adequate. If not, it will be necessary to substitute GI pipe along that section. Ideally, the surveyor has already determined all the places where GI pipe will be needed, but practically speaking there will be sections, not visible from a surface walkover, where additional GI pipe will be needed.

When crossing landslides, gullies, and/or streams, a suspended pipeline may be necessary. Refer to Section 10.11 and Technical Appendix E for further discussion of these special problems.

Experience advises digging the trenchline in sections equal to the length of the coil of pipe to be buried in it. Each worker is assigned a three-meter length of the trench to dig to the proper depth (a villager can typically dig this length in soft, easy soil in one day, or two days if the ground is harder). Pick-axes and crowbars that are provided by the government are not individually owned by the villagers, but should be moved up and down along the trenchline to be used where needed.

The trenchline should be free of all sharp rocks which can cut into the HDP pipe (after the pipe is laid it tends to contract, which can force it to kink around sharp stones). When the entire section is dug, it should be inspected along its full length by the overseer before he allows the pipe to be uncoiled and laid.

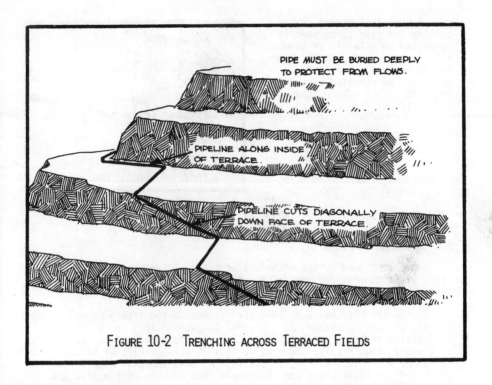

FIGURE 10-2 TRENCHING ACROSS TERRACED FIELDS

PIPE MUST BE BURIED DEEPLY TO PROTECT FROM FLOWS.

PIPELINE ALONG INSIDE OF TERRACE.

PIPELINE CUTS DIAGONALLY DOWN FACE OF TERRACE.

10.4 PIPE LAYING

The HDP pipe is supplied in coils of 25-300 meters in length, depending upon the size and class. The HDP pipe must be uncoiled carefully, otherwise kinks will form which crimp the pipe, as shown in Figure 10-3. Crimped pipe must not be used, since it has been considerably weakened at the crimped point. Such sections should be cut out about 10 cm on either side of the crimp, and the pipe ends rejoined.

FIGURE 10-3
KINKING PIPE BY
IMPROPER UNCOILING

A practical manner of un-
coiling the pipe is to have it
supported by a length of bamboo,
and slowly unwound, as is shown
in Figure 10-4. Larger
coils can be unrolled along
the side of the trench, then
carefully put into position.

FIGURE 10-4 RECOMMENDED
METHOD OF UNCOILING PIPE

10.5 HDP PIPE JOINING

HDP is joined by the technique of butt-welding: using a heated
steel plate to melt the ends of the pipe, which are then pressed together and allowed to cool. This is discussed in detail below:

Once the pipe has been laid out (either in the trench or next
to it), it must be checked for internal blockage   This can be done
by covering the pipe end by mouth and blowing forcefully into it.
If the air flows freely, there is no total blockage. Partial blockages
can occur with dirt, stones, or sticks that have ended up deep inside
the pipe*. A small stone can be dropped into one end of the pipe and
"walked" through the whole length. Its tumbling passage is easily
heard,and therefore can be used to locate blockages. Refer to
Section 10.12 for techniques to minimize such blockages.

When the pipe has been checked and cleared of blockages, it is
prepared for joining as follows:

1)   The pipe ends are cut perpendicular with a hacksaw and
leveled off with a flat file. A pocketknife is then used to trim the
rough plastic filings off. The prepared pipe ends should be clean
and smooth, and when the two ends are mated together, there should be
no gaps of more than one milltmeter.

2)   The pipe-joining crew should make a practice attempt before
actually using the heating plate, so that they are familiar with the
motions necessary to make that specific joint. When making the actual
joint, one person must be positioned to report progress on the under-
side of the pipe as it is being melted. A pocket mirror can help too.

---

* the most common internal blockages are caused by the wooden plugs that
  some HDP manufacturers use to seal the ends of the pipes. These plugs
  sometimes get forced into the pipe.

3)   The temperature of the heating plate is crucial, 220°C on both sides of the plate. To determine this, a white Thermo-Cnrom crayon is used to make a small mark on the hot plate. This mark should turn from white to brown in just two seconds. A hotter plate will turn the mark brown much faster, and a colder plate will take longer (or not change the color at all). A too-hot plate will only melt the plastic it touches, without heating deeply into the pipe which is necessary for the homogeneous, solid fusion of the two pipe ends. A plate that is too cool will also fail to melt enough plastic. Both types of joints will be imperfect and brittle, easily cracked or snapped apart.

4)   When the heating plate is at the proper temperature, it is slipped into a Teflon envelope (which prevents the melted plastic from sticking to the heating plate). The plate is then held between the pipe ends, which are firmly pressed against it. When the pipe is properly heated, there will be a lip of melted plastic around the perimeter of the pipe ends. This lip should be equal and even all the way around.

5)   The pipe ends are separated from the heating plate, which is removed out of the way, and then are carefully brought together. Contact must be even and balanced, and done exactly right the first time: once the melted ends touch, they cannot be taken apart and realigned. The pipe ends should be pressed together firmly but not excessively hard, until the joint has cooled down to where it can be touched by hand, without hurting. It should then be laid on the ground carefully and not moved or disturbed for several minutes more.

6)   The joint is tested by flexing it vigorously and examining it visually. A proper joint is as strong as the rest of the pipe, and cannot be cracked or broken apart. A weak, meek flexing of the pipe serves no purpose. If a weak joint is passed over and buried, it can easily be cracked apart by the earth and water pressures acting on the pipeline once it is in service. It is much easier to re-join the pipe before it is buried, so test it strongly!

7)   When the joint has been successfully tested, the pipe is fully laid in the trench and stretched out. One person can actually walk on top of the pipe, flattening in down into the trench and visually examining to see that no projecting stones will damage the pipe once it is buried.

10.6 BACKFILLING

Backfilling the trench should be done as soon as the pipe has been laid, to minimize exposure to sun and curious villagers, both of which are detrimental to the pipe. Ideally, the backfill should be screened and compacted in 10 cm layers, but practically speaking this is difficult to get the villagers to do. The chief concerns of backfilling should be to prevent any organic materials (such as leaves, sticks, bushes, etc) from being used, and prevent rocks and stones from being dumped directly on the pipeline (after the pipe has been covered with about 50 cm, it is allowable to use rocks in the backfill). Because the backfill will tend to settle, the dirt should be mounded up over the trenchline to compensate, as in Figure 10-5.

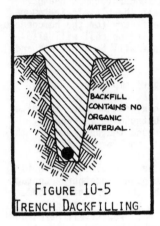

BACKFILL CONTAINS NO ORGANIC MATERIAL.

FIGURE 10-5
TRENCH BACKFILLING

The pipeline should be fully buried except for a three-meter section at each joint. This joint section should only be about half-buried until the pipeline has been filled with water and allowed to stand at full static pressure for 24 hours. This makes it very easy to locate leaking joints, since water will have seeped up to the surface within that time. Once all joints have been tested, they can be fully buried.

Road crossing. When the trench under a road is 120 cm deep or more, it can be backfilled normally except that the backfill should be compacted regularly as it is added, with all large rocks and stones removed.

When the trench is between 100-120 cm deep, the pipe should be laid on a bed of sand, covered with a further 30 cm of sand and then backfilled as above.

When the trench is less than 100 cm deep, the pipe should be bedded on sand, and further covered by 20 cm more of sand. On this, a reinforced-concrete (RCC) slab 10 cm thick should be poured. Once the slab has hardened, backfilling procedes as above. Refer to Chapter 19.12 for details of RCC slabs. Figure 10-6 illustrates backfilling across a road.

Shallow trench and embankments: Along some sections it will not be possible to get the pipeline buried deeply (if at all). If such sections are of HDP pipe, then special earthwork is required for adequate protection of the pipe. Refer to Figure 10-7

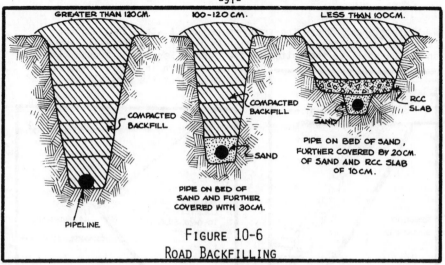

FIGURE 10-6
ROAD BACKFILLING

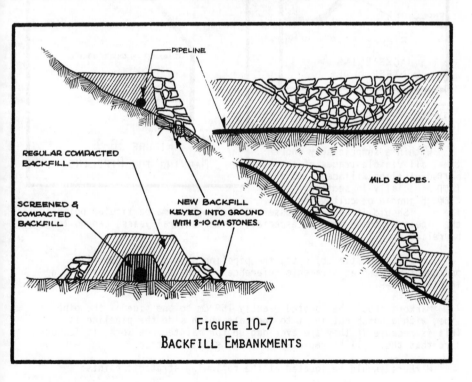

FIGURE 10-7
BACKFILL EMBANKMENTS

Steep slopes: Where the trench cuts down a steep incline, the backfill is vulnerable to easy erosion by rainfall, which will tend to wash all backfill to the bottom of the slope. Facing the trench with stone, as shown in Figure 10-8, will help to protect the backfill.

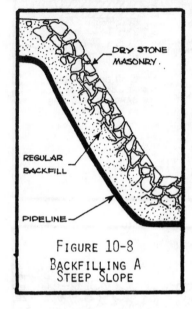

FIGURE 10-8
BACKFILLING A
STEEP SLOPE

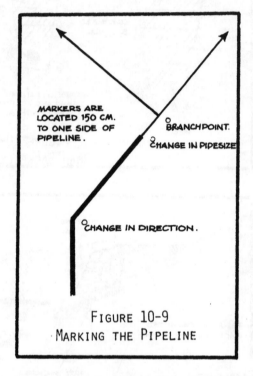

FIGURE 10-9
MARKING THE PIPELINE

10.7 MARKING THE PIPELINE

Within a surprisingly short time, all visible traces of the buried pipeline will cease to exist, especially in sections through jungle or cultivated fields. Should it become necessary to relocate some particular point in the pipeline, human memory, especially after several years, can no longer be relied upon.

To aid relocation efforts, the pipeline should be marked with permanent markers at strategic reference points, similar to that shown in Figure 10-9.

Markers should be located exactly 150 cm to one side of the pipeline, with a notch cut in it to indicate which side the pipeline is. This is because if they are ever dug up for maintenance work, it is not sure that they will be replaced in their exact position.

Markers should be located at the following strategic points:

- at all branchpoints;
- at all reducers (changes of pipe sizes);
- changes in pipeline direction;
- every 200 meters in open terrain, 50 meters in jungle.

A record of each marker should be kept, a copy with the villagers and a copy for the LDD project file.

10.8 REJOINING BURIED PIPE

In special circumstances, it will become necessary to dig up a section of the pipeline to either repair a bad joint or to locate a blockage. At such times, it becomes a difficult task to rejoin the pipe ends. The larger the pipe, the more difficult the job.

There is no easy way of doing this. It requires a lot of excavation to create enough room for the joining crew to work. A standard excavated area is shown in Figure 10-10. The exact dimensions of the area depend upon the size of the pipe being worked on.

The fundamental procedure is to dig up several meters along one pipe end, so that there is a bit of slack. The two pipe ends are cut to a separation of about 30 cm. A new pipe section of about 40 cm is welded onto one pipe end. When it has cooled down and been properly tested, the pipe is flexed and joined to the other end. If this joint fails, there is still enough extra pipe so that by carefully cutting out the bad joint, another joint can be made.

Once the pipe is successfully re-joined, it is flattened down into the trench as deeply as possible and partial-ly reburied until the joints have been tested under 24 hours of static pressure.

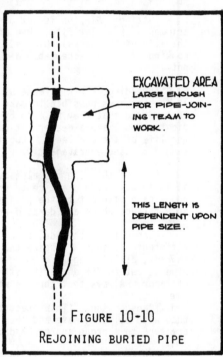

EXCAVATED AREA
LARGE ENOUGH
FOR PIPE-JOIN-
ING TEAM TO
WORK.

THIS LENGTH IS
DEPENDENT UPON
PIPE SIZE.

FIGURE 10-10
REJOINING BURIED PIPE

10.9 FIELD-CONSTRUCTED HDP FITTINGS

Although most HDP fittings are normally available, sometimes out at the project site the overseer may run out of one particular type of fitting. In such cases, it is possible to make the same fitting by using pieces of HDP pipe. Such locally produced fittings, if properly made, are as strong as the regular pipeline.

The "Technical Training Manual #3", published by LDD/UNICEF/SATA in Section 2.4.4 gives excellent diagrams on how to produce elbows, bends, tees, angled branchpoints, and reducers out of HDP pipe.

10.10 GALVANIZED IRON (GI) PIPE

Galvanized iron (GI) pipe is primarily used in the various tanks and tapstands of the system. However, it can be used in the pipeline along sections which will be subjected to excessively high pressures or where proper burial of an HDP pipeline would not be possible.

The GI pipe sizes used for CWS projects in Nepal are 1/2", 1", 1-1/2", 2", and 3" (size refers to inner diameter). The pipe is supplied in lengths up to 6 meters long.

Cutting: GI pipe is cut using a hacksaw, and the rough edges are trimmed with a flat file. Use of oil during the cutting will help prolong the life of the hacksaw blades. If machine oil is not available, then cooking oil is an acceptable alternative. Even water is better than nothing.

Threading: This is done using adjustable pipethreaders. Although it is sometimes possible to make the threads with a single cut, it is recommended that they be made by a series of shallow cuts, adjusting the die teeth to make a deeper cut each time. This technique will prolong the life of the die teeth. Lubricating oil is absolutely necessary and should be used extravagantly.

Even if the pipe has already been cut and threaded in a workshop, it is an advisable practice to bring pipethreaders, extra die teeth, and a pipe vise out to the project site, since inevitably there will be some threads which are damaged and must be cut anew.

When cutting threads, check for a proper fit using several different fittings. Despite the "standardization" of pipe sizes and threads, all fittings are not created equal, and if the entire lot of pipe is cut to fit a misfit fitting, then there will be much repetition of labor. Always test threads with at least three different fittings.

Transporting: To protect threads during transporting, coat them with oil or grease and then screw on a fitting. Exposed threads are sure to corrode and/or be damaged.

Caulking: When a fitting is screwed onto GI pipe, it is necessary to use some method of making the threaded connection watertight, especially if the joint will be under high pressure. Although caulking compounds and pipe dope are useful, it is just as effective to wrap the threads heavily with thin string (such as kite string or thread), and to screw on the fitting tightly.

Caution: When using a pipewrench to tighten fittings, care must be taken not to screw it on so tightly that the fitting is split open! It is not necessary to screw the fitting on as tightly as humanly possible. It is the caulking which makes the connection watertight, not brute strength.

10.11 SPECIAL PROBLEMS

Along certain sections of the pipeline, it is sometimes unavoidable to run through undesirable terrain such as across landslides, over gullies or streams, etc. Where such crossings are short (less than 6 meters), there is usually little technical difficulty. The use of GI pipe, suitably anchored, will usually suffice.

However, for longer spans, where alternate routing of the pipeline is not possible, it may be necessary to use a suspended crossing over the unstable area. Refer to Technical Appendix E for discussion of these crossings.

Landslides: Generally, there is no choice with a landslide area but to use a suspended crossing. The anchor points of the crossing must be on stable ground, and the suspended pipeline must be high enough to avoid being struck by sliding or falling debris.

Gully crossings: Gullies are eroded paths, usually sharp-banked, created (and enlarged) by run-off of rainwater. They are typically dry in clear weather, but may be semi-permanent streams during the monsoon season.

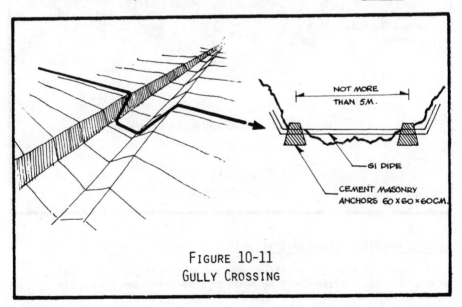

NOT MORE THAN 5M.

GI PIPE

CEMENT MASONRY ANCHORS 60 X 60 X 60CM.

FIGURE 10-11
GULLY CROSSING

Discussion with the villagers will give an idea how extensive the run-off is. Narrow, deep gullies can be crossed by a span of GI pipe above the bottom of the gully, clear of the maximum flood level and anchored in the banks of the gully (similar to the crossing shown in Figure 10-12). Broader gullies should be crossed by GI pipe buried as best as possible, and anchored down using drystone masonry or gabions,as shown in Figure 10-11. Refer to Technical Appendix H for information on gabions.

Stream crossings: Narrow streams can be crossed similarly to narrow gullies, but additional attention must be paid to ensuring that the banks of the stream directly below the crossing point will remain stable. Building dry-stone masonry embankments or gabions (refer to Technical Appendix H) is recommended. Larger or wider streams will require a suspended crossing. In all cases, the height of the pipeline must be sufficient enough to prevent it from being struck by debris floating down the stream, especially at the maximum flood levels. Figure 11-12 illustrates:

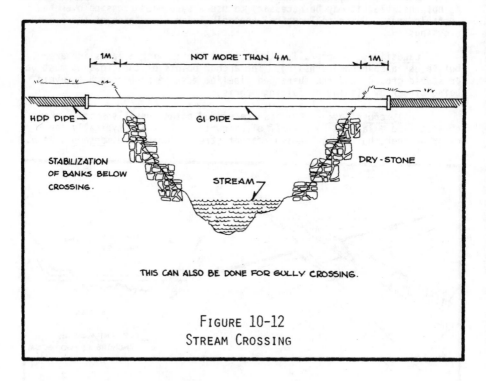

FIGURE 10-12
STREAM CROSSING

10.12   IMPORTANT CONSIDERATIONS

Construction of the pipeline requires more than just technical expertise. The overseer must be aware of human problems frequently encountered in the villages of Nepal.

Children should be considered to be compulsive saboteurs of the system. Although they do not do so deliberately, their curiosity leads to much damage and repetition of work. Open pipe ends, exposed pipeline, fresh masonry all will attract attention, with frustrating results.

Adult villagers, especially strangers passing through, will also be curious about the system and can cause some damage. Exposed fittings can get stolen, and sometimes sections of the pipeline itself are cut out, to be carried off elsewhere.

Heavy animals such as cows and water buffalos can crush or crimp the HDP pipe if they happen to step directly on it. Open trenchlines, expecially along a cowpath, pose a serious danger to these animals, since they can easily stumble into it and break a limb (some animals have even broken their necks and died, resulting in a serious loss for some family).

Some manufacturers of HDP use green (freshly-cut) wooden plugs to seal the pipe mouths of the coils. With the passage of time, these plugs will dry out and shrink and become loose. They can either fall out, or fall into the pipe. If the coil is not tested, these plugs will quickly swell up with water once the pipeline is in service, creating a very tight blockage, not suspected until the water is turned on. At such times, searching a pipeline that is several hundred meters long for a single wooden plug just 10 cm long is a very unhappy task!

The prevention of these problems is not absolute, but the overseer can take some practical steps to minimize their occurence. He should make the villagers understand the difficulties of repairing a damaged or plugged pipeline, and obtain their cooperation in protecting it. The following suggestions are based upon experience in Nepal:

1) NEVER leave a pipe end open and exposed, even for just one night. As soon as the pipe coils have been transported to the village the overseer must seal off every unplugged pipemouth. Simple plugs, cut from branches, can be used for this purpose. They are jammed into the pipemouth, then firmly nailed in place by a few ½" nails, driven directly through the HDP pipe into the plug. The plug is then cut off flush with the end of the pipe, leaving nothing for curious hands to grab and twist. It is especially important to do this for a pipe left overnight in the trenchline. Carrying a small matchbox full of these ½" nails is quite easy and worthwhile.

2) NEVER leave the pipeline exposed in the trench. As soon as it is laid, the pipe should be buried except for a 3-meter stretch at each joint, which should be partially buried until the joint has been tested under static pressure for 24 hours. At the end of the pipeline, where work has ended for the day, the pipe end should be plugged, big rocks should be carefully piled onto the pipe, and the trench filled with thorny bushes.

3) Thorny bushes can be piled around fresh masonry structures, and one or two villagers sleep next to it if necessary, until the cement has set and all pipes are firmly bonded in place.

4) Do not leave control valves exposed. Install them only after the valvebox has been completed and has a secure cover. Removing the valve handle will also discourage tampering.

5) When pipe coils are being transported from the roadhead to the village, and from the village to the worksite, make sure that the villagers do not attempt to re-coil the pipe to a more convenient shape or size.

Many times this has led to excessive amounts of crimping in the pipe, requiring a lot of lost pipe and much labor re-joining it.

11.   INTAKE WORKS

11.1   INTRODUCTION

The first point of flow in a water system is at the source, where water is collected at an intake and funneled into the pipeline. This chapter will discuss various types of intake works, such as spring and stream intakes, dams, source protection, etc.

Due to the uniqueness of a source, there never will be a standard design that can be universally built for every system. However, the intake works should incorporate standard design features, which allow for adequate control of the water, opportunities for sedimentation, and prevention of further contamination. These design features will be the basic theme of this chapter. It is up to the designer to incorporate them into his plan for the intake works. The construction overseer must also be aware of these principles, so that he can make modifications in the event of unforeseen problems.

The fundamental purpose of the intake works is to collect water from one or several points and focus this flow at a single point: the entrance to the pipeline. If the water is dirty, it must be allowed to sit relatively undisturbed for a period of time. The water must be protected as much as possible against further contamination (from rain run-off, grazing animals, and curious villagers). And it must be built in such a way to last for the lifetime of the system.

The number of possible ways to design the intake for a source is infinite, influenced by factors such as available materials, source flow, flood levels, ground stability, topography of the area, etc. This chapter will present several different designs, all of which have been successfully used in the past, and from which the designer can modify and develop a suitable intake for his own system.

The next chapter will present the technical details of sedimentation tanks, which may be required by silty sources such as streams.

11.2   SITE LOCATIONS

Although it is obvious that intake works must be built at the source, there is still flexibility when it comes to locating the actual structures. Water catchments can be built as part of the total intake structure, or can be used as starting points where water is collected and piped down to a nearby site which is more suitable for building settling chambers, sedimentation tanks, or collection tanks.

The most important consideration must be the problems of the monsoon season flooding. Intake structures must be located at points where they will not be threatened directly by flood waters, or indirectly by land erosion over the years. Careful questioning of the villagers must be done to obtain as accurate an idea of monsoon flows as possible.

Intake works should not be built in or near gullies, or at points where unstable ground above them can carry them away in a landslide, or on top of swampy ground (soft dirt saturated by the underground water table).

11.3 EXCAVATION, FOUNDATION, & CONSTRUCTION

The tank site should be staked out with wooden pegs and string, and excavated to a depth of 30 cm (if solid rock is not encountered sooner), and the floor of the excavation leveled off. For a spring intake, the flow should be diverted away from the excavation to keep it as dry as possible. The excavation of catchment walls should be deep enough to cut off underground seepage from the spring (discussed in the next section). The floor of the excavation should be hard and firm. A layer of lean concrete 10 cm in depth is put down, and compacted to ensure proper settling. The cement mortar is put down directly on the concrete, and the masonry footing is laid directly on the mortar. The footing should be 10 cm wider than the wall on each side, and the wall should not be less than 30 cm wide. The height of the footing should be 10 cm. The cement mortar should be of 1:4 cement: sand ratio (refer to Chapter 19 for discussion on cement mortar and masonry). Figure 11-1 illustrates the cross-section of an intake wall.

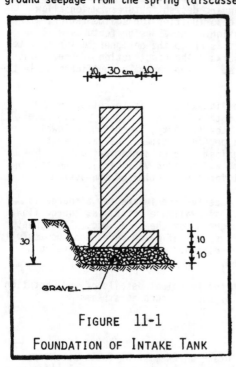

FIGURE 11-1
FOUNDATION OF INTAKE TANK

11.4   CATCHMENT OF FLOW

This is the component where the source flow is captured. In a spring intake, it is typically watertight walls surrounding the source point.

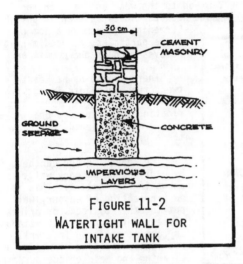

FIGURE 11-2
WATERTIGHT WALL FOR
INTAKE TANK

For a stream intake, it is typically a small pool of water with an intake pipe at its bottom, or a surface channel leading the water to the sedimentation tank.

Where watertight walls must be built to contain the ground flow of a spring, they should penetrate as far into the ground as necessary to cut off seepage flow beneth the intake. Since such foundation trenches will be impossible to keep dry, it is possible to pour a fairly-dry concrete mix into the trenches. As long as the concrete is contained by dirt walls or wooden forms, it cannot be physically washed away and will be alright. Once the concrete has set and hardened slightly, the regular masonry wall can be built on it (refer to Figure 11-2).

For a stream intake, where the depth of the intake point is less than 40 cm, it is necessary to create a basin of water, which will be relatively quiet and therefore allow settlement of the heavier suspended particles (such as sand, leaves, etc). An intake pipe can be located in the bottom of the pool (protected as shown in Figure 11-3). Such an intake should have 40 cm of water depth over it to deter interference from humans and animals, and to protect it from floating debris. An alternative design for such a basin is to dig a channel from the basin to the settling tank. Such a surface channel, unless in extremely sandy or porous soil, does not have to be of masonry, so it is therefore less expensive to built.

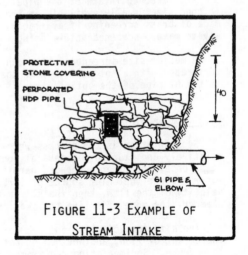

FIGURE 11-3 EXAMPLE OF
STREAM INTAKE

Section 11.12 discusses stream catchments, dams, and basins.

11.5   SCREENING

Suspended particles in the flow can add to the wear and tear on the
HDP pipe, so it is desirable to eliminate such particles as much as possible.
Screening can remove a lot of these particles, and sedimentation removes much of the remainder.

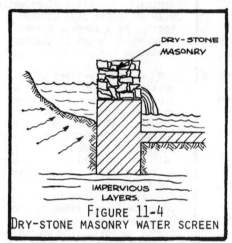

FIGURE 11-4
DRY-STONE MASONRY WATER SCREEN

There should be at least two screening points in the flow: a coarse filter to remove larger floating and suspended debris, and a fine-mesh screened intake over the pipe end.

The coarse screen can be done by a dry-stone masonry wall, as shown in Figure 11-4. This is just a section of masonry wall put together by rocks or bricks closely set together but without any cement mortar. This wall section is easily dismantled for cleaning and maintenance purpose, and then easily reconstructed.

The screened intake of the pipeline should be of a fairly small mesh (a good size usually available in the bazaars is 20 meshes per inch), made of brass screening if available. Chapter 20.2 discusses an easy way to make a screened intake using HDP pipe.

A medium-size screened intake can be made using HDP pipe that is perforated with a hot nail to make dozens of holes. This is then affixed to the GI pipe of the outlet.

11.6   SEDIMENTATION

Sedimentation is the process whereby the water is allowed to sit relatively undisturbed for several hours. In the resulting lack of turbulence, the finer suspended particles sink and settle out of the water. Since the chief source of turbulence in water is due to the velocity of the flow, then the slower the flow through the sedimentation chamber, the more effective the sedimentation process.

The size (capacity) of the chamber depends upon the type of source, the amount of flow, and whether or not there is a reservoir tank further downstream. Sedimentation requirements may be nothing more than a small chamber in the intake structure, or may be a large, separate tank (such tanks are discussed in the next chapter).

Spring sources: These are typically cleaner, and usually such a system will require a reservoir tank. So extensive sedimentation is not usually necessary (unless it is a rather dirty source, or there is no reservoir). A chamber with a dry-stone masonry filter and a screened intake (such as discussed in the proceeding section) is usually sufficient.

Stream sources with reservoirs: A separate sedimentation tank should be built, with a detention time of 15 minutes.

Stream sources without reservoirs: Also require a separate sedimentation tank. A detention time of not less than 60 minutes.

11.7   SERVICE PIPES

Because HDP pipe does not bond to cement mortar or concrete, all pipes set into masonry walls must be of galvanized iron (GI). There are three different service pipes in an intake structure: washouts, overflows, and outlets.

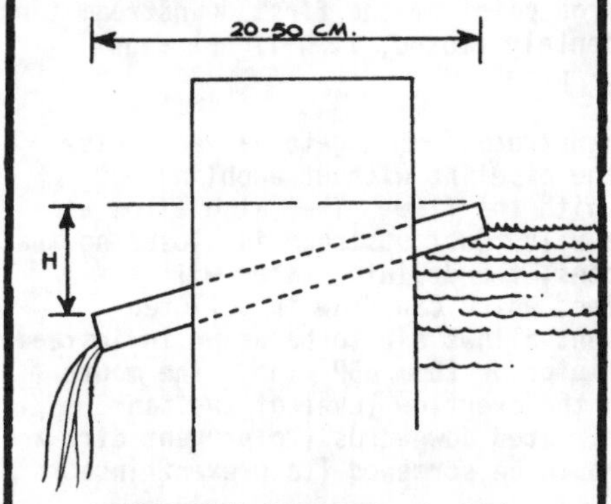

Washouts: allow the draining of the intake so that settled sediments can be washed out, and maintenance work performed. The GI pipe size of the washout should be either 2" or 3". The washouts should be set slightly into the bottom of the chamber, and can be closed with an endcap. Washouts should not be set into masonry walls less than 30 cm wide (to ensure enough bonded strength so that a pipewrench can be used for removing the endcap). Each separate chamber, and the catchment basin, should have its own washout. Water from the washouts must be carried away (by a surface drainage channel) in such a manner that does not cause erosion of the intake foundation.

OVERFLOW CAPACITY (LPS).

GI PIPE SIZE	H=5CM.	H=10CM.
1"	0·62	0·85
1½"	1·4	1·9
2"	2·1	3·0
3"	5·2	7·3

FIGURE 11-5 OVERFLOW DESIGN

Overflows: allow excess water to be safely diverted away from the tank without causing erosion. The size of the overflow must be selected so that it can pass the maximum flood flows during the monsoon season. The typical overflow for small tanks is a short length of GI pipe set into the wall of the tank. Figure 11-5 shows this arrangement, and gives some maximum flows that each size pipe can handle, pitched at 5 cm and 10 cm. Any number of pipes can be used if a single pipe is insufficient. The overflow water must be disposed of in the same manner as the washout flow.

Outlets: The outlet pipe is the starting point of the pipeline.
The size of the outlet can be determined using the information given in
Technical Appendix G, but should not be smaller than the HDP pipe size
for the design at that point. The mouth of the pipe should have a
screened intake. A gate valve is needed, with an air-vent located just
downstream. Figure 11-6 shows the pipe arrangement of a typical tank
outlet.

11.8   CONTROL VALVES & AIR-VENTS

Gate valves should be installed on each outlet pipe, so that the
pipeline can be drained for maintenance purposes.

Globe valves are not necessary when the entire flow of the source
is to be used. A globe valve is needed only when a portion of the source
flow is to be used (as is usually the case with a stream intake). Such
a valve allows only the design flow into the pipeline, and forces the
excess water to overflow and be returned back to the source. This
valve must be located at the discharge point of the first downstream tank,
or at a point where, if it is accidentaly closed, it will not cause
excessive pressures to burst the HDP pipe.

Air-vents are located just downstream from a gate valve. These
serve to allow air to escape from the pipeline without bubbling out
through the intake and interfering with the flow. They also allow air
into the pipeline whenever the gate valve just upstream is closed so that
the pipeline drains (when this happens, the draining water will set
up a suction pressure in the pipeline, which can draw in polluted
groundwater through leaks; an air-vent allows air to be drawn in instead).
An air-vent can be either of ½" GI pipe or 20mm HDP pipe. The mouth
of the air-vent must be higher than the overflow level of the tank.
The end of the air-vent should be directed downwards (to prevent dirt and
dust from settling into it) and should be screened (to prevent insects
from crawling in).

11.9   ROOFING

The roofing on the intake structures must be secure enough to prevent
curious people from interfering with them, and should seal the source
off against any further contamination from surface run-off of rain,
grazing animals, leaves, etc. Accessways are required so that the intake
can be cleaned and repair work performed; an opening to allow a man in
should be at least 60 cm square.

Common roofing schemes in Nepal are:

Slate roofing: constructed by the villagers, if slate is locally
available. Requires a lot of wood for beams and rafters.

CGS roofing: corrugated galvanized steel roofing sheets, nominal
size 3' x 10', effective size 70cm x 320cm. Refer to Technical
Appendix F

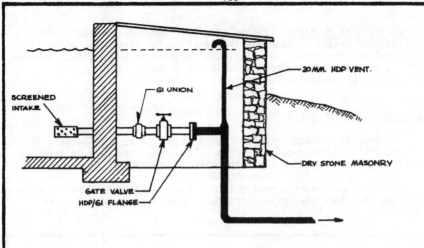

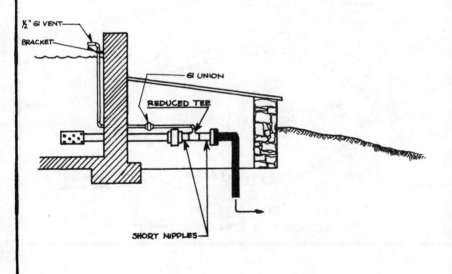

FIGURE 11-6 TYPICAL OUTLET PIPING

Concrete slab roofing: Either of reinforced concrete (RCC) or
reinforced (RF) bricks. These are the ideal roofs, since they will
totally seal off the intake, and last the lifetime of the system. However,
such roofs do require additional materials and costs. Refer to
Chapter 19.13 for technical details.

11.10   PROTECTIVE MEASURES

It is important that, once the source water has been collected, it must
be protected from further contamination. Thus, measures must be taken to
seal off the flow from as much of the external environment as possible.

Surface run-off of rain must not be allowed to flow into the catchment
of springs, therefore the intake structures should be minimally 30 cm

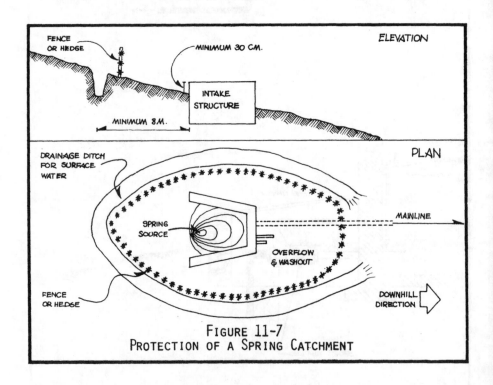

FIGURE 11-7
PROTECTION OF A SPRING CATCHMENT

above ground level. Dirt should be mounded against the tank walls so that
water will be turned away, and the source should have a drainage ditch dug
around its uphill side. This channel should be deep, and can be lined
with dry-stone masonry. Each year, particularly just before the monsoon
season, it should be cleared of accumulated debris.

The catchment of a spring source can be roofed over with a concrete slab, and buried for further protection.

If necessary, retaining walls of gabions or dry-stone masonry should be built to stabilize the land around the intake works, especially if erosion is foreseen to be a major problem over the lifetime of the system.

Re-forestation and planting of grass and bushes directly above spring sources greatly aids in maintaining the flow from the source (vegetation allows surface water to seep into the ground rather than disappear quickly as surface run-off. Such water can add to the yield of the source).

If necessary, fencing should be built around the structures to keep away grazing animals, children, etc. Discuss such measures with the LDD regional engineer.

Figure 11-7   Shows suitable protection for a spring catchment

11.11   MULTIPLE SOURCES

Some systems will actually be supplied by the combined flows from two or more sources (particulary if the sources are low-yield springs). Such multiple sources can be handled in any convenient manner, as determined

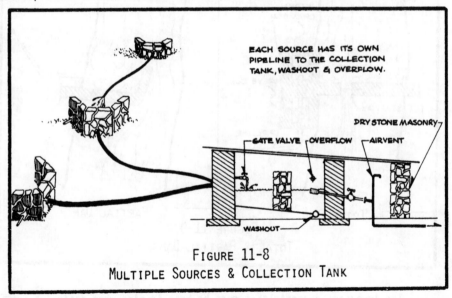

EACH SOURCE HAS ITS OWN PIPELINE TO THE COLLECTION TANK, WASHOUT & OVERFLOW.

DRY STONE MASONRY

GATE VALVE   OVERFLOW   AIRVENT

WASHOUT

FIGURE 11-8
MULTIPLE SOURCES & COLLECTION TANK

by the distances and elevations between the sources. Flow from higher sources can be piped directly into lower sources, or each source may have its own individual pipeline to a single collection tank or

sedimentation tank. Each catchment requires its own washout and overflow
pipes, but a gate valve can be located at the discharge point into the
collection tank. It is not necessary that each catchment have its own
settling chamber, so long as the total flow has the opportunity to settle.

Figure 11-8 shows such a possible arrangement of catchments and
collection tank.

11.12   STREAM CATCHMENTS: Dams and Basins

This section deals with construction of total or partial dams
across streams, to form a sheltered basin of water for a stream intake.
The purpose of the basin is to allow adequate water depth over the
mouth of an intake pipe, and to allow the heavier sediments to settle
out (since turbulent streams carry sand, and even small stones).

Figure 11-9 shows both a total dam, and a partial dam:

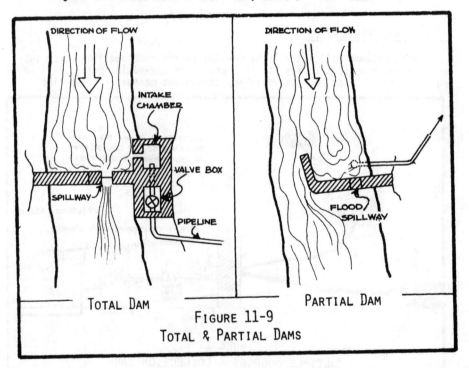

FIGURE 11-9
TOTAL & PARTIAL DAMS

The important concepts that must be kept in mind when designing dams
are as follows:

- when water is backed up to the maximum flood level, it must not
flood the surrounding land;

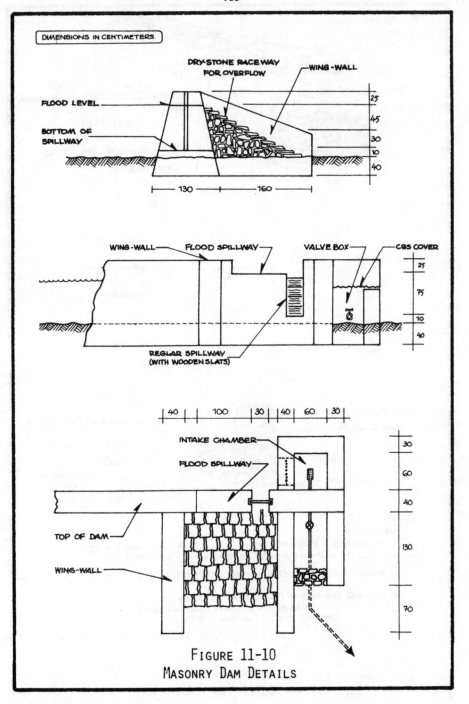

DIMENSIONS IN CENTIMETERS.

FIGURE 11-10
MASONRY DAM DETAILS

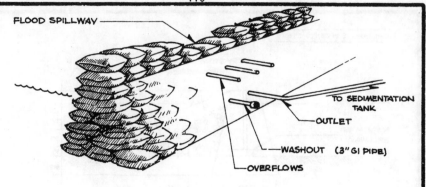

FLOOD SPILLWAY

TO SEDIMENTATION TANK

OUTLET

WASHOUT (3" GI PIPE)

OVERFLOWS

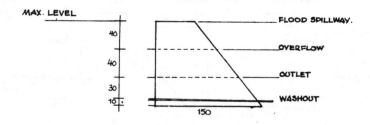

MAX. LEVEL

40

40

30

10

150

FLOOD SPILLWAY.

OVERFLOW

OUTLET

WASHOUT

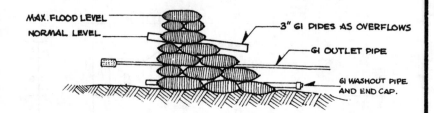

MAX. FLOOD LEVEL

NORMAL LEVEL

3" GI PIPES AS OVERFLOWS

GI OUTLET PIPE

GI WASHOUT PIPE AND END CAP.

NOTES:

1. OVERFLOWS = 3" GI X 150 CM   } MAX FLOW = 15 LPS
   WASHOUTS = 3" GI X 200 CM W/ ENDCAP } FOR EACH.

2. WASHOUTS MUST BE LOCATED DIRECTLY BELOW INTAKE.

3. VOLUME PER BURLAP (JUTE) BAG = 35 LITERS
   { EACH BAG @ 1:6:8 CEMENT·SAND:AGGREGATE.
   { 28 BAGS PER 1·M³ OF DAM.

FIGURE 11-11
BURLAP (JUTE) BAG EMBANKMENT

- excess water (ie- overflow) can be safely handled without causing erosion and collapse of the dam or stream banks;

- a total dam will probably be used as a bridge for human, and possibly animal, traffic across the stream, especially if it is conveniently located.

A dam may be built of cement masonry, or by embankments of concrete-filled burlap (jute) sacks.

Cement masonry dams: A cement masonry dam can only be built when the stream flow is completely diverted away from the fresh masonry. Temporary, diverting dams can be made using sand-filled burlap sacks. Dimensions of a good masonry dam are shown in Figure 11-10. The wooden slates of the spillway are removable, which allows full draining of the basin (which, in turn will carry away much of the accumulated silt in the vicinity of the intake chamber).

Burlap (jute) embankments: An easier type of dam to construct is an embankment of concrete-filled burlap (jute) bags. The bags are filled with a fairly-dry concrete mix (1:6:8 cement:sand:gravel) and sewn shut. They can be placed directly in the water as long as there is no hard current flowing against them (fresh cement bags can have a protective facing of ordinary sand-filled bags in front of them, or a diverting dam can be used to absorb most of the hard currents). The burlap material holds the concrete into position until it has set; the bags will mold themselves tightly together under their own weight, so that they'll interlock solidly. Lengths of 10mm ∅ rebar can be driven vertically through several layers of bags, "spiking" them together. GI pipe can be easily set in place as the bags are being layered. Several washout and overflow pipes (of 3" GI pipe) may be required, depending upon the maximum flood flows of the stream. Washouts should be placed in the vicinity of the intake pipe, so that silt can be washed away whenever the basin is drained. Figure 11-11 shows details of this type of dam.

Spillways: Both type of dams should have emergency spillways. These are low points along the top of the dams which will overflow first with high flooding flows. This overflow will be confined to a special channel, which will carry the excess flows away without causing erosion problems. The spillways should have masonry wing-walls, and a bed of dry-stone masonry to absorb the hard flow currents of the overflowing water. Figure 11-12 presents the overflow capacity of spillways of different depths. For example, a spillway 20 cm deep and 90 cm long can handle an overflow of more than 124 LPS.

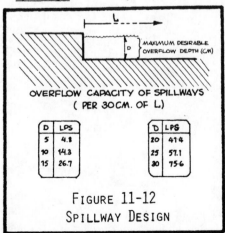

OVERFLOW CAPACITY OF SPILLWAYS
(PER 30 CM. OF L)

D	LPS
5	4.8
10	14.3
15	26.7

D	LPS
20	41.4
25	57.1
30	75.6

FIGURE 11-12
SPILLWAY DESIGN

11.13   EXAMPLE DESIGNS

Figure 11-13 shows different examples of designs and intake structures that have been successfully used for developing stream and spring sources in Nepal.

For futher designs, refer to the "Technical Training Manual No.5" published by LDD/UNICEF/SATA.

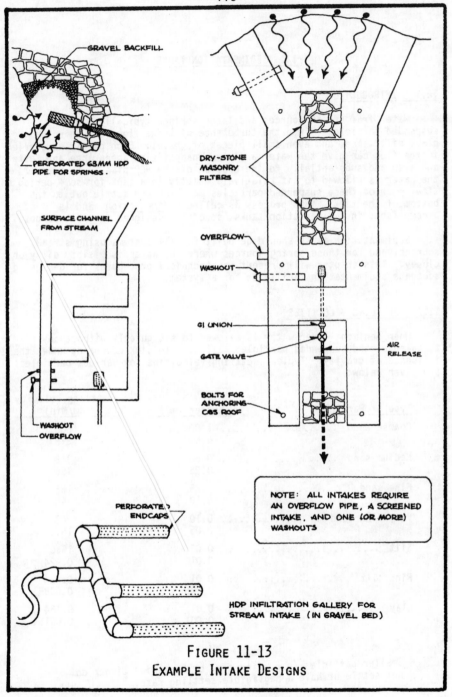

GRAVEL BACKFILL

PERFORATED 63 MM HDP PIPE FOR SPRINGS.

DRY-STONE MASONRY FILTERS

SURFACE CHANNEL FROM STREAM

OVERFLOW

WASHOUT

GI UNION

GATE VALVE

AIR RELEASE

BOLTS FOR ANCHORING CGS ROOF

WASHOUT
OVERFLOW

PERFORATED ENDCAPS

NOTE: ALL INTAKES REQUIRE AN OVERFLOW PIPE, A SCREENED INTAKE, AND ONE (OR MORE) WASHOUTS

HDP INFILTRATION GALLERY FOR STREAM INTAKE (IN GRAVEL BED)

FIGURE 11-13
EXAMPLE INTAKE DESIGNS

12. SEDIMENTATION TANKS

12.1 INTRODUCTION

Water from stream sources and large springs typically contains suspended particles, since the turbulence of large flows can churn up clay, silt, sand, and even small pieces of gravel. Such particles carried in the flow can give the water a dirty, unappetizing appearance and taste, and also add substantially to the erosion of the HDP pipe. If, however, the water is allowed to sit relatively quietly in a tank for some period of time, much of these suspended particles may sink and settle out to the bottom of the tank. This process is called sedimentation, and is accomplished in sedimentation tanks, specially designed for this purpose.

Sedimentation tanks should be built for all systems using stream sources, and for those spring sources where the water is visibly dirty or cloudy. This chapter will present the technical procedures for designing adequate sedimentation facilities for a system.

12.2 SETTLING VELOCITIES

When sediment-laden water is allowed to sit quietly without any turbulence, the suspended particles will tend to sink downwards under the influence of gravity. Typical settling velocities for various particles are given below:

Type of Particle	Diameter (mm)	Settling Velocity (cm/Min)
Coarse sand	1.00	600
	0.50	318
Medium sand	0.50	318
	0.25	156
Fine sand	0.25	156
	0.10	48
Very fine sand	0.10	48
	0.05	15.6
Silt	0.05	15.6
	0.01	0.924
Fine silt	0.01	0.924
	0.005	0.0385
Clay	0.01	0.154
	0.001	0.00154

Smaller particles (e.g. fine clay or bacteria) either do not settle or have a negligible settling rate.

Inlet: The discharge of the flow into the tank should be distributed as evenly as possible across the width of the water path. The depth of discharge should be about halfway between the surface and the floor of the tank, as shown in Figure 12-2. The pipe should be of 1" or 1½" GI, with a perforated length of larger HDP pipe. A globe valve is needed to regulate the flow.

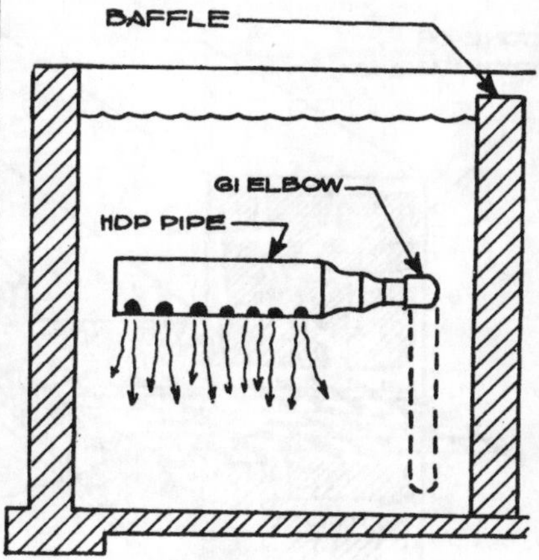

Outlet: The outlet should be designed to collect just the very surface layer of water, from across the full width of the water path. The easiest way to accomplish this is with a collection gutter, as shown in Figure 12-3. The outlet piping should be of GI pipe, according to flow:

FIGURE 12-2
DETAILS OF INLET

GI Size	Flow (LPS)
1"	up to 0.35
1½"	" " 0.85
2"	" " 1.40
3"	greater than 1.40

The outlet should have a gate valve with air-vent.

Washout: The washout should be at least 2" GI pipe with an endcap, set in the bottom of the tank, with suitable drainage for the washout flow.

Overflow: As presented in Figure 11-5.

Flow velocity: The water velocity flowing through the tank should not exceed 0.50 cm/sec. Greater velocity may create turbulent currents which hinder the sedimentation process. The velocity is calculated as follows:

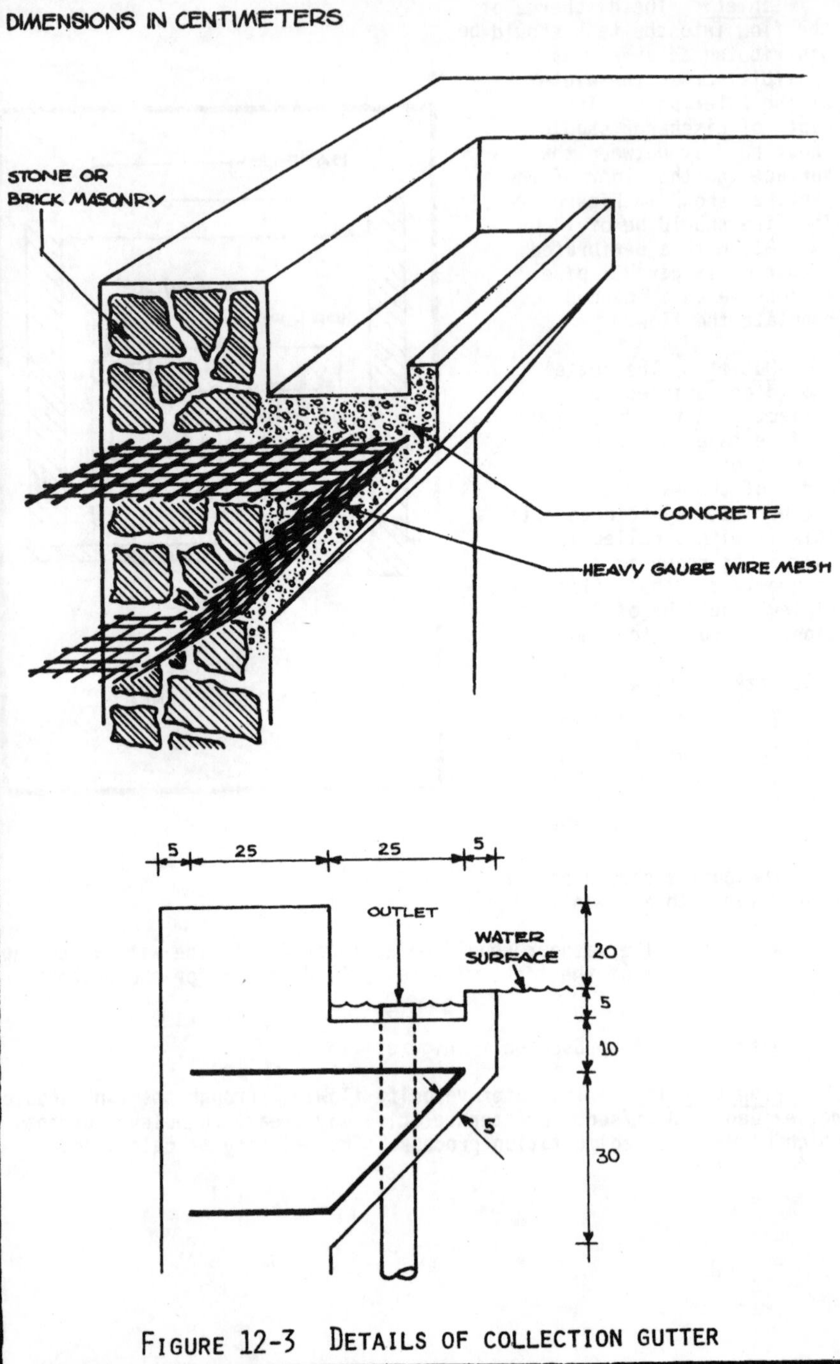
DIMENSIONS IN CENTIMETERS
STONE OR
BRICK MASONRY
CONCRETE
HEAVY GAUGE WIRE MESH
5
25
25
5
OUTLET
WATER
SURFACE
20
5
10
5
30

FIGURE 12-3 DETAILS OF COLLECTION GUTTER

$$V = \frac{1000Q}{WD}$$

<u>where:</u> V = velocity (cm/sec)
Q = flow (LPS)
W = width of water path (cm)
D = depth of water (cm)

Baffles: One or more partitioning walls (baffles) may be used to subdivide the surface of the water so the L/W ratio is improved without increasing the external size of the tank. Baffles should extend the full depth of water, and be of masonry construction.

<u>Excavation, foundation, & walls:</u> The depth of excavation should be enough to half-bury the walls. The floor of the excavation should be level and firm (compacted if necessary). The walls should be built on a masonry footing (as discussed in Chapter 11.3). The walls should be 30 cm thick, of 1:4 cement:sand masonry. The tank floor and plastering is done per specifications in Chapter 19.12 & 19.13.

A <u>recommended design</u> for a sedimentation tank which meets (or exceeds, the above specifications is shown in Figures 12-1, -2, & -3.

13. BREAK-PRESSURE TANKS

13.1 INTRODUCTION

The function of a break-pressure tank is to allow the flow to discharge into the atmosphere, thereby reducing its hydrostatic pressure to zero, and establishing a new static level. Strategic placing of break-pressure tanks can minimize the amount of Class IV and GI pipe which must be used in a system (except where there are U-profiles). In Chapter 8.3, the design example of the mainline included four break-pressure tanks, and discussion was presented about the various strategies to locate them.

It is anticipated that shortly the LDD office will have developed standardized designs for break-pressure tanks, complete with detailed estimate lists. Therefore, this chapter will present just the basic design principles and characteristics of such tanks which have been successfully constructed in Nepal.

13.2 TYPES OF TANKS

Currently, break-pressure tanks can be constructed of cement masonry (with/without float valves) or HDP pipe. Investigation is underway about developing pre-fabricated break-pressure tanks of HDP, GI sheet metal, and ferro-cement.

13.3 MASONRY TANKS

There is no minimum required capacity for a break-pressure tank, as long as water is able to drain from it as fast as it is discharged. The dimensions of the tank are more influenced by the size of the fittings (such as control valves, float valves, etc) which must fit inside of it (and size of the pipewrenches which must be able to swing around inside as well). The tanks can be designed so that they are easily covered by a half-sheet of CGS roofing, or by a small RCC slab, or by slate (if locally available).

Specifications for masonry break-pressure tanks are as follows:

Excavation, Foundation, & Walls: Excavation for a tank should be 30 cm into firm soil, and the floor of the excavation leveled and compacted. A layer of gravel and masonry footing should be built, as specified in Figure 11-1. Minimum height of the wall above ground should be 20 cm; the ground should be pitched away from the tank and have a drainage ditch to divert rain run-off. Drainage provisions must be made for the washout and overflow, and surrounding ground should be stabilized if necessary. Masonry walls should be minimally 20 cm thick (30 cm if there is a GI pipe inbedded in it) of 1:4 cement:sand mortar, plastered accoring to Chapter 19.12.

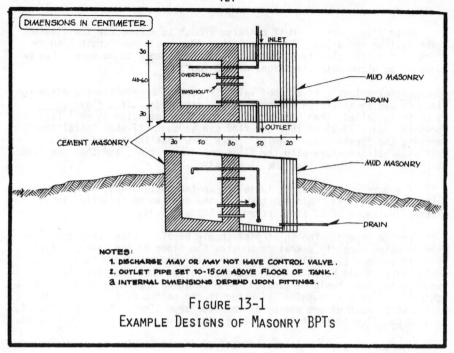

NOTES:
1. DISCHARGE MAY OR MAY NOT HAVE CONTROL VALVE.
2. OUTLET PIPE SET 10-15 CM ABOVE FLOOR OF TANK.
3. INTERNAL DIMENSIONS DEPEND UPON FITTINGS.

FIGURE 13-1
EXAMPLE DESIGNS OF MASONRY BPTs

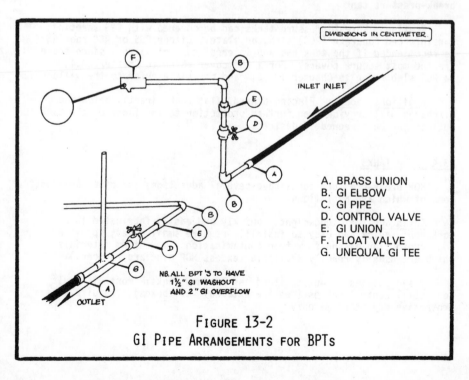

A. BRASS UNION
B. GI ELBOW
C. GI PIPE
D. CONTROL VALVE
E. GI UNION
F. FLOAT VALVE
G. UNEQUAL GI TEE

NB. ALL BPT'S TO HAVE
1½" GI WASHOUT
AND 2" GI OVERFLOW

FIGURE 13-2
GI PIPE ARRANGEMENTS FOR BPTs

Inner dimensions: Must be large enough to accomodate the fittings which will be installed. Minimum width = 40cm; minimum length = 40 cm (80cm if a float valve is to be installed), and depth to be 50cm. Can be adjusted to accomodate dimensions of CGS roofing.

Control valves: If a globe valve is needed to regulate the discharge flow, it can be installed directly on the discharge. If a float-valve is to be installed, then a gate valve should be installed as well (as shown in Figure 13-2) so that the flow can be shut off when installing/ removing the float-valve. NOTE: Make sure that the height of the roof will not interfere with the float-valve operation, and that the tank overflow is set higher than the float-valve.

If a gate valve is to be installed on the outlet pipe, then a valvebox can be built onto the tank, or the gate valve installed in an external valvebox of GI pipe (refer to Chapter 16.8).

Service pipes: The inlet pipe should be of GI pipe, with the discharge flow directed directly downwards towards the floor of the tank (if allowed to spray against the walls, the plaster will soon be eroded away). The outlet pipe should be of GI pipe one size larger than the pipeline it connects to, and should be located 10-15 cm above the floor of the tank (this will create a "cushion" of water in the bottom of the tank, which will absorb much of the energy of the discharge flow). All tanks should have an overflow (refer to Figure 11-5) and also a washout of 1½' GI pipe.

Figure 13-2 gives some specifications of the GI pipe for a masonry break-pressure tank.

Roofing: Break-pressure tanks can be covered with CGS sheeting, a reinforced concrete (RCC) slab, or slate. Either CGS or RCC roofing is recommended if the tank has any internal control valves, since these are the most secure covers. For a CGS cover refer to Chapter 20.4; for an RCC slab refer to Chapter 19.15; and for slate refer to the villagers.

Additional ideas: Placing a hard, flat rock directly below the discharge will provide even further protection to the floor of the tank. Outlets may be screened if desired.

13.4 HDP TANKS

HDP break-pressure tanks have several advantages and disadvantages, some of which are as follows:

Advantages: Lightweight; quickly and easily fabricated in a workshop; quick and easy to install; require small sites; provide good protection of the flow from contamination; made from materials which are usually readily available (excess HDP pipe and reducers).

Disadvantages: Not as sturdy as masonry tanks; more difficult to install control valves (require external valveboxes); require some protective dry-stone masonry.

HDP break-pressure tanks should be installed only where the flow
has been well-screened so that sediments cannot accumulate and clog
the tanks. The "snorkel" of 50mm HDP should have several screens,since
the outermost ones are susceptable to being punctured by children
(refer to chapter 20.2 for ideas on screening HDP pipe). A stone
masonry valve box is needed to protect the snorkel and a drain pipe
and ditch to carry away any overflow.

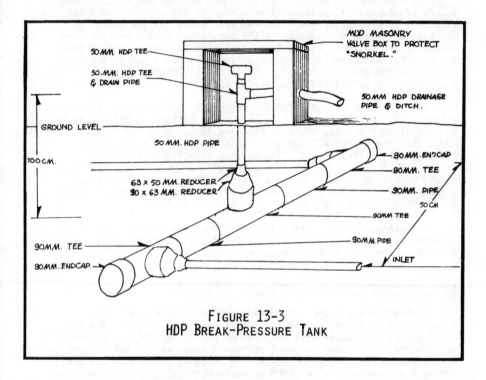

FIGURE 13-3
HDP BREAK-PRESSURE TANK

The rate of flow out of the HDP break-pressure tank will be dependant
upon the head of water acting at the outlet pipe. This head will be
limited by the height of the snorkel overflow tee above the outlet pipe.
Consequently, the HDP break-pressure tank should be at least one meter
below the overflow tee, i.e. about 90cm below ground level.

14. RESERVOIR TANKS

14.1 INTRODUCTION

The construction of the reservoir tank will be the most visible effort of the entire system. It will require the coordinated tasks of dozens of people, ranging from the masons who lay the stone to the assistants who mix cement, to the men, women (and sometimes even children) who collect stones from the fields or porter sand up from the rivers. When completed, the reservoir becomes a public monument of the village and a source of pride to the villagers, especially if the project is considered a successful one.

When it comes to designing the reservoir tank, the most common attitude of the villagers is "the bigger the better!". While this is an understandable idea, there is no point in building any tank so large that the source will never be able to fill it up during the overnight re-filling period. The storage capacity of the reservoir is actually determined by the projected village water needs (as dis- cussed in Chapter 4) and the safe yield of the source. The actual dimensions of the tank are determined by its capacity, the conditions at the site selected, and rules of economical design.

This chapter will present all the procedures and knowledge that is necessary to design and construct practical reservoir tanks. At the end of the chapter is an example design.

14.2 THE NECESSITY FOR A RESERVOIR

Although the village water needs are based upon a minimum re- quirement of 45 liters per person per 24-hour day, in actuality just about all of this water will be demanded during daylight, a period of 10-12 hours. The reservoir tank serves to store water that is provided by the source during low-demand periods (such as overnight) for use during high-demand periods (such as early morning).

A system will require a reservoir when:

- The safe yield of the source will not directly provide 0.225 LPS for each tap;

- The daily water demand is greater than the yield of the source during the daylight hours;

- The pipeline distance from source to village is so far that it is more economical to use a smaller pipe size and build a reservoir tank

14.3   CAPACITY

To determine how large a reservoir tank must be- it is necessary to calculate how much water is demanded at various times during the day, and compare this to how much water is yielded by the source for those same time periods. The difference will either mean that water will be drawn out of the reservoir or will flow into the reservoir.

The maximum size of a tank should not be greater than needed to store the water yielded by the source during the night. It is possible to sometimes design a tank to take advantage of the higher yields during the monsoon season if the dry-season safe yield is not enough.

The daily demand pattern of a typical village would be somewhat similar to either of the schedules below:

Schedule 1

```
6:00 AM - 8:00 AM ......30% of total daily water need
8:00 AM - 4:00 PM ......40% "    "    "    "    "
4:00 PM - 6:00 PM ......30% "    "    "    "    "
6:00 PM - 6:00 AM ......Negligible water demand
```

Schedule 2*

```
 5:00 AM - 7:00 AM ......10% of total daily water need
 7:00 AM -11:00 AM ......25% "    "    "    "    "
11:00 AM - 1:00 PM ......35% "    "    "    "    "
 1:00 PM - 5:00 PM ......20% "    "    "    "    "
 5:00 PM - 7:00 PM ......10% "    "    "    "    "
 7:00 PM - 5:00 PM ......Negligible water demand
```

_____

* This schedule observed by C. Johnson

The first schedule is a general, theoretical pattern that is based upon the traditional Nepali custom of two major meals per day, including pre-meal ritual bathing, cooking, and dish-washing.

The second schedule is based upon direct observation by Johnson of a typical village in Western Nepal, after a water system had been completed for that village. Johnson feels that the other villages he observed generally conformed to that schedule.

In practical applications, use whichever schedule requires the smaller-sized tank, for the villagers will adjust their demand patterns to whatever schedule the tank can provide.

Capacity design example:

The projected population of a village is 400 persons, with no other special water needs. Safe yield of the source is 0.45 LPS, and five tapstands are to be built.

Since the source is not large enough to supply more than two of the tapstands by itself, a reservoir tank is required. Using the two demand schedules, the following water demands are calculated:

TIME PERIODS		SUPPLY	DEMAND	DIFFERENCE	
Schedule 1					
6 AM - 8 AM	(2 hrs, 30%)	3240	5400	-2160	(water withdrawn)
8 AM - 4 PM	(8 hrs, 40%)	12960	7200	+5760	(tank overflows)
4 PM - 6 PM	(2 hrs, 30%)	3240	5400	-2160	(water withdrawn)
			Largest deficiency = 2160 liters		

TIME PERIODS		SUPPLY	DEMAND	DIFFERENCE	
Schedule 2					
5 AM - 7 AM	(2 hrs, 10%)	3240	1800	+1440	(tank overflows)
7 AM - 11 AM	(4 hrs, 25%)	6480	4500	+1980	(" ")
11 AM - 1 PM	(2 hrs, 35%)	3240	6300	-3060	(water withdrawn)
1 PM - 5 PM	(4 hrs, 20%)	6480	3600	+2880	(tank refilling)
5 PM - 7 PM	(2 hrs, 10%)	3240	1800	+1440	(tank overflows)
			Largest deficiency = 3060 liters		

For this example, the required storage capacity is determined by Schedule 1, at 2160 liters. For practical design, consider this 2200 liters (2.2 cubic meters).

Capacity design example:

The projected population of a village is 780 persons, with no other special water needs. Safe yield of the source is 0.45 LPS, and five tapstands are to be built.

Again, a reservior tank is required.

TIME PERIODS		SUPPLY	DEMAND	DIFFERENCE	
Schedule 1					
6 AM - 8 AM	(2 hrs, 30%)	3240	10530	-7290	(water withdrawn)
8 AM - 4 PM	(8 hrs, 40%)	12960	14040	-1080	(" ")
4 PM - 6 PM	(2 hrs, 30%)	3240	10530	-7290	(" ")
			Largest deficiency = 15660 liters		

TIME PERIODS		SUPPLY	DEMAND	DIFFERENCE	
Schedule 2					
5 AM - 7 AM	(2 hrs, 10%)	3240	3510	- 270	(water withdrawn)
7 AM - 11 AM	(4 hrs, 25%)	6480	8775	-2295	(" ")
11 AM - 1 PM	(2 hrs, 35%)	3240	12285	-9045	(" ")
1 PM - 5 PM	(4 hrs, 20%)	6480	7020	- 540	(" ")
5 PM - 7 PM	(2 hrs, 10%)	3240	3510	- 270	(" ")
			Largest deficiency = 12420 liters		

In this example, the required capacity is determined by Schedule 2, at 12420 liters. For practical designing, consider this to be 12500 liters (12.5 cubic meters).

14.4 SHAPE

When the required capacity of the reservoir tank has been calculated, it is then time to begin determining the shape and dimensions of the tank. This is usually a compromise procedure that may have to be repeated two or three times before the optimum design is discovered.

All other factors being equal, the most economical tank shape is circular, then nearly-circular, then square, and then rectangular. For ease of construction, certain shapes are easier than others:

Circular tanks: The most economical shape to use, but not easy to construct, especially for small diameters.

Octagonal (8-sided) tanks: The best shape to use, but not easy to construct for diameters less than 2½ meters (or capacities smaller than 3200 liters).

Hexagonal (6-sided) tanks: Good for tanks between 1700-3200 liters (diameters not less than 2 meters).

Square tanks: This is the traditional shape, and easiest to construct for small capacities (such as mini-tanks, break-pressure tanks, etc).

Rectangular tanks: The least-economical shape, especially as one side becomes much longer than the other. However, due to physical constraints of the site, it may be necessary to use this shape. Keeping it as nearly square-shaped as possible will make a more economical design.

Special note for CGS-roofed tanks: When a square or rectangular tank is to be roofed with CGS, it is easier to slightly adjust the dimensions of the tank so that it is neatly covered by the sheets (such as "5 sheets wide by 1½ sheets long"). This helps to minimize the amount of CGS sheet cutting, which is a relatively difficult task. For the multi-sided tanks this is not so easy to do, but should still be kept in mind.

Figure 14-1 is a table of these various tank shapes, giving the simple mathmatical equations for determining their dimensions once capacity and water depth have been selected.

14.5 WALL DESIGN

The type of walls used in construction of these reservoir tanks are known as "gravity-walls": they resist being overturned (by the hydrostatic water pressure) by virtue of their weight alone. The design of the wall is determined by the material of construction (ie- brick or stone) and the selected water depth.

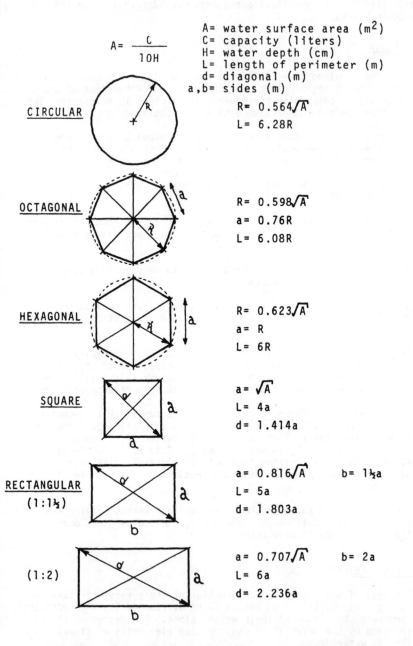

$$A = \frac{C}{10H}$$

A= water surface area (m²)
C= capacity (liters)
H= water depth (cm)
L= length of perimeter (m)
d= diagonal (m)
a,b= sides (m)

CIRCULAR

R= $0.564\sqrt{A}$
L= 6.28R

OCTAGONAL

R= $0.598\sqrt{A}$
a= 0.76R
L= 6.08R

HEXAGONAL

R= $0.623\sqrt{A}$
a= R
L= 6R

SQUARE

a= $\sqrt{A}$
L= 4a
d= 1.414a

RECTANGULAR
(1:1½)

a= $0.816\sqrt{A}$ b= 1½a
L= 5a
d= 1.803a

(1:2)

a= $0.707\sqrt{A}$ b= 2a
L= 6a
d= 2.236a

FIGURE 14-1 SHAPES & DIMENSIONS OF RESERVOIRS

Water depth: Although it is possible to select any depth of water, for the designs presented in this book certain water depths are more economical than others:

     brick masonry: 60, 90, or 105 centimeters depth

     stone masonry: 65, 95, or 115   "   "

These are the water depths that should be first selected and trial designed. Only if the resulting dimensions of the tank cannot be used should other water depths be considered.

Masonry: Stone masonry is generally heavier than brick masonry, and therefore does not require as large a volume to resist the hydrostatic pressures. For the design table of Figure 14-2, the following specific weights were used:

     brick masonry: 2120 kg/m^3

     stone masonry: 2450 kg/m^3

A safety factor against over-turning of 1.5 was used.

External walls: These are the outside walls of the tank. Hydrostatic pressure is exerted on only one side, and they are partially backfilled for additional support.

Partition walls: This is a wall which divides the inside of the tank exactly in half. This allows half of the tank to be drained for maintenance purposes while the other half is still providing some service. In practical use, however, such walls use a tremendous amount of extra material and labor, and their use has never been proven worthwhile in Nepal. Partitioned tanks also must be somewhat larger, to replace the storage capacity displaced by the partitioning wall.

Wall design table: Figure 14-2 allows the quick design of the external and partition (if desired) walls of a reservoir tank. constructed of either brick or stone masonry, for various water depths.

14.6 SERVICE PIPES

The pipe arrangement of the reservoir tank requires some particular attention, especially if the tank is partitioned. A reservoir typically requires an inlet (discharge), outlet, by-pass, overflow, and washout. Refer to Figure 14-3.

Inlet: The inlet can be of 1" GI pipe. Where a free discharge is planned, only a single gate valve is required, but if a controlled discharge is required then a globe valve is also necessary (the globe valve can be located inside the tank, and the villagers warned that it must not be adjusted; the gate valve can be inside the valve box. The actual point of discharge should be on the opposite side of the tank from the outlet, so that maximum opportunity for sedimentation is provided.

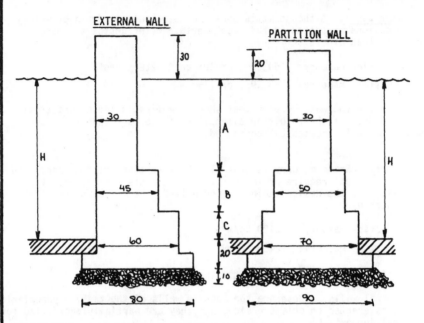

WATER DEPTH H	EXTERNAL WALL stone masonry A B C	brick masonry A B C	PARTITION WALL stone masonry A B C	brick masonry A B C
50	50 - -	50 - -	50 - -	50 - -
55	55 - -	55 - -	55 - -	55 - -
60	60 - -	60 - -	60 - -	60 - -
65	65 - -	50 15 -	65 - -	50 15 -
70	55 15 -	55 15 -	55 15 -	55 15 -
75	60 15 -	60 15 -	60 15 -	60 15 -
80	65 15 -	60 20 -	65 15 -	60 20 -
85	65 20 -	60 25 -	65 20 -	60 25 -
90	65 25 -	60 30 -	65 25 -	55 20 15
95	65 30 -	55 25 15	60 20 15	60 20 15
100	60 25 15	60 25 15	60 25 15	60 20 20
105	65 25 15	60 30 15	60 25 20	60 20 25
110	65 25 20	Not	60 25 25	Not
115	65 30 20	permissible	65 25 25	permissible

Notes: these are gravity-walls with a safety factor of 1.5 against overturning, based upon stone masonry @ 2450 kg/m^3 and brick masonry @ 2120 kg/m^3. All dimensions above in centimeters. Approximate depth of excavation: D= $\frac{1}{2}$H + 30

FIGURE 14-2
WALL DESIGN TABLE

Outlet: For a pipe arrangement similar to that shown in Figure 14-3, the following sizes of GI pipe should be used in the outlet:

GI pipe size	Outlet flow
1"	0.33 LPS
1½"	0.80 LPS
2"	1.30 LPS
3"	3.30 LPS

The outlet should be installed with a gate valve and air-vent (refer to Chapter 11.8).

By-pass: The by-pass line is a direct connection between the inlet and outlet lines, so that when the tank is shut down, at least some of the flow can be diverted into the mainline. A gate valve serves to shut off the by-pass when the tank is in use, and is only open when the flow into the reservoir is cut off for maintenance work. When a by-pass is used, it is important to consider static pressures, since the break-pressure effect of the reservoir has been eliminated.

Overflow: The overflow is sized according to Figure 11-5, but since the reservoir tank will be overflowing frequently, special care must be made to ensure drainage of the overflow water does not cause erosion problems.

Washout: The washout should be of 2" GI pipe, with a gate valve. The floor of the tank should be pitched down to the washout, and the washout pipe imbedded in the bottom of it (refer to Chapter 19.13).

Partitioned tanks: A partitioned tank will require just about complete duplication of control valves, since one sub-tank must be isolated from the system at a time. Figure 14-4 shows the general service pipe arrangements for the necessary cross-connections.

14.7   CONSTRUCTION

This section will present the general steps in construction of a reservoir, listing important considerations of each step.

Site selection: The site selected for the reservoir should be on stable ground which will not be threatened by landslides or erosion.

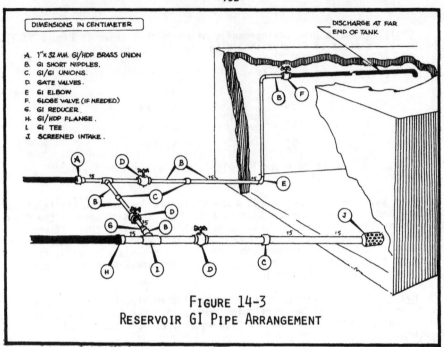

FIGURE 14-3
RESERVOIR GI PIPE ARRANGEMENT

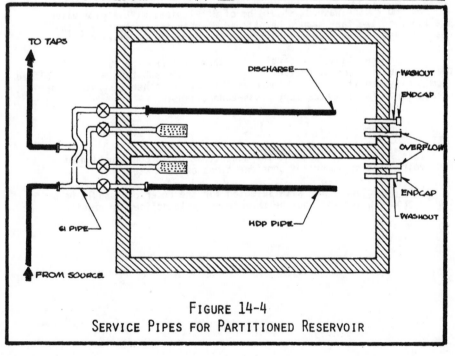

FIGURE 14-4
SERVICE PIPES FOR PARTITIONED RESERVOIR

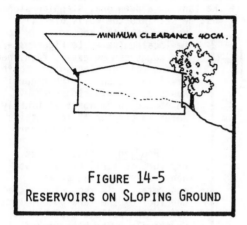

FIGURE 14-5
RESERVOIRS ON SLOPING GROUND

A level ground site is desirable since it will require less excavation, but no site should be used where any wall of the tank will be backfilled too deeply (a minimum of 40 cm of wall must rise above the ground) refer to Figure 14-5. There must be room for stockpiling the construction materials(stone, sand, gravel, etc) and adequate room for the cement-mixing crews to work (for large tanks, the cement-mixing pads can actually be located inside the tank). For a project where many masons will be working, it may be desirable to have two or more mixing pads.

Excavation: The depth of excavation for the tank will depend upon the nature of the soil in the site. Approximate depths of excavation are given in Figure 14-2. In sloping ground, the deepest-buried wall must still rise above the finished ground level by at least 40 cm. Minimum excavation must establish a perfectly level floor, with foundation trenches 30 cm deep for the wall footings. Although gravity-type walls do not require the support of backfill, some excavation is advisable to ensure that the tank is firmly imbedded in the ground, especially if it is on sloping ground. When the excavation is completed, the foundation trenches are staked out (using string and wooden pegs).

Foundations: The foundation trenches should be as wide as the wall footings and 30 cm deep. A bed of gravel or lean concrete 10 cm deep is put down and leveled, then a masonry (or concrete) footing 20 cm high. The regular masonry wall is built up upon this footing. Refer to Figure 14-6.

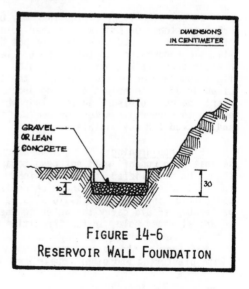

FIGURE 14-6
RESERVOIR WALL FOUNDATION

Wall construction: The masonry walls are of 1:4 cement:sand mortar.
As they are built up, especially if the tank is a deep one, stepping-stones
or foot rungs (made of 3/8" rebar) must be set into the walls directly

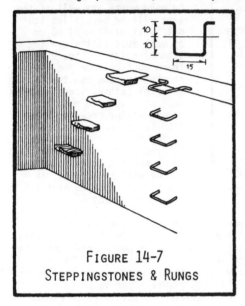

below where the accessway is to
be located (refer to Figure 14-7).
The rungs can be easily fashioned
by the village blacksmith, to the
dimensions shown in the figure.
Rungs or steppingstones should
be spaced 30 cm apart vertically.
Refer to Chapter 19 for details
on cement, mortar, and masonry.

Roofing: Since direct
exposure to sunlight can cause
dehydration of plaster and
concrete, it is recommended that
the roof of the tank be completed
before the walls are plastered
or the floor has been poured.
Having the tank securely locked
will also deter children from
entering it when the plaster
and concrete are still setting.
Chapter 19.14 presents concrete
roof slabs, and Technical Appendix
F discusses other types of roofing.

FIGURE 14-7

STEPPINGSTONES & RUNGS

Plastering: It is recommended that plastering be done before putting
down the floor.   Specifics of plastering are given in Chapter 19.12.

Floor: The floor of the tank may be either of masonry (ie- mortared
brick or stone) or concrete (either reinforced or non-reinforced). A bed
of gravel or crushed stone must be put down, roughly pitched so the floor
will slope downwards to the washout. Technical details of creating
a water-proof tank floor are presented in Chapter 19.13. As soon as the
final concrete or plaster has set, the tank should be filled to a depth
of about 30 cm to help the curing process (a deep depth of water would
exert too much pressure on the floor which the cement would not be strong
enough to support). After two weeks   the tank can be filled completely
and checked for any visible leakage.

Finished grading: The ground around the reservoir should be mounded
so that rain run-off will not head towards the tank. The surrounding land
should be stabilizied against erosion. If there is generally heavy rain
run-off, then suitable drainage channels should be made. The drainage
channel for the overflow should also be carefully constructed, and
perferably should carry the water to where it can be utilized (such as for
an animal water-hole, or for irrigation of a nearby garden).

Maintenance should include a yearly draining and cleaning of the tank.
with plastering and other repair work as necessary.

14.8 DESIGN EXAMPLE

A reservoir tank of 16,000-liter capacity is to be constructed of rubble-stone masonry, with CGS roofing and a non-reinforced concrete floor. This section will present the design calculations and estimates for materials and labor for roofing, masonry, excavation, and floor (excluded are GI service pipes). For specific labor and estimate analysis rates, see REFERENCE TABLE VII at the end of this handbook.

Preliminary calculations:

Water depth selected to be 65 cm   (=0.65m)

Required water surface area = capacity/depth

$$= 16.0m^3/0.65m$$

$$= 24.62m^2$$

Internal dimensions for a square tank = $\sqrt{24.62}$ = 4.96m

$$= 5.0m \times 5.0m$$

The area to be covered by the roof includes the water surface, the top of the tank walls (each 30 cm wide) and a 10cm overhang:

Roofing area = 5.0 + 0.3 + 0.3 + 0.1 + 0.1 = 5.8m x 5.8m

Adjusting these dimensions to accomodate the effective dimensions of a CGS sheet (3.0 x 0.7m):

8 sheets wide = 5.6m

2 sheets long = 6.0m

So the final internal dimensions of the tank are 4.8m x 5.2m (subtracting overhang and walls), which gives a final capacity of 16.22m³ (16,220 liters) which is acceptable.

Wall dimensions: Having selected the water depth, it is possible to select the dimensions of the masonry walls, using Figure 14-2.

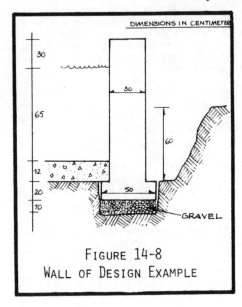

The resulting cross-section of wall and foundation trench are shown in Figure 14-8.

Cross-sect'l areas of:

masonry = 0.42m^2

gravel = 0.05m^2

The final external dimensions of the tank (inclusive of footings) is 5.6m x 6.0m, and excavation dimensions are therefore 7.6m x 8.0m (which allows an extra meter outside of the walls for the masons to work), by 60cm deep.

FIGURE 14-8
WALL OF DESIGN EXAMPLE

Excavations:

volume of main excavation = 7.6 x 8.0 x 0.6 = 36.48m^3
volume of foundation trench excavations:

(5.6 + 5.6 + 6.0 + 6.0) x 0.3 x 0.5 = 3.48m^3

TOTAL VOLUME OF EXCAVATION = 40.0m^3
TOTAL LABOR OF EXCAVATION = 22.0 man-days (unskilled)

Masonry:

total length of masonry walls = 23.2m
cross-sect'l area of walls = 0.42m^2
volume of masonry = 23.2 x 0.42 = 9.74m^3
volume of crushed stone (foundation trenches) = 23.2 x 0.05
therefore TOTAL VOLUME OF CRUSHED STONE = 1.16m^3

Rubble-stone masonry is 65% stone and 35% mortar, and mortar is 100% sand and 25% cement (for 1:4 cement:sand mortar):

Total volume of stone = 0.65 x 9.74 = 6.33m^3
Total volume of mortar = 0.35 x 9.74 = 3.41m^3

Total volume of sand = $3.41m^3$

TOTAL VOLUME OF CEMENT = 0.25 x 3.41 = $0.85m^3$

TOTAL MASON LABOR = 9.74 x 1.4 = 13.64 man-days (skilled)

TOTAL LABOR = 9.74 x 3.2 = 31.17 man-days (unskilled)

Floor slab:

(The floor slab is non-reinforced concrete, 12cm thick of 1:1½:3 cement:sand:gravel mix)

volume of crushed stone foundation = 4.8 x 5.3 x 0.1 = $3.0m^3$

volume of concrete = 4.8 x 5.2 x 0.12 = $3.00m^3$

volume of crushed stone in concrete = 1.0 x 3.0 = $3.0m^3$

TOTAL VOLUME OF CRUSHED STONE = 3.0 + 3.0 = $6.0m^3$

Total volume of sand = 0.5 x 3.0 = $1.5m^3$

TOTAL VOLUME OF CEMENT = 0.33 x 3.0 = $1.0m^3$

TOTAL MASON LABOR = 1.1 x 3.0 = 3.3 man-days (skilled)

TOTAL LABOR = 4.0 x 3.0 = 12.0 man-days (unskilled)

Roofing:

(The roof will require 16 CGS sheets, supported at mid-span by beams (therefore 3 beams required),each beam supported at mid-span by a 1" GI pipe column).

Interior span of tank = 4.8m

Span of each beam = 2.4m

Dimensions of each beam = 5 x 10 x 540 cm

TOTAL VOLUME OF WOOD = 3 x (0.1 x 0.05 x 5.4) = $0.081m^3$

TOTAL CARPENTER LABOR = 0.081 x 18 = 1.46 man-days (skilled)

TOTAL LABOR = 0.081 x 18 = 1.46 man-days (unskilled)

3 pieces 1" GI pipe @ 0.95m

6 pieces 1" GI threaded flanges

20 pieces 3/8" x 5" bolts w/washer & nut

½-kg 2" nails

6 pieces 3/8" rebar @ 0.60m (for anchoring beams to walls)

Plastering:

(Plastering according to specifications of Chapter 19.12, 3 coats @ 1 cm thick)

Plaster area = (4.8 + 4.8 + 5.2 + 5.2) x 0.7 = 14.0m^2 per coat

Spatterdash (1:4 plaster): sand = 14.0 x 0.1 = 0.14m^3

cement = 14.0 x 0.0025 = 0.035m^3

Second coat (1:3 plaster): sand = 0.14m^3

cement = 14.0 x 0.003 = 0.042m^3

Final coat (1:2 plaster): sand = 0.14m^3

cement = 14.0 x 0.005 = 0.07m^3

Total volume of sand = 0.42m^3

TOTAL VOLUME OF CEMENT = 0.15m^3

Total plastered area (ie- 3 coats) = 3 x 14.0 = 42.0m^2

TOTAL MASON LABOR = 42.0 x 0.14 = 5.9 man-days (skilled)

TOTAL LABOR = 42.0 x 0.22 = 9.2 man-days (unskilled)

Total Materials & Labor:

Total volume of crushed stone = 7.16m^3

Labor of crushing stone = 7.16 x 1.4 = 10.0 man-days (unskilled)

TOTAL VOLUME OF CEMENT = 2.00m^3 = 2000 liters = 63 bags

TOTAL UNSKILLED LABOR = 86 man-days

TOTAL SKILLED LABOR = 24.3 man-days

(List of required fittings....)

(List of required tools....)

Figure 14-9 are drawings of the final tank design.

NOTES:

1. GI PIPE SIZES & ARRANGEMENT NOT DETAILED HERE.
2. REFER TO FIGURE 14-8 FOR DETAILS OF WALL DIMENSIONS.
3. EACH ROOF BEAM HAS A 1" GI PIPE COLUMN @ MID-SPAN.
4. CGS ANCHOR BOLTS SPACED AT 65 CM.

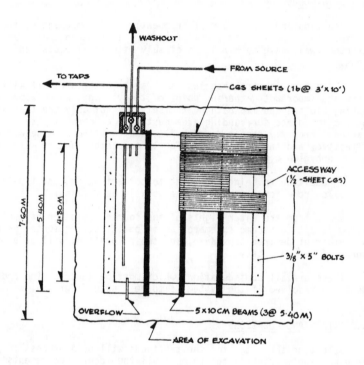

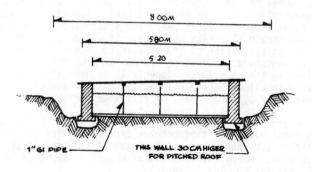

FIGURE 14-9
RESERVOIR FOR DESIGN EXAMPLE

15.   PUBLIC TAPSTANDS

15.1   INTRODUCTION

The tapstands are the most frequently-used component of the entire system. No other structure will face more abuse than these, and no other structure will have to fit in so closely with local social and cultural needs.

A tapstand is more than just a physical structure. It will become a new and important gathering point of the village, where women will be washing clothes and men bathing themselves. Not only the tapstand itself, but the immediate surrounding area must also be carefully selected and planned. Properly designed and built, the tapstand will be a clean, attractive, and inviting place. Poorly completed, and it will be a dirty, muddy, unhygienic eyesore.

In addition to being the point to collect water, the tapstand area must allow room for clothes-washing as well as bathing.

Apart from the water-rights of the source, no other part of the system is apt to become so embroiled in politics, arguments, or disputes. The number of desired tapstands, and their location, will be a frequent source of heated debate.

These are all considerations which must be kept in mind and equitably resolved if the system is to be a successful one.

15.2   TAPSTAND LOCATIONS

Selecting the sites for the tapstands will be a process of compromises, since no single point is apt to meet all the ideal requirements.

The number of taps required in a system will be greatly influenced by the geographical lay-out of the village. Isolated wards, no matter how small, will require their own. The school (if any or several) and health post should also each have one. It would not be unusual for the leading political person of the village to desire his own tap (this can be used to advantage: such a person can be a useful ally in organizing and motivating the work force, especially if he stands to gain a tapstand). It has also sometimes happened in Nepal that certain caste groups will want their own tap, for reasons of religious purity.

These are not all unreasonable requests. While it is not desirable that the total number of taps becomes excessively large, it is generally acceptable to add another one or two taps if the project (as a whole) will gain from this. A small investment of materials may go a long way towards goodwill, motivation, and success.

The location of the tapstands should be based upon a number of considerations: is it well-located to serve those families that will depend upon it, is there an adequate drainage point for the waste-water; is the area large enough to allow for several users at once (washing, clothes, bathing, collecting water, etc).

A site near, but not directly on, a main trail is good. A sunny, sheltered site will encourage bathing (even in the cold season). A small water-hole for animals may be dug nearby to collect waste-water (and prevent the animals from coming directly to the tapstand to get their water). Overflow from the water-hole can be channeled to a nearby garden or field.

15.3   FLOW

The standard tapstand flow is 0.225 LPS (13.5 liters/minute). Such a tap will adequately serve a population of 200-230 persons. Where a tapstand will be serving only just a few households then the flow can be cut down a bit, and conversely the flow may be increased for a more densely-populated area (a double - or triple-faucet tapstand may also be built, refer to Section 15.5).

The design flow is achieved by installing a ½" globe valve at the base of the tapstand, and adjusting it until the desired flow is delivered. This valve is then securely locked up, to prevent furhter tampering. The faucet at the discharge serves only as an on/off control valve.

15.4   RESIDUAL HEAD

The residual head at the tapstand is important: if too high, it will cause accelerated erosion of the interior of the control valve; and if too low, will result in low flows.

The following residual heads are recommended:

Absolute minimum:	7 meters
Low end of desired range:	10 "
Most desirable:	15 "
High end of desired range:	30 "
Absolute maximum:	56 "

These standards are somewhat liberal; Wagner & Lanoix recommend a range of 10-50 meters.*

The static pressure when the tap is closed must not exceed the pressure rating of the tapstand pipe, and tapline.

---

* "Water Supply for Rural Areas & Small Communities" (WHO, 1959)

15.5 STRUCTURAL CONSIDERATIONS

A tapstand may be constructed of brick, stone, or wood, using mortar or dry-stone masonry. Regardless of what it is constructed with, it must be designed and built to survive heavy use and abuse, especially if located in a schoolyard.

A masonry tapstand of cement mortar should have a supporting column 50cm x 50cm around the GI pipe, and should be on a footing imbedded 30cm below ground level. Mortar should be 1:4 and the exterior can be plastered if the villagers so desire. The faucet should protrude far enough so that the water vessels can be easily filled; it need not protrude, however, more than 30cm. Since the water vessels are typically carried by a headstrap, a low bench added to the tap (either of cement, mud mortar, or dry-stone masonry) will be helpful to facilitate lifting the vessel. A concrete or cement-mortared "apron" should provide enough room for several persons to work at once. A non-erodable drainage channel should carry the wastewater to a suitable drainage point.

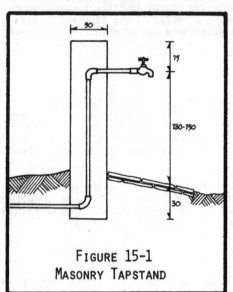

FIGURE 15-1
MASONRY TAPSTAND

Dry-stone tapstands can be used when the tapstand can be built into an embankment, or where there are skilled rock-cutting masons who can carefully fit together a solid tapstand structure; these types require minimal (if any) cement mortar. Both of these types are shown in Figure 15-2.

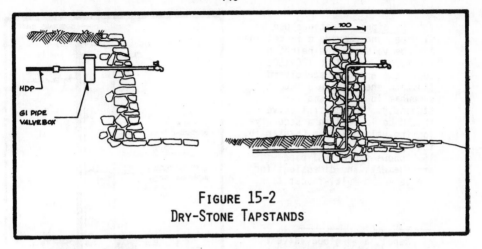

FIGURE 15-2
DRY-STONE TAPSTANDS

<u>Wooden tapstands</u> do not have such a long lifetime as masonry

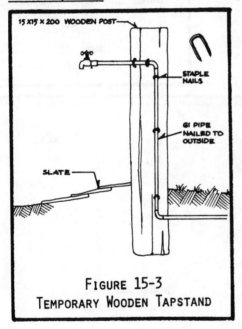

FIGURE 15-3
TEMPORARY WOODEN TAPSTAND

tapstands, due to the moist environment which promotes rotting. However, occasionally some projects will temporarily require such tapstands until cement can be obtained to build the proper one. In such cases, a wooden post, 15cm square minimally by 100cm longer than the height of the faucet, can be quickly installed. The village blacksmith is able to make a few iron staple-nails with which the GI pipe can be firmly nailed to the post. This type of tapstand is shown in Figure 15-3.

A more permanent wooden tapstand can be made with a post of the same size, but a channel cut in the back of it so that the GI pipe can be installed inside of it, as shown in Figure 15-4. A wooden cap over the top of the post will prevent rainwater from seeping into the wood, and the surrounding area around the post should be slated to minimize seepage into the ground. The post should be set into a bed of gravel, and backfilled with more gravel, so that water drains freely downwards and doesn't soak the post. The post itself should be thoroughly painted with a wood preservative or varnish, to inhibit rot.

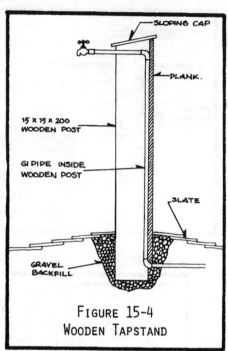

GI pipe: Tapstands use ½" GI pipe, and require a faucet and a globe valve.* The height of the faucet should be 120-150cm above the apron (a schoolyard tapstand should have a faucet somewhat lower for smaller students). The control valve should be located in a securely-locking valvebox (see Chapter 16) that prevents tampering. Figure 15-5 shows typical GI pipe arrangements and dimensions for single - and multi-faucet taps:

*In Nepal, a ½" globe valve is known as a "corporation cock"

FIGURE 15-4
WOODEN TAPSTAND

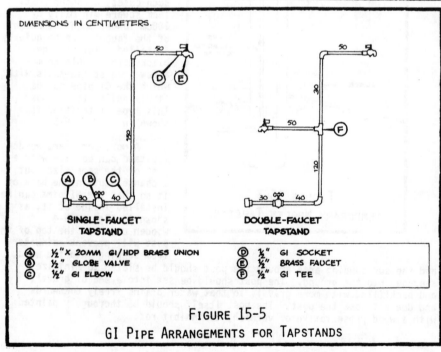

DIMENSIONS IN CENTIMETERS.

SINGLE-FAUCET TAPSTAND

DOUBLE-FAUCET TAPSTAND

Ⓐ ½" X 20MM GI/HDP BRASS UNION Ⓓ ½" GI SOCKET
Ⓑ ½" GLOBE VALVE Ⓔ ½" BRASS FAUCET
Ⓒ ½" GI ELBOW Ⓕ ½" GI TEE

FIGURE 15-5
GI PIPE ARRANGEMENTS FOR TAPSTANDS

Multi-faucet tapstands: Where the population density of a village
is quite high, it is possible to economize on the number of tapstands
by constructing ones with two or three faucets. In such cases, one faucet
should be set about 30cm lower, and the control valve adjusted so that
not less than 0.20 LPS flows from each tap when all taps are open. Multi-
faucet tapstands are not required anywhere except where it is expected
that there will be more than 200 persons using the tap, or where an
unusual water demand schedule will result in a great number of persons
trying to use the tap at once (such as bathing at a bazaar tapstand).

Drainage: The waste-water from tapstands must not be allowed to
collect in muddy puddles, where it can stagnate and become a breeding

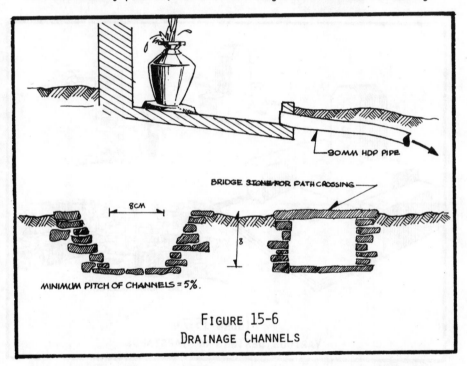

FIGURE 15-6
DRAINAGE CHANNELS

place for mosquitoes and disease. Waste-water should be carried away by
a non-erodible channel (or 90mm HDP pipe) to a suitable drainage point
(such as a water-hole for animals, or a nearby garden or field). Such
channels do not have to be made of mortared masonry but should be made
of brick or stone that is carefully fitted. Drain channels should be
bridged at path crossings. The drainage point must definitely be at
a lower elevation, and the minimum slope of the drain channel should be
5%. Refer to Figure 15-6 for drawings of some drainage channels.

Finishing: The ground around the tapstand should be finished
in such a way that it is stable, quick-draining, and quick-drying.
Animals should be precluded from walking over, or through, the tapstand
area, and therefore some fencing may be needed.

The tapstand may be plastered or left natural, depending upon the quality of the masonry and village desires. In fact, much of the tapstand construction should be according to the wishes of the villagers, with the overseer providing guidence along those lines discussed in this chapter.

Some villagers may be content with just an open pipeline. Such arrangements invariably create problems that for outweigh the expense and labour of building a sound tapstand.

Various drawings of tapstands are shown in Figure 15-7.

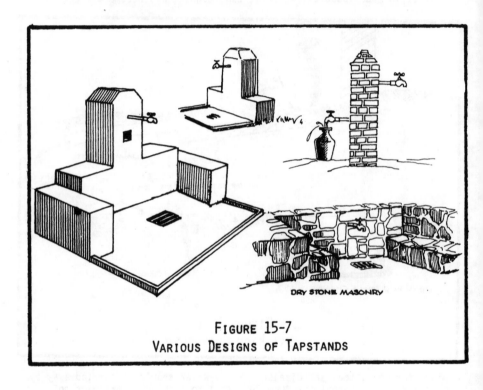

DRY STONE MASONRY

FIGURE 15-7
VARIOUS DESIGNS OF TAPSTANDS

16. VALVEBOXES

16.1 INTRODUCTION

The purpose of a valvebox is to protect a control valve from undesirable tampering which can upset the hydraulic balance of the system and disrupt flows.

Valveboxes can be attached to the structures (as is common with tanks) or located independently along the pipeline (such as at strategic branchpoints or near tapstands). They can be constructed of masonry, GI pipe, HDP pipe, or reinforced concrete (RCC), depending upon the materials available, size and number of valves, how often they will be operated, etc.

16.2 DESIGN CHARACTERISTICS

Regardless of what they are constructed with, all valveboxes must be built with the following characteristics:

Secure cover: The valve must be protected by a strong and secure cover which cannot be undone or opened by ordinary persons. Covers can be bolted down, nailed down, buried, or even welded down (as is the case with a HDP pipe valvebox). Valvebox covers can be RCC slabs (see Chapter 19.15), GCS sheeting (refer to Chapter 20.6) or wooden planks.

Free-draining: No valvebox should have a solid floor, so that any leakage or ground seepage can quickly drain away. A bed of gravel or crushed stone is recommended.

Adequately large enough to allow the valves to be removed easily and replaced, without having to tear down the valvebox. If constructed of masonry, it must be large enough so that wrenches and pliers can swing freely. If constructed of GI or HDP pipe, they must be easily removable.

16.3 MASONRY VALVEBOXES

Masonry valveboxes are of either stone or brick. The lower portion of the box may be of dry-stone masonry, but cement-mortar masonry should be used for the top 40cm. The box should protrude about 10cm above ground level. The interior dimensions of the box must allow the valves(s) to be unscrewed from the pipe; in a box with two or more valves, staggering them will leave some more room. The pipeline should not be

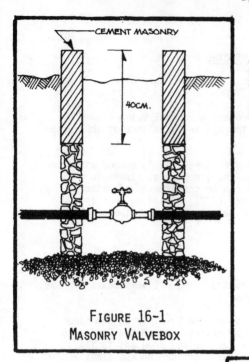

FIGURE 16-1
MASONRY VALVEBOX

cemented into the walls of the box, and the box should be built on a bed of gravel or crushed stone several centimeters deep to allow quick drainage of leakage or moisture. Refer to Figure 16-1.

16.4   RCC VALVEBOXES

Valveboxes made of reinforced concrete are not generally worth the effort for just a single box. However, when several boxes of the same dimensions are to be built, then a wooden form can be made and RCC valveboxes easily produced. The RCC valvebox can rest upon a lower portion of dry-stone masonry. The reinforcement should be of 3/8" rebar, the concrete should be 1:2:4 mix (with small-sized gravel), and the walls should be about 5cm thick. Bolts should be imbedded in the top for bolting down the cover (refer to Chapter 20.4). The dimensions of the interior are the same as for masonry valveboxes. Refer to Chapter 19 for details of RCC cementwork.

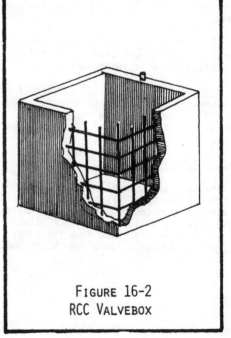

FIGURE 16-2
RCC VALVEBOX

16.5   GI PIPE VALVEBOXES

For a single valve, it is possible to use a length of GI pipe as the valvebox, as shown in Figure 16-3. The size of the GI pipe depends upon the size of the control valve; for valves used in Nepal, the following sizes can usually be used:

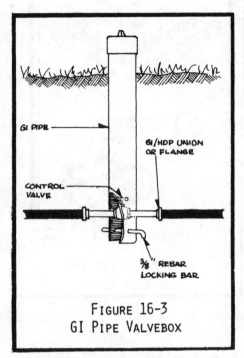

VALVE SIZE	GI PIPE SIZE
½"	2"
1"	3"
1½"	3"
2"	4"

It is recommended, however, that the overseer personally check that the control valves will actually fit inside the GI pipe.

The base of the GI pipe is slotted to allow it to slip over the pipeline, and locked into place with a 3/8" bolt or hooked rebar (these are passed through two ½" holes drilled in the bottom of the pipe). An endcap screwed down with a pipewrench will be a secure cover.   For operating the valve, a "key" of ½" or 1" GI pipe is used: the ends of this key are slotted so it can be slipped onto the valve handle and turned. Dry-stone masonry walls and gravel backfill are recommended, and painting the GI pipe will help to retard corrosion.

**FIGURE 16-3
GI PIPE VALVEBOX**

16.6   HDP PIPE VALVEBOXES

These are best suited for the ½" control valve of a tapstand, since these are valves that are not frequently adjusted. An HDP valvebox is of 90mm HDP pipe, secured to the pipeline in the same slotted manner as described above, but not extending to the ground surface. They are closed by welding on a 90mm HDP endcap, with enough clearance so that the cap may be cut off without damaging the valve inside. The same cap can be re-welded back on once the maintenance work is completed. Refer to Figure 16-4.

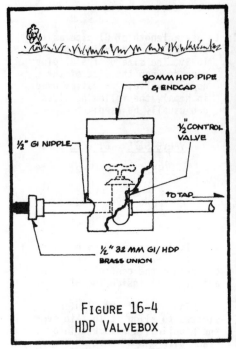

FIGURE 16-4
HDP VALVEBOX

FIGURE 16-5
VALVEBOX WITH KEY

16.7   FREQUENTLY-ADJUSTED VALVES

For valves which must be operated fairly frequently, it may be better to leave a hole in the valvebox cover that is located directly over the valve handle. Then the valve can be operated using the "key" (described in Section 16.5) instead of repeatedly removing the cover. The hole in the cover should be just a few centimeters larger than the key pipe, and the cover should be high enough so that hands cannot reach down through the hole and operate the valve manually. Refer to Figure 16-5. A dis-advantage of this type of valve box is that the hole is open, which leaves the valve liable to being tampered with by using a hand-made key.

16.8   ATTACHED VALVEBOXES

These are valveboxes attached to, or built into, some structure, such as intake tanks, break-pressure tanks, or reservoirs. Such boxes will usually consist of three masonry walls (of which the wall of the tank may be one) with a dry-stone masonry wall as the fourth. This dry-stone wall can be dismantled and the pipeline below it dug up without destroying any part of the valvebox.

Various drawing of some valveboxes are presented in Figure 16-6:

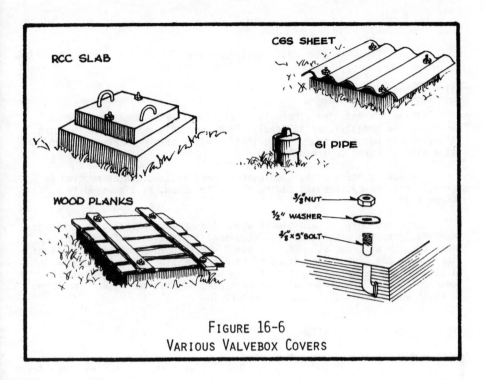

FIGURE 16-6
VARIOUS VALVEBOX COVERS

17. WATER QUALITY

17.1   INTRODUCTION

At the current time, there is no practical water treatment system which can be broadly used in Nepal. Thus, emphasis must lie in locating the cleanest possible source of drinking water, then properly securing it against further contamination.

Physical contaminants, such as suspended matter, can be removed or greatly reduced by allowing sedimentation to occur, as discussed in Chapter 12.

There are only two additional steps that can be practically employed towards improving water quality: slow-sand filtration, and aeration. This chapter will not attempt to present the technical details for these: the reader can find an abundance of such information among the sources listed in the Reference section of this handbook. Instead, general description and discussion will be presented so that the reader can gain a basic understanding of these procedures.

17.2   SLOW-SAND FILTRATION

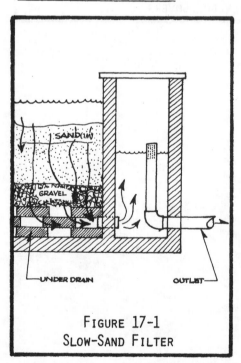

FIGURE 17-1
SLOW-SAND FILTER

A slow-sand filter is a large tank that has an under-drain system which is covered by a base layer of gravel and then a bed of filtering sand. The filter works by mechanically straining the water as it flows through the sand, and also by biologically attacking the organic impurities (the filter bed develops a "slime" of bacteria, which feed upon the organic impurities carried in the flow).

These filters are relatively simple to build and do not require highly-trained personnel for maintenance. However, a slow-sand filter has several serious drawbacks: at best efficiency, it can only filter about 0.002-0.003 LPS (7-11 liters/hour) per square meter of filter surface area. Thus, a large areas is required for providing even a minimal flow for the system. Additionally, although simple to maintain, they do require regular, reliable attention or else they can become sources of bacterial pollution rather than removers.

The decision to install such a filter involves much serious consideration and consultation with the villagers, the overseer, and the LDD engineers. Technical design of such a filter is best left to professional people.

17.3   AERATION

Aeration is the process of thoroughly mixing the water with air. Oxygen-enriched water loses its acidity (which is due to the presence of dissolved carbon dioxide) and reduces undesirable tastes and colors due to the presence of iron or other dissolved gases.

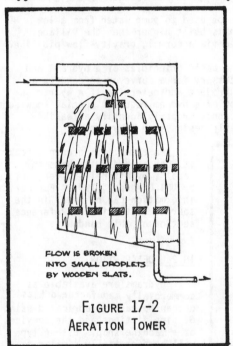

FLOW IS BROKEN INTO SMALL DROPLETS BY WOODEN SLATS.

FIGURE 17-2
AERATION TOWER

The easiest method of aeration is to build a tower, as shown in Figure 17-2, which has several tiers of plastic screens or wooden slats. These mechanically break the water flow into small droplets, which, because of their increased surface area, can absorb oxygen quicker. Such a tower can be built as part of a sedimentation tank or collection tank, or even the reservoir.

17.4   FURTHER REFERENCE

For quick, basic information on slow-sand filters and aeration techniques, refer to "Water Supply for Rural Areas and Small Communities", Lanoix & Wagner (WHO, 1959), pages 175-180.

18. HYDRAULIC RAMS

18.1 INTRODUCTION

Hydraulic rams (hydrams) are coming into greater and greater use
Nepal, allowing many villages that earlier could not use a gravity-flow
water system (because the source was too low) to now have a drinking
water system which is still economical to construct. Although the hydram
is a pump, it requires no fuel or electricity. Instead, it operates by
using the gravitational energy contained in a large amount of water
falling a short distance to pump a small amount of water up a high distance.

This means that the hydram can be used to pump water from a low
source up to a reservoir tank which is built higher than the village.
From there, the water is distributed via a normal, gravity-flow pipeline.

This chapter will introduce the basic principles of a hydram, and
present the technical knowledge necessary for a surveyor to conduct a
field survey of a potential hydram project and determine if a hydram is
feasible. Although the installation of a hydram requires special knowledge,
there is no reason why a surveyor cannot properly identify a feasible
hydram project, or a designer properly design such a system.

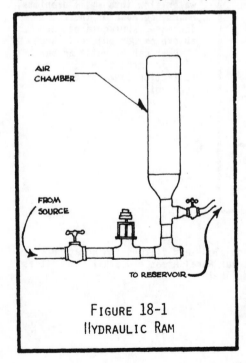

FIGURE 18-1
HYDRAULIC RAM

An excellent reference book
is "Use of Hydraulic Rams in
Nepal", by Mitchell Silver, printed
by UNICEF/Nepal, 1977. Further
information can be found in the
sources listed in the Reference
section of this handbook.

18.2 DESCRIPTION

Hydrams are available as
commercially manufactured kits,
or can be easily fabricated using
GI pipe fittings and the services
of a machine shop. Either type
will be essentially similar to
the one shown in Figure 18-1.

A large amount of water
flowing from the source down
the drivepipe compresses the
air in the chamber, which then
expands and drives a small
amount of water up the delivery
pipe. The quantity and height
that the hydram can push water
up to depends upon the quantity

and height of the water "falling" in the drivepipe.

A typical installation of a hydram system is shown in Figure 18-2:

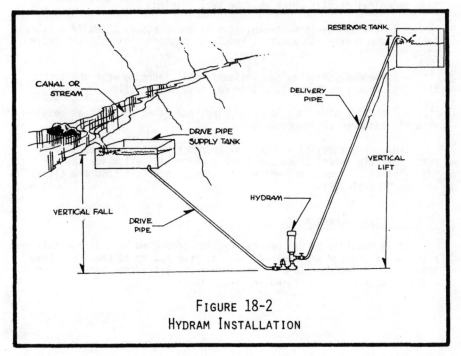

FIGURE 18-2
HYDRAM INSTALLATION

18.3   OUTPUT CALCULATION

A hydram, under optimum conditions, can rarely pump more than 25% of the source flow to a higher elevation. Thus, usually only very large springs, or streams, will be able to provide enough flow to serve a village. The higher the water must be pumped, the smaller the flow will be.

To calculate the approximate delivery flow of a hydram:

$$Qp = \frac{2 \times Hd \times Qd}{3 \times Hp}$$

Where:

Qp = delivery flow (LPS)
Hd = "falling" head (meter)
Hp = "lifting" head (not to exceed 100 meters)
Qd = "falling" flow (LPS)

These variables are indicated in Figure 18-2.

18.4   TECHNICAL CONSIDERATIONS

When studying a village for a potential hydram project, there are some technical details which must be kept in mind:

- If the source is a stream, it will be necessary to build a storage tank for the hydram (to ensure a regular, constant flow into the drive pipe)·

- Suspended particles and sediments will increase wear and tear on the pump, thus a sedimentation tank may have to be built;

- The drive pipe must be of GI pipe, and be as straight as possible, securely anchored or imbedded;

Thus, when studying a potential hydram project site, the surveyor must carefully select sites and terrain which will allow for the installation of tanks, drivepipe, etc, and must obtain accurate elevations and ground distances.

18.5   SPECIAL ARRANGEMENTS

It is possible to use several hydrams connected to a single delivery pipe; or to use the waste-water from an upper hydram to operate a lower hydram; or to incorporate a hydram into a break-pressure tank. These possibilities are illustrated in Figure 18-3.

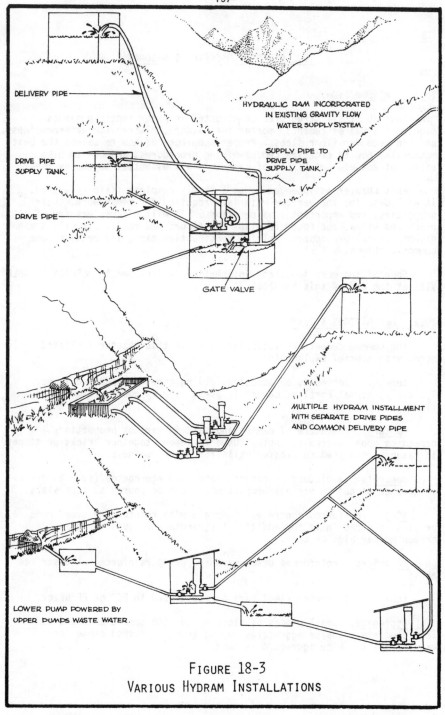

DELIVERY PIPE

HYDRAULIC RAM INCORPORATED
IN EXISTING GRAVITY FLOW
WATER SUPPLY SYSTEM.

SUPPLY PIPE TO
DRIVE PIPE
SUPPLY TANK.

DRIVE PIPE
SUPPLY TANK.

DRIVE PIPE

GATE VALVE

MULTIPLE HYDRAM INSTALLMENT
WITH SEPARATE DRIVE PIPES
AND COMMON DELIVERY PIPE

LOWER PUMP POWERED BY
UPPER PUMPS WASTE WATER.

FIGURE 18-3
VARIOUS HYDRAM INSTALLATIONS

19. CEMENT, CONCRETE, & MASONRY

19.1 INTRODUCTION

Just about all structures constructed in water supply projects require the use of cement: mortar for masonry, plaster for waterproofness, and concrete for floor slabs. Proper knowledge of how to select the best materials, how to organize cement-mixing procedures, and how to make efficient and economical use of cement is all essential to the overseer.

This chapter is intended to be a fairly complete field reference. It will describe the various materials required for cementwork, their properties, and important considerations. It will discuss masonry of brick and stone, and concrete slabs for floors and roofs. It will present organizational procedures, helpful construction tips, and mention some common problems.

Some of the more important information is included in REFERENCE TABLE VIII at the end of this handbook.

19.2 DEFINITIONS & TERMS

The common cementwork vocabulary used in this chapter is listed here, with a brief explanation:

cement: serves as an adhesive, gluing together sand and stone. Typically, normal Portland cement is used: a gray powder, similar to flour.

mortar: a mixture of cement and sand in various proportions, depending upon desired strength. Used to cement together bricks or stones in masonry, and used to plaster walls for waterproofness.

concrete: a mixture of cement, sand, and aggregates (such as gravel or crushed stone) in various proportions. Can be poured to form slabs.

RCC: reinforced concrete. Concrete with reinforcing steel rods or bars imbedded in it for additional strength and support. Wire screening may also be used.

RF bricks: reinforced brick masonry, using reinforcement described above.

rebar: reinforcing steel bars or rods, used in RCC or RF brick.

aggregate: small pieces of stone mixed with cement and sand to form concrete. Coarse aggregates may be gravel, crushed stone, or crushed brick. Fine aggregate is sand.

gravel: usually found along rivers and streams: small pebbles and stones, worn fairly smooth and rounded by the action of water.

crushed stone: large pieces of rock or stone broken down to aggregate size, by manual labor using sledge hammers.

crushed brick: pieces of broken-up brick.

19.3 CEMENT

Cement is a mixture of chalk or limestone, and clay, which is fired and then ground into a fine powder. Additional materials may be added to impart certain properties to the cement (such as to make it quick-setting, low-heat, rapid-hardening, etc). Ordinary cement is a gray powder, commonly known as "Portland cement". This is the type commonly provided for water supply projects in Nepal.

Properties of cement: Portland cement is used for ordinary construction projects. Cement mortar or concrete has high compressive (crushing) strength, but relatively low tensile (stretching) strength. When water is added to a mortar or concrete mixture, it forms a fluid mass which is easily worked and placed into position. Within an hour (depending upon temperature and mix) the cement begins to set, losing its plasticity. Within 4 hours it has finished setting and can no longer be worked. From the time that setting begins, the cement is undergoing a chemical hardening process which will continue for at least a year, although it most-rapidly hardens during the first few days.

STRENGTH OF PORTLAND CEMENT CONCRETE
(Per cent of ultimate strength
at various ages)

3 days	approx.	20%
7 days	"	45%
28 days	"	60%
3 months	"	85%
6 months	"	95%
1 year	"	100%

Hydration: When water is added to a dry cement mixture (for either mortar or concrete), it begins a chemical reaction with the cement known as "hydration". This reaction causes the cement to set and harden, giving off heat in the process. The rate of hydration is accelerated by heat and humidity, therefore cement will set and harden faster at warmer temperatures, and vice versa for colder temperatures (freezing of cement completely kills the hydration reaction, which will not continue even if the cement is thawed out. Refer to Section 19.18). The hydration reaction requires moisture, but the heat generated by hydration tends to cause evaporation of the moisture in the mix. Thus it is necessary to prevent the rapid drying-out of the cement, especially during the first few days. Once hydration ceases, the cement will gain no further strength.

Setting: When water is added to a cement mix, there is a period of about 30-60 minutes in which the mix is plastic and easily worked into position. However, after that period, the mix begins to set, becoming stiffer and stiffer. Within a few hours, the setting should be complete. Once setting has begun, the mix should not be disturbed, which would weaken the mix. Onset of setting can be determined by pressing the blunt end of a stick or pencil into the mix: resistance to penetration will suddenly increase when setting begins.

Hardening: This is the process whereby the cement mix gains strength. Hardening begins as soon as setting begins, but continues for at least a year.

Both setting and hardening are influenced by temperature: heat accelerates the rates of both.

Curing: Curing is the process of keeping the cement mix properly wetted, to ensure that there is enough moisture for the hydration reaction to continue. It is especially important during the first few days after pouring a concrete mix, when the cement most rapidly gains its strength.

Packaging of cement: One liter of Portland cement weighs approximately 1.44 kgs. Cement is typically factory-packed in bags of 50 kgs each, so therefore each bag should ideally contain nearly 35 liters of cement. However, some cement is lost during shipping and portering. For practical purposes, the amount of cement per bag should be considered as follows:

    burlap (jute) bags :   32 liters

    paper bags :   34 liters

Storage of cement: Cement easily absorbs moisture from the air, and as a result loses strength during long periods of storage. Typical losses are as follows:

Period of storage	Loss of strength
3 months	20%
6 "	30%
12 "	40%
24 "	50%

When storing cement at the project site, it should be stacked in a closely-packed pile, not more than 10 bags high (to keep the bottom bags from bursting). Close-packing also reduces air-circulation between the bags, which is good. The pile of cement should be raised on a platform above the floor. The room or storage shed should have as little air circulation as possible, and if a long storage period is anticipated, the pile should be further covered by plastic or canvas tarpaulins. Paper bags of cement will resist aging much better than burlap bags, thus paper bags should be on the outside of the pile, and the burlap bags should be the first used in construction.

Aged cement will form lumps. All lumps should be screened out of the cement, and no lumps should be used which cannot be easily crumbled by the fingers. If old cement (ie- field stored for more than 6 months) must be used, increase the amount of cement in the mix by ½-1 parts (depending upon how lumpy it is).

19.4   WATER

Water in the cement mix serves two purposes: first, to take part in the hydration reaction of the cement; and secondly, to make the mix fluid and plastic enough so that it can be easily worked and placed.

Quality: Water that is fit for drinking is usually fit for mixing cement. Water unsuited for drinking may still be used, if tested as follows:

Using water of known suitability (ie- drinking water), make 3 cakes of cement paste, each approximately 1-2 cm thick by 6 cm in diameter. At the same time, make 3 identical cakes using the unknown water. Comparing the two types, observe the setting time, the "scratchability" (using a fingernail) and strength after a few hours, 24 hours, and 48 hours. Only if both types of cakes are equally strong should the unknown water be used.

Quantity: Water is necessary for the hydration of the cement, but too much water added during mixing results in a weaker strength. The quantity of water generally needed to make the mix easily workable is much more than is needed for the hydration reaction. Therefore, no more water should be added than necessary to make the mix easily workable. The ideal quantities of water depend upon the amount of cement in the mix, and approximate guidelines are given along with the mix proportions for concrete, in Section 19.11.

Once the cement has finished setting, further addition of water does not weaken it. In curing concrete, this is a necessary action to prevent the surface of the slab from drying out too quickly.

19.5   SAND

Sand is used in both mortar and concrete (in the latter, it is sometimes referred to as "fine aggregate"). Proper sand is well-graded (ie- containing grains of many sizes mixed together). Sand of a uniform size, such as beach sand or very fine sand, is not suitable (but can be mixed into coarser sands).

Sources of sand: Sand found in land deposits is known as "pit sand" Such grains are generally irregular, sharp and angular. Sand carried by water, such as found along banks of rivers or lakes, is known as "river sand". Such grains are generally rounded and smooth, due to the action of water.

Both types of sand are suitable for cementwork, so long as they are well-graded and clean.

Quality: Sand containing clay, silt, salt, mica, or organic material is not good, since such contaminants can weaken the strength of the cement if they are present in large quantities. There are easy field tests which can be conducted to determine the quality of a sand source:

a) A moist handful of the sample sand is rubbed between the palms of the hands. Suitable sand will leave the hands only slightly dirty.

b) Decantation test: a drinking glass (or other clear glass container) is half-filled with the sample sand, and then filled 3/4-full with water. The glass is then shaken vigorously, and allowed to sit undisturbed for an hour or so. The clean sand will settle immediately, and the clay and silt will settle as a dark layer on top of the sand. The thickness of the clay/silt layer should not be more than one-seventeenth (6%) of the thickness of the sand.

Dirty sand can be washed by rinsing repeatedly with water.

Bulking of sand: Damp sand that contains up to 5-6% water will swell up and occupy a greater volume than if it were perfectly dry. This is known as "bulking". A moisture content of 5-6% can increase the volume by over 30%. Additional water content reduces the bulking, until saturated completely (saturated sand occupies nearly the same volume as it does when dry). Thus when using slightly damp sand, it is necessary to use an extra amount of sand in the mix if it is to be proportioned by volume. Very damp sand (such as freshly washed) is measured as if it were dry. If the mix is proportioned by weight, the bulking is of no consequence.

19.6 AGGREGATES

Aggregates is the general term for the material mixed with cement and water to form concrete. Sand is a fine aggregate, and larger material is a coarse aggregate.

Coarse aggregates may be gravel (generally river-worn, rounded rocks) or crushed rock and brick.

Stones of granite, quartzite, basalt, or having rough non-glossy surfaces are best. Hard limestones are good, soft sandstones are not. Limestones and sandstones are porous and therefore not good for water tank floor slabs, but can be used for roof slabs (same applies for crushed brick).

Aggregates must be clean and well-graded. Smaller rounder aggregates (such as river gravel) are better for waterproof floor slabs.

Sizes of aggregates: Aggregates should be well-graded so that air voids between pieces are minimal. Largest sizes should be:

For roof slabs: 3/8" (10mm)

For unreinforced or lightly reinforced slabs: 3/4"-1" (20-25mm)

Crushed brick: Pieces of broken-up brick may be used as aggregate in concrete, but due to their porous nature should not be used for floor slabs of water tanks. When using crushed brick aggregate, pieces should be thoroughly soaked in water prior to mixing, to prevent absorption of moisture from the mix (which will interfere with the hydration reaction).

19.7   REBAR REINFORCEMENT

Reinforcement of concrete is only needed for slabs which are large in area or will be put under great hydrostatic pressure (ie- deep water depth). An RCC slab can be thinner than a non-reinforced slab. The presence of the reinforcement helps to distribute the stresses and forces uniformly over the entire mass of concrete.

Reinforcing bar (rebar): Is available in many sizes, but for typical water supply projects only the following diameters are needed: ¼", 5/16", or 3/8" (6mm, 8mm, or 10mm).

Wire-mesh screen: (also known as "wire-mesh fabric") can also be used as reinforcement in slabs. The size of aggregate in the concrete mix should be smaller than the size of the mesh (using a piece of the screen to sift the aggregate is the best way of ensuring this).

Spacing of rebar: The spacing of the rebar must distribute the cross-sectional area of steel uniformly across the cross-sectional area of the slab. For a floor slab, the area of rebar must not be less than 0.225% of the total cross-sectional area of the slab, and for a RCC roof slab is must not be less than 0.30%. The following table can be used:

Type of slab	Thickness (cm)	Spacing of Rebar (cm)		
		6mm	8mm	10mm
floor	8	15	30	40
roof	8-9	12	21	33
roof	9-11	10	17	27
roof	11-13	8	14	22
roof	13-15	7	12	19
roof	15-17	6	11	17

Placing of rebar: The reinforcement is made as a grid, with the size of the squares according to the table above. The rebar rods can be tied together with thin wire or string. The rebar must have a minimum of 3 cm of concrete covering. For a roof slab, the rebar is set 3 cm from the bottom of the slab, and for a floor slab the rebar is set 3 cm from the top of the slab (Refer to Figure 19-1).

The rebar must be securely fastened so that it cannot be shifted around while the concrete is being placed (the rebar can be supported on pieces of non-porous rock, but NOT brick or wooden stakes).

Reinforced (RF) brick slabs: When a roof slab is to be of reinforced brick, different rebar spacing is required, depending upon the thickness of the slab, and the size of the bricks. Refer to Section 19.14 for technical details of this type of roof slab. A floor slab of brick requires no reinforcement (refer to Section 19.13).

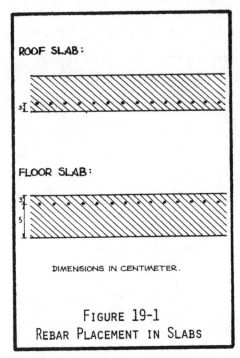

ROOF SLAB:

FLOOR SLAB:

DIMENSIONS IN CENTIMETER.

FIGURE 19-1
REBAR PLACEMENT IN SLABS

19.8   CEMENT MIXING

For convenience, it is usually easiest to mix cement at the construction site, so it is necessary to ensure that there is an organized system for delivering cement, sand, aggregates, stone or brick, and water. It is particularly important when mixing and pouring concrete that it be done in a continuous operation, without long delays caused by lack of materials.

Mixing pad: Cement should never be mixed on the ground. A mixing pad of brick, slate, concrete, or even a CGS sheet should be made. It should be large enough to allow mixing of convenient-sized batches, without overflowing: 1.5 square meters is adequate. If possible, build a small lip around three sides of the pad so that materials may not get accidently washed off.

When a number of masons are working at once, or concrete is being mixed, it is usually better to have two or more pads.

Proportioning: Although the most accurate method of proportioning cement, sand, and aggregates is by weight, in a field site this is not so easy to arrange. The common method is to mix by volume, using a small bucket. Measuring by shovelfuls is not accurate. Mortar should be mixed in smaller batches than concrete, but no batch should be so large that it is not used in 30 minutes.

Dry-mixing: All ingredients are first thoroughly dry-mixed together, using shovels and trowels, until the mix is of a uniform color and consistancy.

Wet-mixing: Water is added slowly, a small quantity at a time. Each time water is added, the mix is thoroughly "turned over" a few times with shovels. Water is added until the mortar or concrete is at the desired consistancy. The wet-mix can be adjusted as follows:

Too wet: add sand (and aggregate)

Too dry: add water

Too stiff: add sand

Too sandy: add cement

Tools & Manpower: A cement-mixing team should minimally have three persons: two for mixing, one for adding water and ingredients. Each team should have two shovels and two trowels, a small bucket (for measuring proportions) and a large bucket (for transporting the mix to the masons).

19.9   MORTAR

Cement mortar is used for masonry construction of walls, and for plastering. Grout is used to cement rebar anchor rods into rocks and imbedding GI pipes into the masonry.

Typical mixes: Proportions of cement to sand, by weight or by volume:

Type of mortar	Cement:sand
Ordinary masonry	1:4
Reinforced brick roof slabs:	1:3
Spatterdash (1st coat plaster)	1:4
Rough plaster (2nd coat)	1:3
Final plaster (3rd coat)	1:2
Grout:	1:1 - 1:1½

Volumes of mortar: The total volume of mortar is equal to the total volume of sand in the mix. The cement mixes with water to form a paste which fills in the voids in the sand. Thus, a 1:4 mix requires 100% sand and 25% cement; a 1:3 mix requires 100% sand and 33% cement, etc.

Quantities required to make one cubic meter (1 m^3) of various mortar mixes:

Mortar mix	Sand (m^3)	Cement (m^3)
1:4	1.0	0.25
1:3	1.0	0.33
1:2	1.0	0.50
1:1½	1.0	0.67
1:1	1.0	1.00

19.10   MASONRY

Because the masonry walls of the tanks are required to be as waterproof as possible against the hydrostatic pressure of the water inside, particular attention must be paid to the workmanship of the masons. It must be made clear to them that a masonry wall built the same as walls for their houses is not adequate, and that the walls of the tanks must be carefully laid down according to directions.

Brick masonry: Bricks are usually locally manufactured in Nepal, and are of various shapes and quality. The exact dimensions of local bricks should be obtained for making the estimated requirements. The total volume of brick masonry is approximately 25% mortar and 75% brick. Bricks should be soaked in water for several minutes prior to being used (this prevents them from absorbing too much moisture from the mortar) but not soaked excessively.

Masons who are experienced at building houses with brick and mud mortar will be inclined to build tank walls in the same manner; laying down a bed of mortar, then placing the bricks tightly together on top of it, then laying down another mortar bed for the next course. The result is a network of unobstructed channels between the bricks where water will have easy leakage. Proper brick masonry for water-proof walls requires spacing the bricks one centimeter apart, and carefully filling in the joints with mortar. Bricks should be laid in patterns that do not result in a straightline joint from the inside to outside of the wall. Refer to Figure 19-2 for various points on brick masonry.

The top course of bricks should be completely clean and wetted before putting down the mortar bed for the next course. If the mortar on the top course has begun to set, the joints should be scraped down approximately one centimeter deep and refilled with fresh mortar. The walls should be built up evenly, so that the weight is distributed uniformly: no section of a wall should be more than 15 courses (approximately 1 meter) higher than the lowest section.

Once the mortar has set, the masonry should be wetted regularly (several times per day) for several days.

Dressed-stone masonry: Also known as "Ashlar masonry". In this type of masonry, the stones are carefully cut to rectangular dimensions, making "stone bricks". Such masonry requires skilled masons, and much

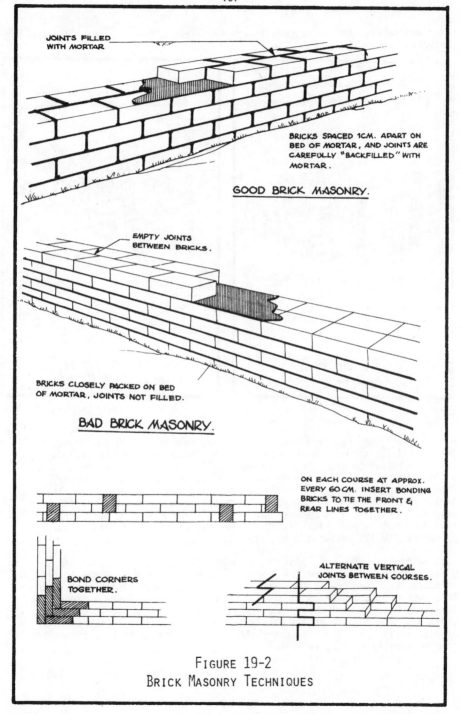

JOINTS FILLED
WITH MORTAR

BRICKS SPACED 1CM. APART ON
BED OF MORTAR, AND JOINTS ARE
CAREFULLY "BACKFILLED" WITH
MORTAR.

GOOD BRICK MASONRY.

EMPTY JOINTS
BETWEEN BRICKS.

BRICKS CLOSELY PACKED ON BED
OF MORTAR, JOINTS NOT FILLED.

BAD BRICK MASONRY.

ON EACH COURSE AT APPROX.
EVERY 60 CM. INSERT BONDING
BRICKS TO TIE THE FRONT &
REAR LINES TOGETHER.

BOND CORNERS
TOGETHER.

ALTERNATE VERTICAL
JOINTS BETWEEN COURSES.

FIGURE 19-2
BRICK MASONRY TECHNIQUES

time and labor. Ashlar masonry is approximately 30% mortar and 70% stone. Refer to Figure 19-3:

FIGURE 19-3
DRESSED-STONE MASONRY

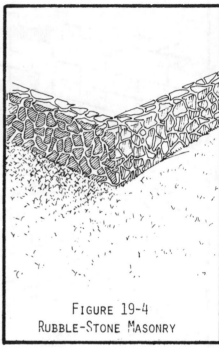

FIGURE 19-4
RUBBLE-STONE MASONRY

Rubble-stone masonry: This is the most common type of masonry used in Nepal. The stones are roughly shaped by the masons, and the resulting wall is similar to that shown in Figure 19-4. The stones should be lightly tapped down into the mortar, then securely fixed using mortar and pieces of crushed gravel. No stone should span completely from the inside to the outside of the wall. With this type of masonry, it is very easy to leave air voids between the stones, so care must be taken that this does not happen. For estimate purposes, this type of masonry is approximately 35% mortar and 65% stone.

Setting GI pipe: GI pipe is set into masonry walls on a bed of grout (1:1 or 1:1½ mortar). A minimum length of 30cm of pipe should be imbedded, and the more the better. Once the pipes have been placed, they must not be disturbed at all for several days. Building a protective dry-stone masonry wall will protect against accidental dislodgement (this can happen quite easily otherwise, for the worksite is the scene of much activity). The pipemouths should be plugged up to keep any mortar from accidently falling into them.

19.11   CONCRETE

Concrete is used for pouring floor and roof slabs of tanks. The size and type of aggregates depends upon the purpose of the slab, its reinforcement, and its thickness (all discussed in Section 19.6).

Typical mixes: The following proportions are recommended for concrete, proportions by either weight or volume:

Normal RCC work (roof slabs):   1:2:4 (cement, sand, aggregate)

Waterproof slabs (tank floors):   1:1½:3

The concrete is proportioned and mixed as already discussed in Section 19.8.

Water: For the above mixes, the approximate amount of water needed is 3/4 parts water per part of cement (1:3/4 cement:water) by volume.

Volumes of concrete: The total volume of the concrete mix is never less than the total volume of aggregates. Typically, air voids make up 50% of the aggregate volume, and these voids must first be filled by the mortar. Excess mortar then adds to the volume of the concrete.

For the above mixes, the following volumes of cement, sand, and aggregate are necessary to produce one cubic meter (1 m^3) of concrete:

Concrete mix	cement (m^3)	sand (m^3)	aggregate (m^3)
1:2:4	0.25	0.5	1.0
1:1½:3	0.33	0.5	1.0

Segregation: This is the separation (due to gravity) of the aggregates in the concrete. The heavier aggregates will tend to sink to the bottom, and water will rise to the surface. The result is a poorly mixed concrete which will be weak. Segregation usually happens transporting the concrete from the mixing pad to the work site, therefore the mixing pad should be as close to the final pouring point as possible, and the concrete should be re-mixed with a trowel before pouring.

Placing the concrete: A bucket of concrete should never be dumped from any height since segregation of the aggregates will occur. Concrete should be placed in strips about 15-20 cm wide, never as piles (refer to Figure 19-5). If a fresh layer is to be put down on top of an earlier layer, then the second layer should be put down before the first has begun to set (within 30 minutes). Rough leveling of the concrete can be done, but extensive trowelling will cause the cement paste to rise to the surface of the slab.

Before it sets, the concrete must be thoroughly compacted.

Compacting: This is the process of settling the concrete so that it contains no air voids. This is accomplished by "rodding" the concrete: poking a length of rebar into the concrete and stirring it up and down.

WRONG

CORRECT

FIGURE 19-5
PLACING CONCRETE

The concrete should be carefully rodded in all corners and around reinforcement. Over-rodding, however, will cause segregation. After rodding, the concrete should be tamped level again, using a flat board of wood. Sprinkling loose cement on the surface of the slab (to absorb excess water) is not good: such a layer will easily crack, crumble, and powder.

Waterproofing floor slabs: A day after the concrete has been placed, a water proofing plaster may be put down. A grout mixture of 1:1 proportions should be worked into the surface of the slab with a wooden float. Only a thin layer of plaster is needed, just enough to seal the surface pores of the slab and smooth it over. Water-proofing compound can be added to the grout (refer to Section 19.17).

Curing: As soon as the concrete has set (within a few hours), the floor slab should be flooded with a few centimeters of water. More than this will put too much hydrostatic pressure on the concrete, which may not be strong enough to support it. After one day, the water may be drained off for waterproofing (as described above), but once the water-proofing plaster has set it should be re-flooded and kept that way for several days (after 3 days, if all else is finished, the tank may be filled fully and put into service).

When first flooding the slab, care must be taken that the discharge flow doesn't erode the fresh concrete.

If the slab is being poured over a period of several days, the surface of each section must be covered over with a tarpaulin and constantly wetted. This method must also be used for drying a roof slab.

Improper curing will allow the surface of the slab to dry out and shrink, while the interior mass remains unchanged. The resulting tensions will cause the surface to crack, reducing waterproofness. Too much loss of moisture will stop the hydration reaction, and no further strength will develop (even if the concrete is thoroughly flooded again).

19.12   PLASTERING

Plastering masonry walls adds to their waterproofness. Several thin coats of increasing richness (ie- cement content) are better than one or two thick coats.

All walls will receive three coats of plaster, each 1 cm thick; and should be plastered at least 5 cm above the overflow level.

Spatterdash: This first coat is a rough plaster of 1:4 mortar. It is applied by spattering the plaster against the walls, using a trowel. This coat is NOT troweled smooth, and the resulting surface is extremely bumpy and irregular. This provides a good rough surface for the next layer to adhere to.

Second coat: A mortar mix of 1:3, applied to the spatterdash coat. That coat is left with a rough surface.

Third coat: The final coat is a 1:2 mortar mix, which is finally troweled smooth and clean.

Only one coat of plaster per day should be applied.

Volumes of plaster: For a plaster coat 1 cm thick, the following quantities of cement and sand are needed for each square meter of plastered surface:

Plaster mix	Cement (m^3)	Sand (m^3)
Spatterdash (1:4)	0.0025	0.01
Second coat (1:3)	0.0030	0.01
Third coat	0.0050	0.01

19.13   FLOOR SLABS

Tank floors may be of mortared brick or stone, or concrete (either non-reinforced or reinforced). The floor slabs of tanks must be as waterproof as possible. Concrete slabs should use carefully-selected aggregate, and mortared slabs should be plastered.

Foundations: Tank floors are put down on a bed of gravel or crushed stone, averaging 10cm deep. This gravel bed should be pitched down towards the washout pipe. An easy way of accomplishing this is to radiate several strings from the mouth of the washout pipe to various points around the perimeter of the tank, as shown in Figure 19-6. Each string is at the desired slope, and the gravel bed is set down according to the nearest string. The gravel should be several centimeters below the washout pipe (otherwise it will not be possible to fit the floor slab underneath it !).

Mortared brick: A brick floor slab should consist of two layers of brick, laid flat on beds of mortar, carefully spaced with good mortared joints in between. The mortar should be 1:4 mix. The line of bricks should be different between the two layers. The floor is then plastered with two coats (the first at 1:3 mix, and the second at 1:2 mix,

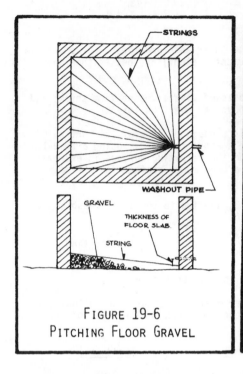

**FIGURE 19-6
PITCHING FLOOR GRAVEL**

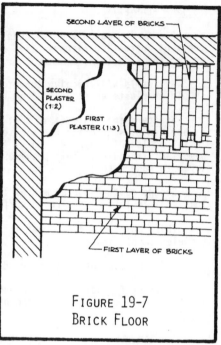

**FIGURE 19-7
BRICK FLOOR**

no spatterdash coat needed). As soon as the second plaster coat has set, the tank should be flooded a few centimeters deep (for curing the mortar) for several days. Refer to Figure 19-7.

Mortared stone: This type of flooring is more difficult to put down, especially with rubble-stone masonry. Care must be taken to prevent air voids in the masonry. This type of floor should be 15 cm thick, mortared and plastered as prescribed above.

Reinforced (RCC) concrete: The aggregate for concrete slabs should be small and well-graded, maximum size being 18mm. Rounded river gravel is excellent for this type of slab. A reinforced slab should be 8cm thick, with the reinforcement according to the specifications of Section 19.7, and the concrete work according to Section 19.11.

19.14   ROOF SLABS

Although roof slabs of concrete or reinforced brick require extra materials and labor, such roofs are structurally quite strong, and should never need replacing during the lifetime of the system. A slab roof also effectively seals off the tank from external contamination.

An accessway must be left in the roof, approximately 60cm x 60cm. Bolts should be imbedded for securing the accessway cover.

Structurally, the roof slab must be "tied" into the masonry walls of the tank. This is done by imbedding rebar rods in the walls, then bending them over and securing the roof reinforcement to them. This is shown in Figure 19-8:

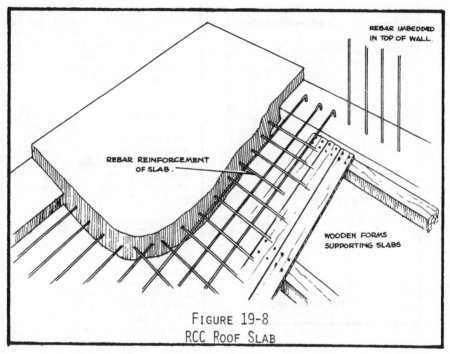

REBAR IMBEDDED IN TOP OF WALL.

REBAR REINFORCEMENT OF SLAB.

WOODEN FORMS SUPPORTING SLABS

FIGURE 19-8
RCC ROOF SLAB

Columns: No unsupported span should be more than 4 meters. Support can be made using GI pipe as columns:

GI pipe size	Max height of column
1½	178 cm
2"	278 cm

The ends of the column must be threaded and have flanges (which act as bearing plates). The bottom flange of the column should rest on the floor slab, with additional concrete on it to hold it firmly in place (rebar studs can be left protruding from the floor slab to help anchor the concrete cover).

A "beam" of 1" GI pipe spans the interior, supported directly on the column. This GI pipe beam should be in the exact centre of the roof slab.

-174-

Figure 19-9 shows the arrangement of a GI pipe column and beam.

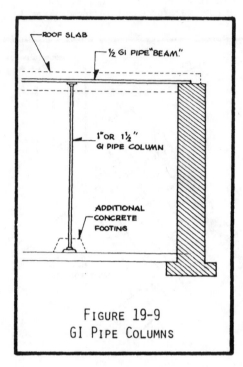

FIGURE 19-9
GI PIPE COLUMNS

RCC slabs: The amount of rebar in an RCC roof slab must not be less than 0.30% of the cross-sectional area of the slab. The thickness of the slab should not be less than 1/30 (3.33%) of the longest span of the tank, but the thickness should not be less than 8 cm. The concrete mix should be 1:2:4, aggregates should be well-graded of crushed stone or brick (if crushed brick is used, the roof should be plastered with a 1 cm coat of 1:3 mortar). Largest size of aggregates should be 10mm. Refer to Section 19.7 for details of rebar.

Reinforced (RF) brick slabs: Roof slabs of RF brickwork offer considerable savings in cement, compared to an RCC slab. The thickness of an RF brick slab should not be less than 1/30 (3.33%) of the longest span of the tank. The size of the rebar should be either 5/16" (8mm) or 3/8" (10mm), and is spaced between the bricks. Bricks are laid in one direction, spaced 4 cm apart. The rebar must not touch any brick (such contact would allow moisture from the brick to corrode the rebar). The cement mix is 1:3 mortar, with enough water to make it easily worked into position around the rebar and between the bricks. A second pouring of mortar may be required,to bring the slab to the proper thickness (due to settlement of the mortar). Figure 19-10 shows different brick arrangements for roof slabs of various thickness.

Curing: Curing the roof slab is very important, since otherwise it may not develop the full strength it needs to support its own weight (and the weight of those who will stand upon it). Unfortunately, curing a roof slab is not so easily accomplished as for a floor slab. Direct exposure to sunlight will greately hasten the drying-out of the slab if care is not constantly taken to prevent this.

The rim of the slab should have a low wall (of brick or dirt) around the edge of it, about 20 cm high. The slab itself should be covered with several centimeters of sand, which is then thoroughly wetted using several buckets of water. The sand is then covered using a plastic or canvas

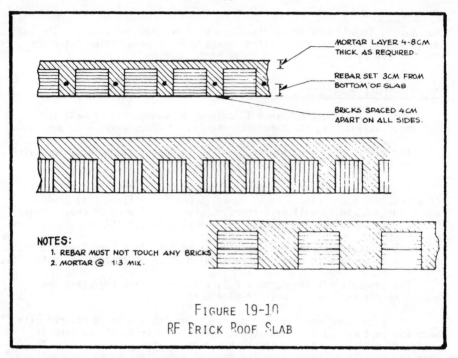

FIGURE 19-10
RF BRICK ROOF SLAB

NOTES:
1. REBAR MUST NOT TOUCH ANY BRICKS
2. MORTAR @ 1:3 MIX.

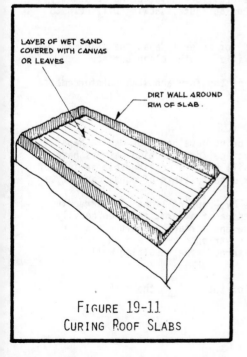

FIGURE 19-11
CURING ROOF SLABS

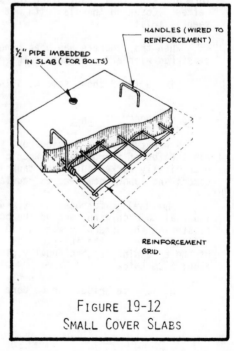

FIGURE 19-12
SMALL COVER SLABS

tarpaulin, straw mats, or several layers of banana tree leaves. The sand is re-wetted at least three times per day, for a week, after which the surface can be cleared off and forms stripped away.

19.15   SMALL SLAB COVERS

Small RCC slabs (less than 100cm square) can easily be made for covers of valveboxes, break-pressure tanks, or accessways in larger tanks.

For such slabs, the reinforcement is best done using large-mesh wire screen, but small size rebar can also be used.

A simple wooden form can be constructed. The rebar is firmly set in place, and short pieces of ½" GI or 20mm HDP are fixed into position where the 3/8" bolts will pass through. Handles of wire or rebar should be tied to the reinforcement, so that the slab can be lifted.

The thickness of the slab should not be less than 5 cm, and not more than necessary to cover the rebar with 2½ cm of concrete on both sides.

The concrete mix should be 1:2:4, with small-size aggregate small enough to fit through the mesh if wire screen is used.

After the concrete has been poured, the slab should be covered with sand and kept wetted for three days. After that time, if the form is needed to make more covers, the slab can be carefully removed from the form and kept in a shady place for several more days, being constantly wetted. Covering the slab with wet burlap (jute) sacking will help to keep it moist.

When the concrete has been cured for several days, the slab may be plastered with a 1:3 mortar, to give it a smooth, clean surface.

Figure 19-12 shows some details of the form and slab reinforcement.

19.16   FERROCEMENT TANKS

A new type of tank is currently being developed for use in Nepal, constructed of ferrocement. When practical construction methods have been finally worked out, such tanks will offer a considerable savings of cement and labor, compared to regular masonry tanks of equal capacity.

Essentially, ferrocement is made by wrapping light wire screening (such as chicken-wire) around the outside of a form, and then heavily plastering the screening with a 1:3 cement mortar. When the plaster has strengthened, the interior form is stripped away, and the inside of the screening is then equally plastered. The resulting wall is about 5 cm thick.

The same technique can be done for the roof of the tank. .

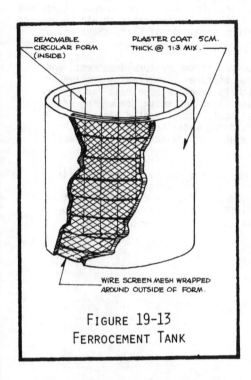

REMOVABLE
CIRCULAR FORM
(INSIDE)

PLASTER COAT 5CM.
THICK @ 1:3 MIX.

WIRE SCREEN MESH WRAPPED
AROUND OUTSIDE OF FORM.

FIGURE 19-13
FERROCEMENT TANK

For quick technical reference, see "Ferrocement Water Tank" by Frans Dubbeldam, printed by the German Volunteer Service in Nepal. For general reference, refer to "Ferrocement Water Tanks and their construction", by S.B.Watt, . printed by the Intermediate Technology Publications, London, UK.

19.17 WATER-PROOFING COMPOUNDS

Commercially-manufactured additives may be mixed into the mortar or concrete dry-mix, to improve the imperviousness of the resulting plaster or concrete. Such compounds are generally packaged in the quantity that should be mixed into a full 50-kg bag of cement. However, typical construction work of CWS projects rarely calls for mixing an entire bag of cement at once, which means that the compound must be sub-divided into smaller portions. This is most accurately done by weight, which is not easily done in the field.

No amount or type of additives will make a poorly-mixed or poorly cured plaster or slab waterproof. Therefore, the most improtant procedure is to see that the cementwork is properly done. Additional compounds are helpful, but not essential.

19.18 COLD WEATHER CONCRETING

When cementwork must be done where temperatures are expected to drop down to freezing levels, special precautions must be taken to protect the cement.

When concrete or mortar freezes, the hydration reaction is stopped permanently. Even when the cement is thawed and re-wetted, the chemical process does not resume, and the concrete develops no further strength than it had when it first froze.

Since the hydration reaction generates heat, the single best strategy is to insulate the cementwork to prevent the loss of this heat. especially during the first two days (when the rate of heat loss would be highest).

Padding the cementwork with straw and covering with mats or tarpaulins will be of special help. When re-wetting the cement (during curing), heated water should be used if possible. Protecting the cementwork against the wind is extremely important, and all protruding rebar should be wrapped with cloth (since steel is an excellent conductor of heat, these would be major points of heat loss).

The setting and hardening of cement is temperature-dependent, and will proceed more slowly at lower temperatures. Increasing the amount of cement in the mix by 20-25% will help generate more heat and earlier strength. Heating the aggregates and using hot water for mixing will improve the setting time (aggregate should not be heated hotter than can be touched by the hand, nor should the water be hotter than 140°F/60°C. Never heat the cement alone, or add hot water to cement alone).

The freezing point of the mix may be reduced by dissolving salt into the heated mixing water. Salt is added by weight, and should not exceed 5% of the weight of the cement. Each percentage of salt lowers the freezing point by about 1½°F (0.8°C), but salt cannot be used effectively for temperatures lower than 25°F (-4°C).

20. PRACTICAL TECHNOLOGY

"Necessity is the mother of Invention"

20.1   INTRODUCTION

Technical theory is useless without effective and practical methods of applying it. Years of experience in the field have yielded many practical construction techniques to supplement and implement the theory of CWS construction. This chapter will present some of these ideas.

20.2   SCREENED INTAKES

Screened intakes can be quickly made using light wire mesh or ordinary window screening, and HDP pipe.

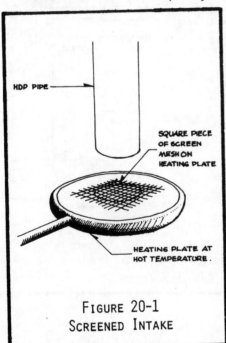

HDP PIPE

SQUARE PIECE OF SCREEN MESH ON HEATING PLATE

HEATING PLATE AT HOT TEMPERATURE.

FIGURE 20-1
SCREENED INTAKE

The size of the HDP pipe should be one or two sizes larger than the outlet pipe. A square piece of screen, slightly larger than the mouth of the HDP pipe, is laid onto the hot heating plate. The HDP pipe is then pressed against the screen and heating plate until the melted lip is formed. The HDP is then given a slight twist, and removed from the plate. The screen will be perfectly welded across the end of the pipe. When it has cooled, the excess screening is trimmed away.

This screened intake takes a few seconds to make (indeed, it is possible to make several without reheating the plate), and the villagers can easily make new ones to replace those worn out.

20.3   JOINING HDP & GI PIPE

At points of low pressure, HDP and GI pipes can be joined without using flanges or brass unions.

Threading: Depending upon the size of the HDP pipe, it can sometimes be threaded (just like GI pipe) and screwed in GI fittings. This is particularly possible with Class IV pipe, which has thicker walls. A short "nipple" of Class IV HDP can be threaded into a GI fitting, and regular Class III HDP pipe welded on.

Expanding: The HDP pipe can be heated and softened over a fire, and then a threaded GI pipe or nipple can be jammed/screwed into it.

The HDP/GI joints should only be used at low-pressure points. They are useful for making a discharge pipeline of tank washouts and overflows, and for putting HDP screened intakes onto the outlet pipes, and for air-vents, etc.

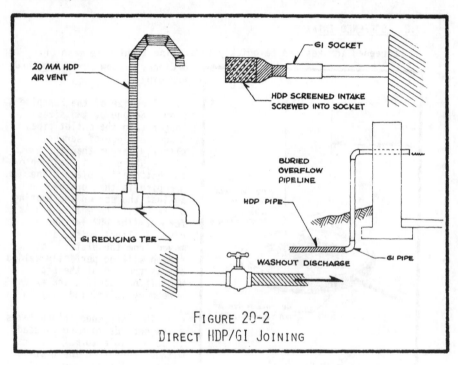

FIGURE 20-2
DIRECT HDP/GI JOINING

20.4   IMBEDDING BOLTS IN MASONRY

The best size of bolts to use is 3/8" x 5" (10mm x 15cm) with two washers and nut. Clamp the head of the bolt into a vise, and slip a length of ½" GI pipe (75-100cm long) over it. Using the pipe as a lever, bend the bolt over 90°. Set the bolt into the fresh mortar or concrete, leaving about 4 cm protruding (a longer bolt may have to be used if a thick RCC slab cover is to be bolted down).

This type of imbedded bolt will never "spin" when a wrench is used to remove the nut.

Refer to Figure 20-3.

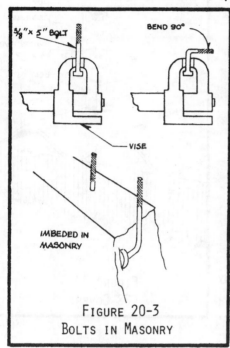

FIGURE 20-3
BOLTS IN MASONRY

20.5   ANCHORING BEAMS TO MASONRY

Using the same technique as described above, a 60cm length of 3/8" (10mm) rebar is bent 90° and imbedded in the top of the masonry walls. A ½" (12mm) hole is drilled in the wood beam, which is then slipped over the protruding rebar. The rebar is then hammered over, locking down the beam to the wall.

Beams anchored in this manner are easily removed when it comes time to replace them.

Refer to Figure 20-4.

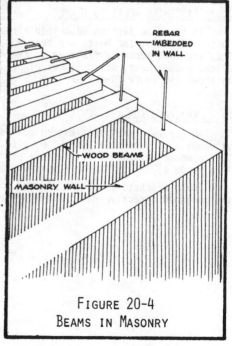

FIGURE 20-4
BEAMS IN MASONRY

20.6 LOCKING DOWN CGS COVERS

Valvebox or accessway covers of CGS roofing are quite quick and easy to construct. However, they suffer from one serious weakness: where holes have been cut in them (for bolts), it is very easy for someone to enlarge the hole and then slip it over the washer and nut that are supposed to be locking it down.

To prevent this, a special washer can be made by the village blacksmith. It is made from a piece of flat iron, and measures 5 cm across. This special washer is large enough to completely protect the hole in the CGS and prevent people from enlarging it. The nut should be tightened down so that there is no way of shifting around the CGS cover.

Refer to Figure 20-5.

20.7 FASTENING BOLTS TO BEAMS

In·the same fashion described already in Section 20.5, the bolts are bent 90°. They are then securely fastened to the side of the wooden beam, using 1½" or 2" nails, as shown in Figure 20-6.

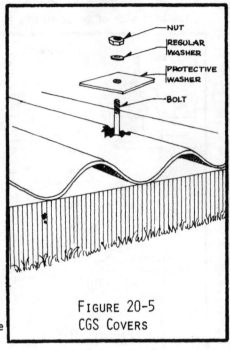

FIGURE 20-5
CGS COVERS

20.8 BRACKETS FOR AIR-VENTS

An air-vent that must extend outside the protective confines of the valvebox should be made with ½" GI pipe, firmly mounted to the tank wall. Such a mounting bracket can be made using small-size rebar, fashioned into shape by the village blacksmith (refer to Figure 20-7).

These brackets should be mounted about one meter apart; the brackets are imbedded directly into the masonry at the time of construction.

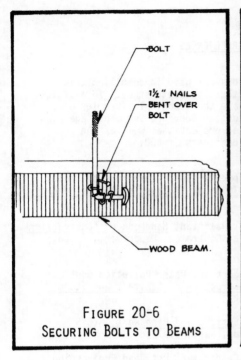

FIGURE 20-6
SECURING BOLTS TO BEAMS

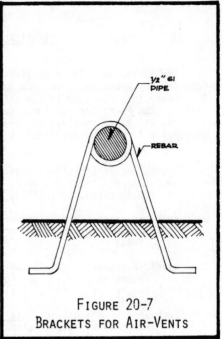

FIGURE 20-7
BRACKETS FOR AIR-VENTS

TECHNICAL REFERENCES

The following list of publications was used in compiling this handbook, or would be useful for further, in-depth study. In addition, the reader is encouraged to investigate the technical libraries of UNICEF, LDD, Peace Corps, German Volunteer Service, and other agencies in Nepal which are involved in similar projects, as well as the personal reference materials of the engineers of LDD.

1. Agency for International Development (AID), Department of State, Communications Resources Division, Village Technology Handbook (Washington, D.C. 1964)

2. American Peace Corps Volunteers, Pakistan, Handbook of Construction (Basic Democracies and Local Government Department, Dacca, 1965)

3. American Society of Civil Engineers and Water Pollution Control Federation, Design and Construction of Sanitary and Storm Sewers, (New York, 1969).

4. Bachmann, A., Manual for Water Systems and Pipe Work, (BYS Plumbing Division, Kathmandu, Nepal 1974)

5. Calder, L.E. and Calder, D.G., Calder's Forest Road Engineering Tables, (Calders, Eugene, Oregon, USA, 1957)

6. California Agricultural Experiment Station Extension Service, Measuring Irrigation Water, (Davis, California, USA 1959)

7. Daugherty, R.L. and Franzini, J.B., Fluid Mechanics with Engineering Applications, Sixth Edition, (McGraw-Hill, 1965)

8. Davis, R.E. and Foote, F.S. and Kelly, J.W., Surveying: Theory and Practice, Fifth Edition, (McGraw-Hill, 1966)

9. Dubbeldam, Frans, Ferrocement Water Tank, German Volunteer Service, (Kathmandu, Nepal, 1979)

10. Dutta, B.M., Estimating and Costing in Civil Engineering, Ninth Edition, (Lucknow, India 1969)

11. Eckenfelder, W.W. Jr, Water Quality Engineering for Practicing Engineers, (Barnes and Noble, 1970)

12. Huisman, L. and Wood, W.E., Slow Sand Filtration, (WHO, 1974)

13. Husain, S.K., Water Supply and Sanitary Engineering, (Oxford and IBH Publishing Co, 1974)

14. Johnson, C.R., Village Water Systems Technical Manual, (UNICEF/Nepal, 1977)

15. Khanna, P.N., Indian Practical Civil Engineer's Handbook, (Engineers' Publishers, 1971)

16. King, H.W. and Brater, E.F., Handbook of Hydraulics, Fifth Edition, (McGraw-Hill, 1963)

17. Lowndes, W.S., Building Stone-Foundations-Masonry, (International Textbook Co, 1942)

18. Rubey, H., Route Surveys and Construction, Third Edition, (Macmillan Co, 1956)

19. Silver, M., Use of Hydraulic Rams in Nepal, (UNICEF/Nepal, 1977)

20. Singh, G., Water Supply and Sanitary Engineering, (Standard Publishers Distributors, India, 1976)

21. Singh, G., Standard Handbook on Civil Engineering, (Standard Publishers Distributors, India, 1976)

22. Swiss Association for Technical Assistance (SATA), Published by UNICEF, Kathmandu, Nepal (1979):

    Technical Training Manual No. 1: Hydrology
    "   "   "   No. 2: Stone Masonry
    "   "   "   No. 3: Pipe and Fittings
    "   "   "   No. 4: Concrete
    "   "   "   No. 5: Construction Design

23. Teng, W.C., Foundation Design, (Prentice-Hall, 1962)

24. Tuladhar, K.R. and Sharma, R.K., Manual of Sanitary Engineering, Ministry of Public Works, Communication, and Irrigation, HMG, Nepal, 1961)

25. Tuladhar, K.R., and Sharma, R.K., Manual of Water Supply, Ministry of Public Works, Communication, and Irrigation, (HMG, Nepal 1961)

26. United Nation's Children's Fund (UNICEF), UNICEF Guide List OLGA: Rural Water Supply and Sanitation in the Developing Countries, (UNICEF, New York, 1975)

27. United States Department of the Army, Technical Manual Series, (Headquarters, DOA, Washington, D.C.)

    TM 5-270 Cableways, Tramways, and Suspension Bridges (1964)
    TM 5-335 Drainage Structures, Subgrades, and Base Courses (1962)
    TM 5-460 Carpentry and Building Construction (1960)
    TM 5-461 Engineer Handtools (1966)
    TM 5-742 Concrete and Masonry (1964)

28. United States Department of Health, Education, and Welfare, Public Health Service, Manual of Individual Water Supply Systems, (USPHS, Washington D.C., 1963)

29. United States Department of Health, Education, and Welfare, Public Health Service, Manual of Septic Tank Practice, (USPHS, Washington, D.C., 1958)

30. United States Department of the Interior, Bureau of Reclamation, Hydraulic and Excavation Tables, Eleventh Edition (Washington, D.C., 1957)

31. Volunteers for International Technical Assistance, Inc, (VITA), Low-Cost Development of Small Water-Power Sites, (Schenectady, New York, 1967)

32. Volunteers for International Technical Assistance, Inc., (VITA), Village Technology Handbook, (Schenectady, New York, 1970)

33. Volunteers for International Technical Assistance, Inc, (VITA), Water Purification, Distribution, and Sewage Disposal, (Schenectady, New York, 1969)

34. Wagner, E.G. and Lanoix, J.N., Excreta Disposal for Rural Areas and Small Communities, (WHO, 1958)

35. Wagner, E.G., and Lanoix, J.N., Water Supply for Rural Areas And Small Communities, (WHO, 1959)

36. Watt, S.B., Ferrocement Tanks: Their construction and use, (Intermediate Technology Publications, London)

37. Wright, F.B., Rural Water Supply and Sanitation, Second Edition, (John Wiley & Sons, 1956)

TECHNICAL APPENDIX A

Equation of Continuity

Bernoulli's Equation

In reference to Chapter 6, page 40

The two mainstay principles of all hydraulic behavior are expressed in the Equation of Continuity, and Bernoulli's Equation.

Bernoulli's Equation is used in any fluid calculations, and can be applied to determine the lift of an airplane wing, the height that a column of mercury will rise in a barometer due to atmospheric pressure, or even the rate at which a sinking ship will flood. It is as easily applied to a system of several different fluids, or a single fluid only. And it is equally valid on Earth, the Moon, or Jupiter!

The Equation of Continuity, although much more easy to comprehend, is no less important. It allows one to determine the velocity of a fluid flowing through a pipe, or a series of different sized pipes.

Each of these equations will be presented and explained, and their specific applications to gravity-flow water systems demonstrated.

EQUATION OF CONTINUITY

The Equation of Continuity, when applied to water flowing through a pipeline, relates flow, velocity, and pipe size together. It can be used as follows:

When known....   Can calculate....

flow, pipe size.........flow velocity

flow, velocity..........pipe size

velocity, pipe size......flow

This equation can be applied to any non-compressible fluid flowing through a pipe of any shape. In the case of gravity-flow systems, the fluid is water, flowing through circular pipes of HDP or GI.

Mathematically written, the equation is:

point A   point B   any point

$$Q = V \times A = V \times A = V \times A = \text{constant}$$

where: Q = flow
        V = velocity
        A = cross-sect'l area of pipe

Explained, the equation means that for a constant flow through a pipeline, at any point the flow must be equal to the flow at any other point. If the pipe size changes, then the velocity of the flow will change until the flow is once again constant.

The most commonly used units for the equation are:

Variable	Metric units
Q (flow)	cm^3/sec
V (velocity)	cm/sec
A (area)	cm^2

The use of the equation is demonstrated using the pipeline section shown in Figure A-1 below:

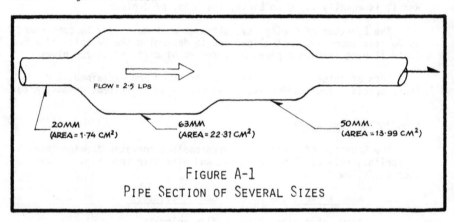

FLOW = 2·5 LPS

20MM (AREA=1·74 CM²)   63MM (AREA=22·31 CM²)   50MM. (AREA=13·99 CM²)

FIGURE A-1
PIPE SECTION OF SEVERAL SIZES

Knowing the flow (2.5 LPS = 2500 cm^3/sec) and the cross-sect'l areas of the pipe sizes, the Equation of Continuity can be used to calculate the velocity of the flow through each pipe size:

$$if \; Q = V \times A$$

$$then \; V = \frac{Q}{A} = \frac{2500}{cross\text{-}sect'l \; pipe \; area}$$

Therefore 20mm section velocity = 1437 cm/sec = 14.37 m/sec
           63mm section velocity = 112 cm/sec = 1.12 m/sec
           50mm section velocity = 178 cm/sec = 1.78 m/sec

A direct application of the Equation of Continuity is determining maximum and minimum desirable flows for each HDP pipe size. The maximum desirable flow velocity is 3.0 m/sec, and the minimum flow velocity is 0.7 m/sec, and since the cross-sect'l areas of the pipe can be calculated, it is possible to determine the corresponding flows for these velocities.

BERNOULLI'S EQUATION

To understand Bernoulli's Equation, it is necessary to realize that energy exists in many different forms, such as light, heat, sound, electrical, etc. In a gravity-flow water system, energy is present in four forms: potential, pressure, velocity, and frictional. Bernoulli's Equation is simply an energy equation which relates each of these different energy forms together, for any fluid(s) in a gravitational field. In a gravity-flow water system, the specific fluid is water, in the Earth's gravitational field.

In this discussion of Bernoulli's Equation, it will first be applied to an "ideal system", that is, a system without frictional losses. Once the principles of the equation are understood, it will then be applied to a "real system", where frictional losses occur.

Bernoulli's Equation for an Ideal System:

In this sort of system, energy is present in just three forms: potential, velocity, and pressure. As water flows through the frictionless pipeline, it posesses energy in each of these forms, in various quantities. From point to point along the pipeline the amount of energy in each form will fluctuate, but the total sum of the energies will remain constant at all points along the pipeline. This is what Bernoulli's Equation states.

Thus, at some point A, the water may possess 30% pressure energy, 10% velocity energy, and 60% potential energy, while at some other point B it may have 50% pressure energy, 15% velocity energy, and 35% potential energy. However, at both points the total sum of energy would be equal.

Mathematically, Bernoulli's Equation expresses this principle as follows:

$$H = \frac{p}{r} + h + \frac{V^2}{2g} \quad = \quad \frac{p}{r} + h + \frac{V^2}{2g} = \frac{p}{r} + h + \frac{V^2}{2g} = \text{constant}$$

point A   point B   any other point

where: H = total sum of energy
p = pressure at points A, B...
r = specific weight of the fluid
h = height above reference level
V = velocity of flow
g = gravitational acceleration

In hydraulics, energy is measured as "head" (in metric units, as "meters of head"). Each term in Bernoulli's Equation is the amount of energy in one particular form. The first term is the measure of pressure energy, and is called the pressure head. The second term is called the potential head, and the third term is called the velocity head. The sum of all three terms must be equal at every point along the pipeline.

The relevant units are given below:

Terms	Metric units
H (total energy head)	meters
p (pressure)	kg/cm^2
r (specific weight of water)	$1 gm/cm^3$
h (height)	m/sec
g (Earth's gravitational acceleration)	$9.8 m/sec^2$

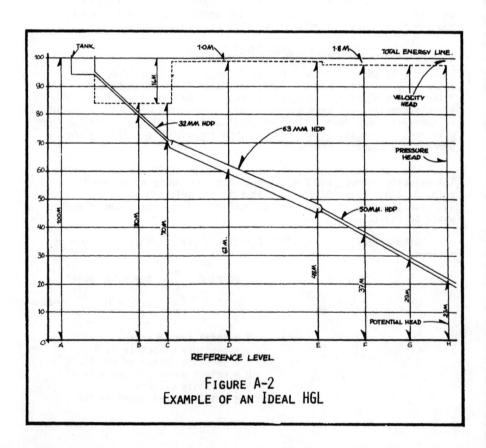

FIGURE A-2
EXAMPLE OF AN IDEAL HGL

Consider the example pipeline shown in Figure A-2, where a flow of 10 LPS leaves the tank, which is 100 meters above some reference elevation. The water flows through a section of 32mm HDP pipe, then 63mm HDP pipe, then 50mm HDP pipe.

Using Bernoulli's Equation, it is possible to determine the amount of energy in each form at the various points along the pipeline:

Point	Total Head μ	Potential Head h	Velocity Head $\dfrac{v^2}{2g}$	Pressure Head $\dfrac{p}{r}$
A	100 m	100 m	0 m	0 m
B	100 m	80 m	16 m	4 m
C	100 m	70 m	16 m	14 m
D	100 m	61 m	1.0 m	38 m
E	100 m	48 m	1.0 m	51 m
F	100 m	37 m	2.6 m	60.4 m
G	100 m	29 m	2.6 m	68.4 m
H	100 m	23 m	2.6 m	74.4 m

The flow velocity was calculated using the Equation of Continuity; multiplying the pressure head by r will yield the water pressure in the pipe at that point.

The sum of the potential head and pressure head, connected in a line from point to point along the pipeline, forms the hydraulic grade line (HGL), shown as a dashed line in Figure A-2.

Where gravity-flow water systems are concerned, certain simplifications become allowable:

1) Since the potential head contributes nothing directly to the internal pressure of the pipeline, it can be disregarded (but can be used for certain calculations, shown later);

2) The maximum desirable flow velocity in HDP pipe is 3.0 m/sec, which yields a velocity head of 0.5 meters. This is such a small amount of head compared to the other terms that it is negligible. Thus, practically speaking, the total energy line and the hydraulic grade line (HGL) become the same. In a frictionless system, this means that the static line and HGL would always be equal.

3) Atmospheric pressure acts equally at every point along the pipeline, thus canceling itself out of consideration.

Example application:

An example of applying Bernoulli's Equation to an ideal, frictionless system is shown, using Figure A-3. Bernoulli's Equation will be used to calculate the discharge flow into the tank:

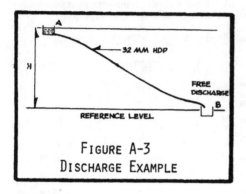

FIGURE A-3
DISCHARGE EXAMPLE

Since the equation can be applied to any points along the pipeline, we shall apply it at the two atmospheric points: the water surface of the upper tank, and the discharge at the lower tank. The equation would be written as follows

$$\underbrace{\frac{p}{r} + h + \frac{v^2}{2g}}_{\text{upper point A}} = \underbrace{\frac{p}{r} + h + \frac{v^2}{2g}}_{\text{lower point B}}$$

Some calculations can be made: since both points are at the same atmospheric pressure and under no water pressure, then the pressure head cancels out equally. The height of the upper water surface is "H" above the reference line, whereas it is zero for the lower point. Furthermore, the water surface at the upper tank has zero velocity, therefore the velocity head for that point is also zero. The modified equation now is:

$$\frac{\cancel{p}}{\cancel{r}} + \cancel{h} + \frac{\cancel{v^2}}{\cancel{2g}} = \frac{\cancel{p}}{\cancel{r}} + \cancel{h} + \left(\frac{v^2}{2g}\right)$$

$$H = \frac{v^2}{2g}$$

This can be rearranged to determine the discharge velocity:

$$V = \sqrt{2gH}$$

Knowing the pipe size and the discharge velocity, it is possible to use the Equation of Continuity to determine the discharge flow. Suppose that in this example, H = 50 meters, and the pipe size was 32mm HDP (cross-sect'l area = 5.68 cm²). The discharge velocity would then be 3130 cm/sec, and the discharge flow therefore would be 17778 cm³/sec or 18 LPS.

Similar calculations will reveal that to produce most flows commonly used in gravity-flow CWS systems, only a mere 30-40 cm of head would be required if the pipe were only frictionless!

Bernoulli's Equation for a Real System:

It was shown that for an ideal, frictionless system, the energy possessed by the water would change form from point to point, but that the total quantity would remain constant. Also, it was said that a frictionless system possessed energy in only three forms.

In a real system, however, these are not true: some amount of energy is converted into heat (by the friction and turbulence of the flow) which is absorbed by the pipe walls and is lost from the system (ie- the water no longer holds the energy, since it has been transferred into the pipe).

Bernoulli's Equation can be modified to this real situation by adding another term, which represents this lost frictional energy:

$$\overbrace{\frac{p}{r} + h + \frac{v^2}{2g}}^{\text{point A}} = \overbrace{\frac{p}{r} + h + \frac{v^2}{2g} + f}^{\text{point B}}$$

where: f = the frict'l headloss from points A to B

This new term, "f", represents the total frictional headloss of the flow between the two points under consideration. This includes frictional losses of the water rubbing against the pipe, the high frictional losses of flow through valves and fittings, and the internal turbulence of the water molecules against each other.

Once again, in the case of gravity-flow systems certain simplifications are allowable. In addition to the ones already mentioned, frictional losses from fittings in a pipesection ..ore than 1000 diameters long are negligible. The <u>velocity head</u> is still negligibly small, but now the HGL is separated from the total energy line by the amount of frictional head lost. The new HGL is similar to that shown in Figure A-4 below:

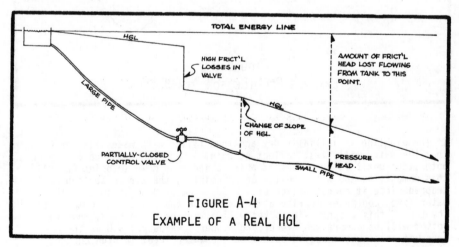

FIGURE A-4
EXAMPLE OF A REAL HGL

TECHNICAL APPENDIX B

Analysis of Air-blocks

In reference to Chapter 7.2, page 54

This technical appendix will deal with the mathematical analysis of determining whether or not a pipeline section will contain interfering air-blocks. The first section will explain how air-blocks are created, the second section will present a step-by-step procedure of analysis, the next section includes strategies to overcome or minimize such air-blocks, and the final section will illustrate with a design example.

Formation of Air-blocks

Refer to Figure B-1 below. When pipe is laid in the ground, very often the topography of the land will create high and low points along it.

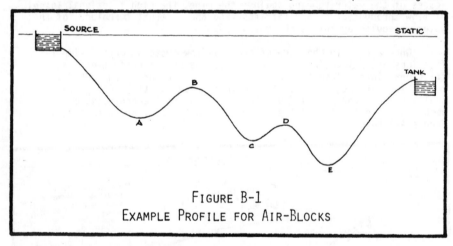

FIGURE B-1
EXAMPLE PROFILE FOR AIR-BLOCKS

If the pipeline is initially dry and then filled with water, it can be seen that the water will first collect at point A, and then rise up evenly on both sides until it overflows at point B and runs down to point C. At this moment, as the water builds up at point C, the air in section BC is trapped since it cannot escape either upstream or downstream. As the water level continues to rise at point C, the trapped air is compressed. The top of this trapped air pocket will always be at point B, and the bottom will be compressed higher and higher towards point B as the pressure continues to build up. When the water level is high enough, it will overflow at point D down to point E, creating a second trapped air pocket in section DE. From point E, the water level will rise in the pipeline (towards the tank) only as long as there is additional pressure (from the source) to push it higher. The final equilibrium of the system would be as shown in Figure B-2:

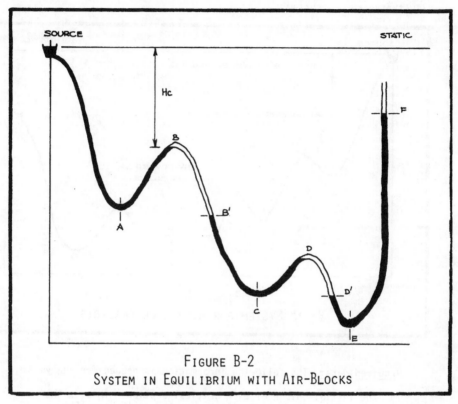

FIGURE B-2
SYSTEM IN EQUILIBRIUM WITH AIR-BLOCKS

The head between the source and top of the first air-block shall be called the compression head, Hc; the sections of pipe containing the initial, uncompressed volumes of trapped air shall be the critical sections (sections BC and DE in Figure B-2); the top of an air-block will be the high point (points B and D); the bottom of an air-block will be the low point (points B' and D'); and the height to which the water will rise shall be called the maximum elevation (point F).

Although the figure above shows a pipeline with only two air-blocks, the procedural analysis described herein is equally applicable to a pipeline with any number of air-blocks.

Procedure of Analysis

This step-by-step procedure will allow a pipeline with any number of potential air-blocks to be examined and analysed. Figure B-3 below illustrates such a system:

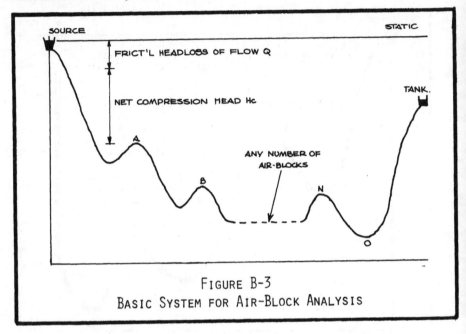

FIGURE B-3
BASIC SYSTEM FOR AIR-BLOCK ANALYSIS

Required data: The following information is needed for analysis:

1) The initial volume of each critical section. This is the uncompressed volume of air that will be trapped in the pipeline at each air-block. Can be calculated knowing the pipe size and length (refer to Reference Table IV, where the "volume per length of pipe" is given for HDP pipe).

2) A carefully plotted profile. Working from the graphed profile will be more accurate than working from blueprint.

Procedure: Even if the desired design flow cannot initially make it through the pipeline (due to air-blocks), it is still possible that some smaller flow will be able to. As long as some flow is getting through, the water will gradually absorb the trapped air and carry it out of the pipeline*.

---

* This will happen by the same process by which carbon dioxide is dissolved into a carbonated drink such as coca-cola.

As the air is absorbed, the air-blocks will shrink, which allows the flow to gradually increase. Within a day or so, all trapped air will be carried out and the full design flow will be possible.

Therefore, it is necessary to determine some minimal flow that can initially make it through the pipeline past the air-blocks. For this type of analysis, assume that this minimum desired flow is 0.1 LPS.

The designer has already designed the pipeline to achieve the desired HGL for the desired design flow. Analysis will begin at the first air-block downstream from the source (or some other break-pressure point) and progress downstream.

All pressures are in kg/cm^2, all heads and pipelengths are in meters, and all volumes are in liters.

Step 1

Determine the frict'l headloss of the 0.1 LPS flow between the source and first air-block. Substract this from the static pressure head on the air-block. The result is the net compression head, Hc.

$$Hc = \text{static head - frict'l headloss}$$

Step 2

Use the net compression head, Hc, to calculate the compressed air pressure of the first air-block:

$$P = (0.1 \times Hc) + 1.0$$

Step 3

Use Boyle's Law to determine the compressed air volume of the air-block:

$$V = \frac{\text{initial volume of critical section}}{\text{compressed air pressure}}$$

Step 4

Using the "volume per meter" column of Reference Table IV or V, calculate the length of pipe necessary to contain the air-block:

$$L = \frac{\text{volume of compressed air}}{\text{length per liter}}$$

Step 5

On the graph profile, measure this distance "L" downstream from the high point of the air-block. This locates the low end of the air-block. Determine the elevation of this point.

Step 6

With this information, it is possible to calculate the compressed air pressure of the next downstream air-block (refer to Figure B-4):

Pb = compressed air pressure of air-block B

Hb = hydrostatic head

Pd = compressed air pressure of air-block D

Hd = hydrostatic head

The equilibrium of pressures at point C can be written:

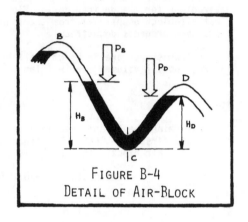

FIGURE B-4
DETAIL OF AIR-BLOCK

$$Pb + 0.1 (Hb) = Pd + 0.1 (Hd)$$

$$Pd = Pb + 0.1 (Hb - Hd)$$

Step 7

With the air pressure of this new air-block, repeat steps 3,4,5 and 6 continuously, proceeding downstream for each air-block, until the last one is reached. Determine the air pressure and elevation of the low end of this last air-block.

Step 8

Calculate the equivalent head, He, of this last air-block:

$$He = 10 (P - 1.0)$$

(where "P" is the compressed air pressure of the last air-block)

Step 9

Calculate the frictional headloss of the 0.1 LPS flow from the first air-block to the downstream tank. Subtract this from the equivalent head, He, to determine the final head, Hf:

$$Hf = He - frict'l\ headloss$$

Step 10

Add "Hf" to the elevation of the low end of the last air-block. The result is the highest elevation that the 0.1 LPS flow will reach. If the downstream tank is lower than this elevation, then this minimal flow will be able to get through the pipeline, and eventually will eleminate all air-blocks so that the design flow will be able to make it. Nothing needs to be done about the air-blocks.

Step 11

If the downstream tank is higher than the point that the 0.1 LPS flow will reach, then the pipeline must be re-designed to minimize (or eliminate) the air-blocks.

Strategies to overcome air-blocks

To minimize air-blocks, pipe sizes must be specially arranged. To eliminate an air-block, an air-valve must be installed (which will eliminate the air-block automatically), or some other air releasing device must be installed (as discussed in Chapter 7.5).

The higher air-blocks (ie- those closest to the static level) are the more critical ones. Concentrate efforts first on them (the "deeper" air-blocks have more pressure available for compression):

1) Arrange the pipe sizes to minimize frictional headlosses between source and first air-block.

2) Arrange the pipe sizes so that the upper portion of a critical section is large-diameter pipe while the lower portion of the section is small-diameter pipe.

3) If calculations show that the above strategies still will not work, install an air-valve on the highest air-block, and repeat the analysis. Install another air-block on the next highest air-block, repeat analysis, etc, until the minimal flow of 0.1 LPS will get through. It is unlikely that every single high point in the pipeline will require its own air-valve.

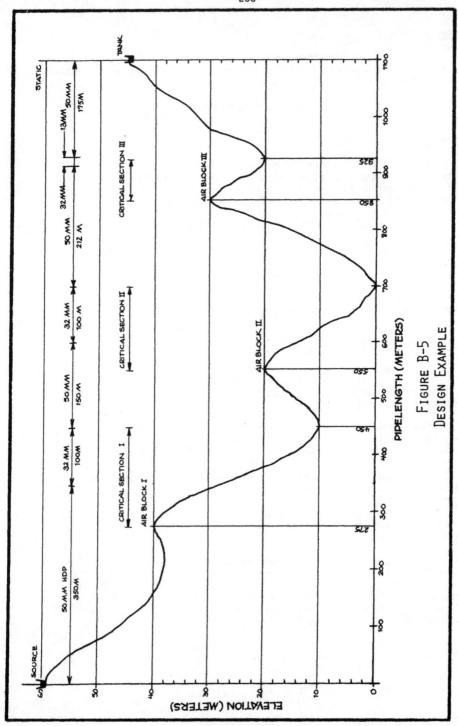

FIGURE B-5
DESIGN EXAMPLE

Design Example

Figure B-5 shows an example profile with three potential airblocks. In the preliminary design, a desired flow of 0.5 LPS was used, and pipe sizes were selected to leave a residual discharge head of 5 meters at the tank (this was accomplished by selecting 213m of 32mm HDP and 887m of 50mm HDP pipe). The pipe was arranged in accordance with the above strategies: 50mm HDP was used from the source to the first air-block, and also used in the upper portions of each of the critical sections.

Critical section I   (points A-B):   75m @ 50mm HDP + 100m @ 32mm HDP
Critical section II (points C-D):   50m @ 50mm HDP + 100m @ 32mm HDP
Critical section III (points E-F):   62m @ 50mm HDP + 13m @ 32mm HDP

The initial volume of these critical sections was calculated:

Air-block I:

75m of 50mm HDP @ 1.4 liters/meter = 105 liters
100m of 32mm HDP @ 0.57 liters/meter =   57 liters
_____

TOTAL = 162 liters

Air-block II: 127 liters

Air-block III: 94 liters

The frictional headloss of the 0.1 LPS flow from source to the first air-block is 0 (zero) meters. Thus, the net compression head:

$$Hc = 20 - 0 = \underline{20 \text{ meters}} \qquad (Step 1)$$

Analysis of Air-block I:

compressed air pressure = P_1 = 0.1 (Hc) + 1.0 = 0.1 (20) + 1.0

$$P_1 = \underline{3.0 \text{ kg/cm}^2} \qquad (Step 2)$$

compressed air volume = $V = \dfrac{\text{initial volume}}{\text{air pressure}} = \dfrac{162}{3.0}$

$$V = \underline{54 \text{ liters}} \qquad (Step 3)$$

required pipelength of 50mm HDP (@1.4 liters/meter) = $\underline{39 \text{ meters}}$
(Step 4)

elevation of low end of air-block (from profile) = $\underline{36 \text{ meters}}$
(Step 5)

Calculating compressed air pressure of the next air-block (Step 6):
$$P_2 = 3.0 + 0.1(26 - 10) = \underline{4.6 \text{ kg/cm}^2}$$

Proceeding to analysis of Air-block II: (Step 7)

$P_2 = 4.6$ kg/cm^2 (calculated above)

$$V = \frac{127}{4.6} = \underline{28 \text{ liters}}$$

required pipelength of 50mm HDP = 20 meters

elevation of low point of Air-block II = 19 meters

calculating pressure of next air-block (Air-block III):
$$P_3 = 4.6 + 0.1(19 - 30) = \underline{3.5 \text{ kg/cm}^2}$$

Going on to tne last air-block (Air-block III):

$P_3 = 3.5$ kg/cm^2 (calculated above)

$$V = \frac{94}{3.5} = \underline{27 \text{ liters}}$$

required length of 50mm HDP pipe = 19 meters

equivalent head of P_3 (Step 8):
$$He = 10(3.5 - 1.0) = \underline{25 \text{ meters}}$$

headloss of 0.1 LPS flow = 0 meters, therefore final head:
$$Hf = 25 - 0 = \underline{25 \text{ meters}} \quad \text{(Step 9)}$$

elevation of low point of Air-block III = 28 meters

Maximum elevation that 0,1 LPS will reach (Step 10):

elevation of low point = 28 meters
final head = 25 meters

Max elevation= 53 meters
(tank elevation= 45 meters)

Since the 0.1 LPS flow will reach an elevation of 53 meters, and the discharge point of the tank is only 45 meters, then this flow will be able to get through. Within a few hours, this initial flow will have absorbed all the trapped air, thus eliminating the air-blocks and allowing the final desired flow of 0.5 LPS to get through.

TECHNICAL APPENDIX C

Derivation of
Combination Pipes Equation

In reference to Chapter 8.6, page 71

This is the derivation of the equation used to determine the
lengths of two pipe sizes used to produce an exact headloss when either of
the two sizes alone will not accomplish that.

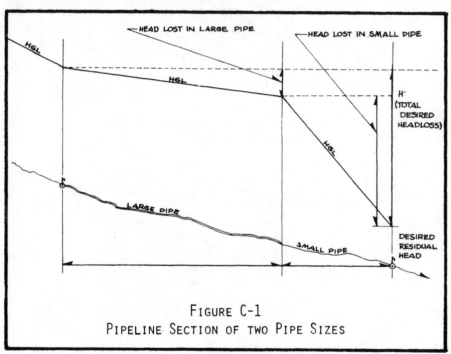

FIGURE C-1
PIPELINE SECTION OF TWO PIPE SIZES

L = total pipelength   Fs = frict'l factor of small pipe   }   for
X = small-size pipelength   Fl = frict'l factor of large pipe   }   desire
L - X = large-size pipelength   H = total desired headloss   flow

$$Fl \times \frac{L - X}{100} = \text{head lost in large pipe section}$$

$$Fs \times \frac{X}{100} = \text{head lost in small pipe section}$$

The total desired headloss, H, is the sum of the headlosses in the two pipe sections:

$$H = Fs \times \frac{X}{100} + Fl \times \frac{L - X}{100}$$

$$100H = Fs \times X + Fl \times (L - X)$$

$$100H = (Fs \times X) + (Fl \times L) - (Fl \times X)$$

$$100H = X \times (Fs - Fl) + (Fl \times L)$$

$$100H - (Fl \times L) = X \times (Fs - Fl)$$

$$\frac{100H - (Fl \times L)}{(Fs - Fl)} = X$$

TECHNICAL APPENDIX D

Frictional Diffuser

In reference to Chapter 8.7, page 73

This is the general equation for calculating the flow through a small orifice:

$$Q = CA\sqrt{2gH}$$

Where: Q = flow

C = coefficient of orifice

A = cross-sect'l area of orifice

g = gravitational acceleration

H = headloss through orifice

For the frictional diffuser shown in Figure 8-9, the orifice is made by melting a hole in the plastic endcap, using a 3" nail. The approximate coefficient of such an orifice is 0.6, the approximate diameter of the hole is 5mm, so the cross-sect'l area is about $1.96(10^{-5})$ m^2. In the metric system, the gravitational acceleration is 9.8 m/sec^2. The flow is in m^3/sec, and the headloss in meters.

Substituting these values, including a conversion factor for a flow given in LPS, the above equation can be rearranged to give the headloss for any flow:

$$H = 369Q^2 \qquad (Q = \text{flow (LPS)})$$

For a normal tapline flow of 0.225 LPS, the headloss becomes approximately 18 meters. If a second orifice is made, the flow through each orifice becomes 0.113 LPS, and the headloss then is approximately 5 meters.

If a different size of nail is used, then the new cross-sect'l area of the orifice must be calculated (the coefficient, however, for all these types of orifices is approximately 0.6).

TECHNICAL APPENDIX E

Suspended Crossings

In reference to Chapter 10.11, page 95

Suspended pipelines may be required to cross over a wide stream, or across unstable terrain which is subjected to erosion and landslides.

Although there are many possible designs for a particular situation, there are certain fundamental principles which must be used, and each possible design contains several common characteristics:

- The suspended pipeline must be high enough not to be snagged by debris floating down the stream at its maximum flood level, or by landsliding rocks and boulders;
- The cable supporting the pipeline must be adequately anchored on stable ground at both ends;
- The suspended crossing must be level or nearly so (ie- at the same elevations on either end);
- The cable supporting the pipeline must be strong enough to support the weight of itself, the pipe, the water in the pipe, as well as the forces generated by wind and swaying;
- The pipe is securely fastened to the suspending cable, either by wire or clamps of some sort.

The suspended pipe may be either of GI or HDP, depending upon costs and availability of materials. An HDP pipe, however, will require a protective covering wrapped around it, as this pipe will deteriorate quickly under exposure to sunlight, and within a few years would be likely to break.

Several possible designs of successful suspended crossings are shown in Figure E-1.

Basic Calculations

The calculations outlined below lead to the determination of the tension in the suspension, which governs the size of the suspending cable, and the design of the anchors at each end.

Figure E-2 shows a typical suspended crossing, and lables the variables needed for the calculations:

W_c = weight per length of cable (kg/m)

W_p = weight per length of pipe (kg/m)

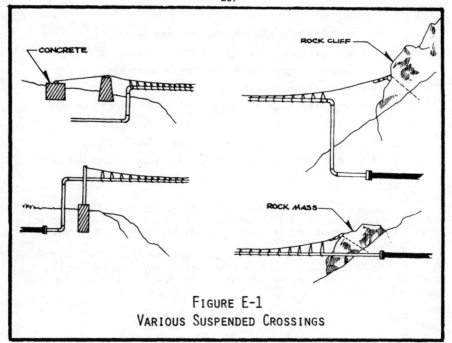

FIGURE E-1
VARIOUS SUSPENDED CROSSINGS

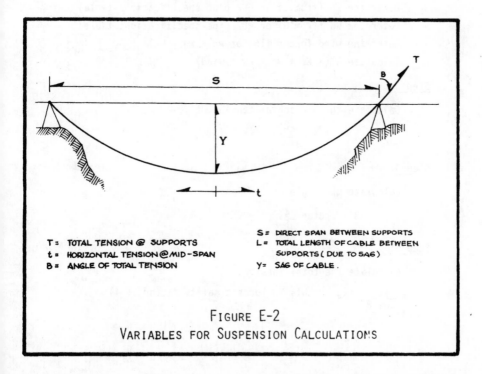

T = TOTAL TENSION @ SUPPORTS
t = HORIZONTAL TENSION @ MID-SPAN
B = ANGLE OF TOTAL TENSION

S = DIRECT SPAN BETWEEN SUPPORTS
L = TOTAL LENGTH OF CABLE BETWEEN SUPPORTS (DUE TO SAG)
Y = SAG OF CABLE.

FIGURE E-2
VARIABLES FOR SUSPENSION CALCULATIONS

Ww = weight per length of water in pipe (kg/m)

W = total weight per length of crossing (Wc + Wp + Ww)

S = length of span (between anchors) (meters)

Y = vertical sag of cable (meters)

L = total length of cable (including anchoring) (meters)

t = horizontal tension in cable at mid-span (kg)

T = total tension in cable at anchors (kg)

B = angle between the horizontal & tension vector (degrees)

Step 1:

Select the amount of vertical sag, Y, desired. The cable must not sag so much that it will be snagged by floating debris or landsliding rocks. A sag of 8%-10% of the span is good, if there is adequate clearance

Make an arbitrary selection of the cable (for trial calculation). Refer to the "USS Tiger Brand Wire Rope Engineering Handbook" or "Standard Handbook of Civil Engineering (Chapter 11)". 8mm Ø wire rope is a good selection to begin with.

Step 2:

Determine Wc (from wire rope handbook)

Determine Wp (from GI or HDP pipe specifications table)

Determine Ww (from GI or HDP pipe specifications table)

Determine wind forces (15% of Wc + Wp + Ww)

Calculate W (= Wc + Wp + Ww + wind)

Step 3:

Calculate the horizontal tension, t :

$$t = \frac{WS^2}{8Y} \quad (kg)$$

Step 4:

Calculate the angle of tension, B :

$$B = \arctan \frac{4Y}{S} \quad (degrees)$$

Step 5:

Calculate the total tension, T:

$$T = \frac{4t}{\cos B} \quad (kg; \quad this\ includes\ a\ safety\ factor\ of\ 4)$$

Step 6:

Compare the total tension, T, with the allowable tension of the selected cable. Select a larger or smaller cable size if necessary, and repeat the calculations.

Step 7:

Calculate the required length of cable, L:

$$L = S \times (1 + \frac{8Y^2}{3S^2}) + \text{extra for anchoring}$$

DESIGN OF ANCHORS

There are a number of different ways to secure the suspending cable at either end, as discussed below:

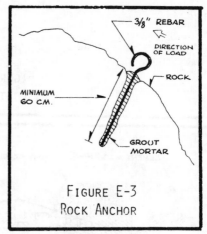

FIGURE E-3
ROCK ANCHOR

Rock Anchor: Using a rock drill or rock pick, a hole 60cm deep is drilled into a massive rock boulder or cliff. The hole is then filled with cement grout, and the 3/8" rebar anchor rod is driven in.

Maximum tension, T, is not more than 890 kg for 3/8" Ø rebar, or 1583 kg for ½" Ø rebar.

Refer to Figure E-3.

GI Post: A length of GI pipe securely imbedded in a ground block of concrete will make a sturdy securing point. If necessary, two such posts can be used. Refer to Figure E-4.

Maximum allowable horizontal tension, t, is:

1" GI pipe:	68 kgs
1½" GI pipe:	151 kgs
2" GI pipe:	270 kgs
3" GI pipe:	678 kgs

Masonry Block Anchors: Where it is not possible to dig a posthole deep enough for a GI post, then a cement masonry block anchor can be used. Such an anchor functions by its frictional resistance to sliding.

The anchor should be built into an excavated pit, as deeply as possible. Refer to Figures E-5 and E-6. The 3/8" rebar should be hooked around the ½" GI pipe, and both rebar and pipe placed as indicated.

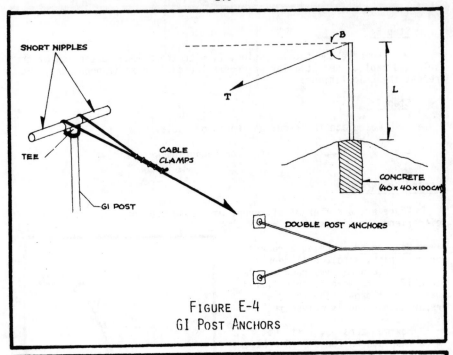

FIGURE E-4
GI POST ANCHORS

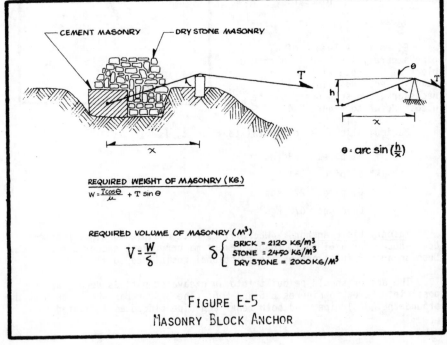

$$\theta = \arcsin\left(\frac{h}{x}\right)$$

REQUIRED WEIGHT OF MASONRY (KG.)

$$W = \frac{T\cos\theta}{\mu} + T\sin\theta$$

REQUIRED VOLUME OF MASONRY (M³)

$$V = \frac{W}{\delta} \qquad \delta \begin{cases} \text{BRICK} = 2120 \text{ KG/M}^3 \\ \text{STONE} = 2450 \text{ KG/M}^3 \\ \text{DRY STONE} = 2000 \text{ KG/M}^3 \end{cases}$$

FIGURE E-5
MASONRY BLOCK ANCHOR

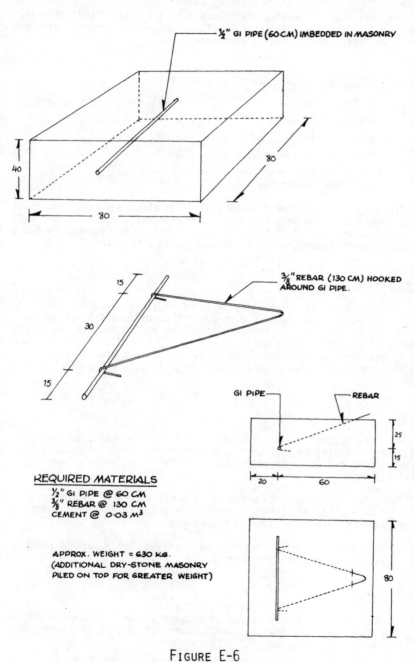

REQUIRED MATERIALS

½" GI PIPE @ 60 CM
⅜" REBAR @ 130 CM
CEMENT @ 0·03 M³

APPROX. WEIGHT = 630 KG.
(ADDITIONAL DRY-STONE MASONRY
PILED ON TOP FOR GREATER WEIGHT)

FIGURE E-6
MASONRY BLOCK ANCHOR (CON'T)

The total weight required is governed by the type of soil that the anchor is imbedded in, and the angle of the suspension cable. Different soils have different frictional characteristics:

Soil type	u
coarse-grain (w/o silt/clay)	0.55
coarse-grain (with silt/clay)	0.45
silt or clay	0.35
firm rock (roughened surface)	0.60

u = Greek letter "mu"

The weight of the cement masonry block is about 630 kgs. The total weight required can be calculated from the equation given in Figure E-5. The remaining weight (if the masonry block alone is not enough) is added using dry-stone masonry, which is approximately 2000 kg/m^3.

CLAMPING

The pipeline must be securely fastened to the suspending cable, and the fastenings must be secure enough not to be worked loose during the swaying motions of the pipeline. HDP pipe must especially be evenly supported (ie- fastenings regularly and closely spaced). Fastenings may be ordinary wire, or 3/8" rebar shaped by the village blacksmith, or special clamps manufactured in a metal shop. These are shown in Figure E-7.

SHEATHING

When the suspended pipe is to be of HDP, it must be covered with some outer sheathing to protect it against the ultra-violet radiation of sunlight (this radiation rapidly "ages" the HDP pipe, which causes brittleness).

Sheathing may be done by wrapping the HDP pipe with two or more layers of burlap (jute) sacking material, or using split bamboo slats secured by wire. This is shown in Figure E-8.

A suspended GI pipeline requires no sheathing, but a coat of paint will provide some weathering protection.

DESIGN EXAMPLE

A suspended crossing is needed to cross a stream, as shown in Figure E-9. The pipeline along that section is 50mm HDP, but it is desired to use GI pipe for the crossing (1½" size).

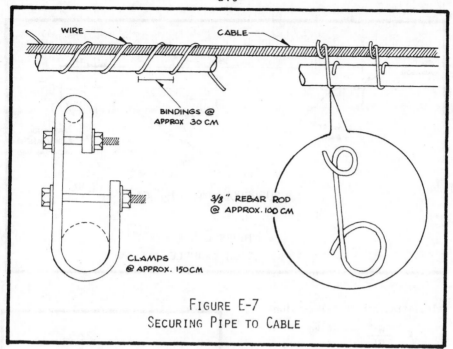

WIRE

CABLE

BINDINGS @
APPROX 30 CM

3/8" REBAR ROD
@ APPROX. 100 CM

CLAMPS
@ APPROX. 150CM

FIGURE E-7
SECURING PIPE TO CABLE

Known variables:

W_p = 3.65 kg/m

W_w = 1.26 kg/m

S = 25 meters

Y = 2.5 meters

From the "Handbook of Civil Engineering", a cable size is selected: <u>8mm Ø Round Strand 6 x77 group</u>, nominal breaking strength of 3500 kgs, and weight of 0.21 kg/meter:

W_c = 0.21 kg/m

wind force = 15% of
$W_p + W_w + W_c$ = 0.77 kg/m

Therefore, total loading:

$W = W_p + W_w + W_c + wind$ = 5.89 kg/m

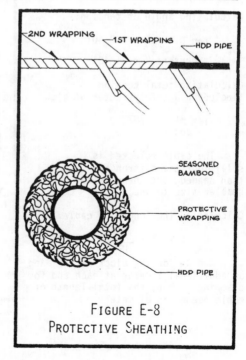

2ND WRAPPING   1ST WRAPPING   HDP PIPE

SEASONED
BAMBOO

PROTECTIVE
WRAPPING

HDP PIPE

FIGURE E-8
PROTECTIVE SHEATHING

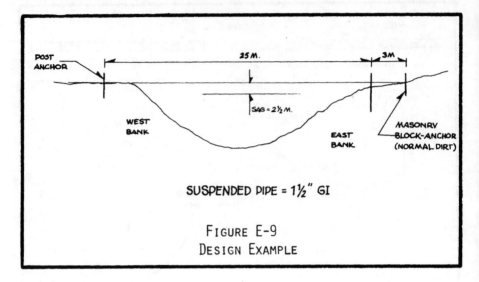

SUSPENDED PIPE = 1½" GI

FIGURE E-9
DESIGN EXAMPLE

Calculating horizontal tension:

$$t = \frac{WS^2}{8Y} = 184 \text{ kg}$$

Calculating angle of tension:

$$\tan B = \frac{4Y}{S} = 0.40;$$
therefore $B = 21°48'$

Calculating total tension
(including a safety factor of 4):

$$T = \frac{4t}{\cos B} = 792 \text{ kg}$$

The cable selected is still four times stronger than needed, but there is no smaller size to use.

Calculating the length of cable:

$$L = S \times (1 + \frac{8Y^2}{3S^2}) = 25.7 \text{ m}$$

Add 3m for the block anchor, and an additional 1 meter at each end for clamping. Thus, the total length of cable needed is 31 meters.

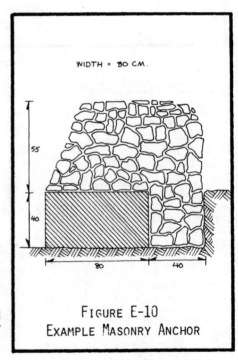

WIDTH = 80 CM.

FIGURE E-10
EXAMPLE MASONRY ANCHOR

Designing the masonry block anchor (east bank)

$$\sin \theta = \frac{0.5}{3.0} = 0.1667$$

therefore $\theta = 9°36' = 9.59°$

for normal dirt, $u = 0.45$

$$W = \frac{T \times \cos \theta}{u} + T \times \sin \theta$$

$$= 1735 + 132 = \underline{1867 \text{ kgs}}$$

weight of masonry block = 630 kgs, therefore 1237 kgs of dry-stone masonry is required additionally (this is about 0.618m^3).

Refer to Figure E-10.

Designing the post anchor (west bank)

It was previously calculated that the horizontal tension, t, was 184 kgs. From the information on page 209, it is seen that a single post of 2" GI pipe would be used (or two posts of 1½" GI).

TECHNICAL APPENDIX F

Roofing

In reference to roofing for tanks.

GENERAL NOTES

The roofing of a tank will depend upon its size, and whatever materials are available locally or from the regional office.

The basic structural requirements for a tank roof are strength and waterproofness. Since the tanks are relatively low structures, their roofs become accessible playgrounds for children. Additionally, the roof will become dirty with dust, leaves, bird-droppings, etc, which must not be washed into the tank by rain.

The roof must be pitched (sloped) so that rainwater runs off it quickly: no roof should be perfectly flat. The minimum pitch should be 5% (ie- 5cm vertical for each 100cm horizontal). A roof may be single-pitched, double pitched, or multi-pitched (as illustrated in Figure F-1). Although a multi-pitched roof may fit a hexagonal or octagonal tank better, it requires a great deal of extra roofing material, and the ridges are difficult to make waterproof. Double-pitched roofs also require extra roofing and masonry (for gables). A single-pitched roof, especially of CGS sheeting, is both fast and economical to construct.

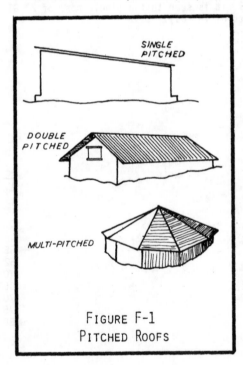

FIGURE F-1
PITCHED ROOFS

The roof should overhang outside the walls by at least 10 cm. An accessway should be built into the roof itself or into a gable (of a double-pitched roof). The accessway opening should be at least 60cm x 60cm, with a secure cover.

BEAMS AND COLUMNS

Beams span the tank and support the roof. A CGS roof requires the minimum amount of wood (and the simplest structure), and a slate roof requires the most.

Figure F-2 shows a beam across a tank. The <u>span</u> of the beam is the unsupported length(s). The <u>length</u> of the beam also includes overlap and overhang. The tank may be spanned by one continuous beam, or by two or three shorter beams supported by columns.

The table below gives the maximum allowable spans for wooden beams of the given dimensions. The most economical beams are those that span the tank without relying upon a column for additional support.

To prolong its lifetime all wood should be thoroughly painted or varnished. The beams should be anchored to the masonry walls in a secure manner (see Chapter 20.5).

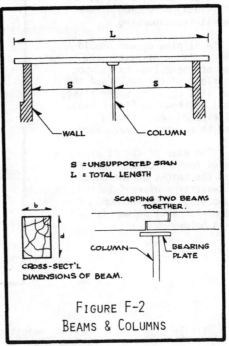

S = UNSUPPORTED SPAN
L = TOTAL LENGTH

CROSS-SECT'L
DIMENSIONS OF BEAM.

FIGURE F-2
BEAMS & COLUMNS

Maximum Span (cm)	b x d (cm x cm)	Cross-sect'l Area (m²)	Maximum Span (cm)	b x d (cm x cm)	Cross-sect'l Area (m²)
102	3 x 8	0.0024	307	4 x 12	0.0048
129	3 x 9	0.0027	323	5 x 11	0.0055
137	4 x 8	0.0032	360	4 x 13	0.0052
160	3 x 10	0.0030	384	5 x 12	0.0060
173	4 x 9	0.0036	450	5 x 13	0.0065
213	4 x 10	0.0040	523	5 x 14	0.0070
258	4 x 11	0.0044	600	5 x 15	0.0075
267	5 x 10	0.0050	683	5 x 16	0.0080

These calculated using maximum allowable extreme fiber stress of <u>sal</u> wood @ 168 kg/square centimeter, with a mid-span load of 210 kgs.

Beams may be supported by using a column of wood or GI pipe, although the latter is recommended. The dimensions of the wood column should be square, equal to the "b" (width) dimension of the beam it is supporting.

A GI pipe column should have a flange at either end. The base of the column rests upon the floor of the tank, and the beam sits upon the upper flange (this is shown in Figure F-3). All exposed metal should also be painted or varnished.

The size of the GI pipe needed for the column depends upon the height of the column, and what type of roof it is supporting. The maximum height for a GI column is given below:

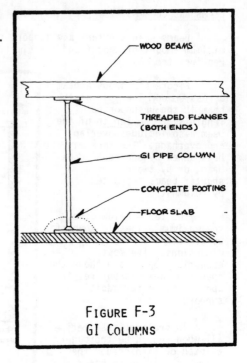

FIGURE F-3
GI COLUMNS

| GI Pipe size | Maximum height of column (cm) | |
	RCC slab	CGS sheets
1"	67	170
1½"	178	316
2"	278	480

These calculated for supporting roof weight plus 700 kg of human load plus safety factor of 2.0

SLATE ROOFING

This type of roofing depends upon the local availability of slate. It requires a lot of supporting woodwork (beams, rafters, purlins etc) which will increase the cost and construction time of the roof. If a slate roof is to be used, the main beams are sized according to the table above; the villagers can be relied upon to construct the remaining woodwork and proper installation of the slate.

Slate roofs are not recommended for break-pressure tank or valvebox covers, since it is not a secure roofing material. A CGS or RCC slab cover is better.

CGS ROOFING

Roofs of corrugated galvanized steel (CGS) sheets are the best and easiest to construct, requiring a minimum of supporting wood. The standard size available in Nepal is 3' x 10', and its effective size (with one corrugation overlap) is 300cm x 70cm, and weighs approximately 25 kgs.

CGS sheets can be easily cut by hammer and chisel, or using tin snips (which are not so easy). If a tank is to be roofed with CGS, it is best to adjust its dimensions so that there is a minimum of CGS cutting or wastage.

CGS roofs need only to be supported by beams which run across the corrugations. Maximum unsupported spans should be 150cm. CGS sheets are fastened to the beams with roofing nails or J-hooks and can be bolted to masonry walls (see Chapter 20.6).

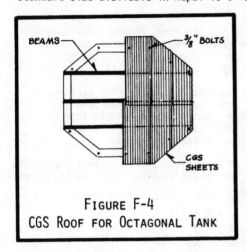

FIGURE F-4
CGS ROOF FOR OCTAGONAL TANK

Figure F-4 is of an octagonal tank, showing arrangement of beams, bolts, and CGS sheets.

CEMENT SLAB ROOFS

Roof slabs of either reinforced concrete (RCC) or reinforced (RF) brick have been discussed previously in Chapter 19.14.

Construction of these types of roofs requires a lot of wood for temporary forms, supporting the concrete while it is curing. Coating the inner surfaces of these forms with old motor oil will make it easier to remove them from the concrete.

THATCHED & MUD-ROOFS

Although commonly used to roof houses and barns in Nepal, these are not acceptable roofing methods for water tanks. They require frequent maintenance, and will quickly become dirty and harbor insects.

TECHNICAL APPENDIX G

Headlosses of a Tank Outlet

As explained earlier in Chapter 6.10, frictional losses caused by fittings such as elbows, reducers, unions, etc are considered negligible when the distance between individual fittings is at least 1000 pipe diameters.

Whereas this applies to most of the pipeline, special note must be made for the outlet piping of water tanks. For these, often several fittings are located closely together. Under these circumstances, the headloss generated by these cannot be considered negligible.

Flow through a fitting creates turbulence, which often persists for quite some distance downstream from the fitting. When several fittings are located closely together, their turbulences mix together and the combined effective headloss will be greater than the sum of each individual headloss had they been located far apart.

When calculating the headloss of an outlet, the equivalent pipelength of the fittings are used, given as the length/diameter (L/D) ratio. Typical L/D ratios for various fittings are:

Fitting	L/D ratio
Tee (flow from run-to-run)	27
Tee (flow from run-to-side)	68
Elbow (90° short radius)	33
Union	7*
Gate valve (fully open)	7
Free entrance (at intake)	29
Screened intake	150**

* assumed to be same as gate valve
** assumed to be 5x more than free intake

Example: The equivalent pipelength of a 1½" GI elbow is:

1½" x 33 = 50" = 126 cm

The amount of head available to push the flow through the outlet piping is exactly equal to the depth of water in the tank above the outlet level. Of this head, it will be assumed that not more than 20 cm is desired to be lost due to the frictional headloss of the outlet flow.

An example for applying these principles is illustrated, using the outlet of 1½" GI pipe shown in Figure G-1. The pipe section from the screened intake to the GI/HDP union will be analysed:

Total up the L/D ratios of the fittings:

screened intake = 150

gate valve = 7

tee (run-run) = 27

union = 7

TOTAL = 191

Therefore, the equivalent pipelength of these fittings is:

191 x 1½" = 287" = <u>728 cm</u>

The length of GI pipe and nipples is 130 cm, so the total pipelength of the piping is 858 cm. The maximum desired headloss is 20 cm, therefore the maximum desired frictional factor is:

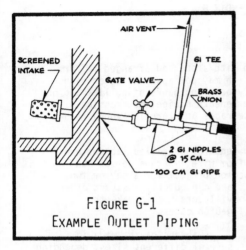

FIGURE G-1
EXAMPLE OUTLET PIPING

20/858 x 100% = 2.33%

Thus, the maximum outlet flow must not have a frictional headloss factor greater than 2.33% for 1½" GI pipe. The same technique is used to determine the maximum outlet flow for different pipe sizes. For the above pipe arrangement, these maximum flows are:

GI Pipe size	Maximum allowable frict'l factor	Maximum flow
½"	5.36%	<0.10 Lps
1"	3.25%	0.33 LPS
1½"	2.33%	0.80 LPS
2"	1.32%	1.30 LPS
3"	1.26%	3.30 LPS

From the above table it can be seen that 1/2" pipe is unsuitable as a tank outlet because of the low flow.

TECHNICAL APPENDIX H

Gabions

Gabions are wire-mesh cages filled with stone and arranged to form retaining walls for banks and cliffs which may collapse due to erosion. Their use in CWS projects will primarily be along banks of gullies and/or streams, directly supporting the ground beneath a pipeline crossing. Gabions can also be used to stabilize terraces and terrain around intake tanks, etc.

The actual construction of gabions requires a skilled laborer who already knows how to "weave" the cages from wire. Such a person can usually be borrowed from a road construction project for a day or two, and can quickly instruct other villagers how to make the gabion cages.

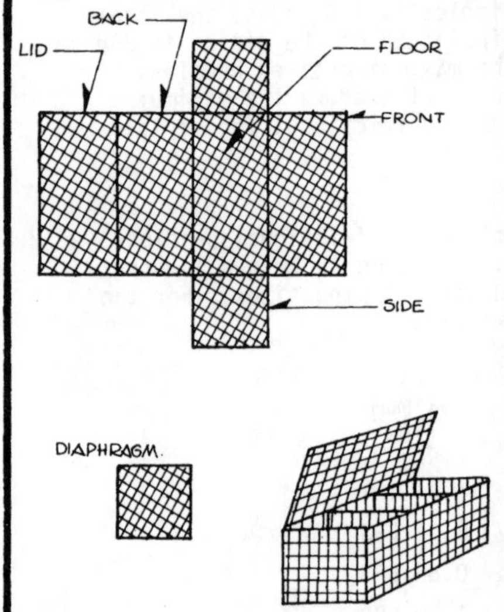

Gabions can be made in several different sizes, depending upon the needs of the embankment. A rectangle is woven and then folded up to form the four sides of the box. The two end pieces are woven separately and wired into position. They are carefully filled with stone (as dry-stone masonry) and their lids are wired shut.

Some large gabions are sub-divided into two or three compartments by partitions called "diaphragms". When the gabions are folded into shape, their edges are wired together (these edges are called selvedges). An embankment of gabions under construction is shown in Figure H-2.

Gabions are very expensive to construct, and should be used only in extremely unstable conditions where there is no alternative plan. The actual design of an embankment of gabions should be done in consultation with knowledgable engineers.

FIGURE H-1
UNFOLDED GABION

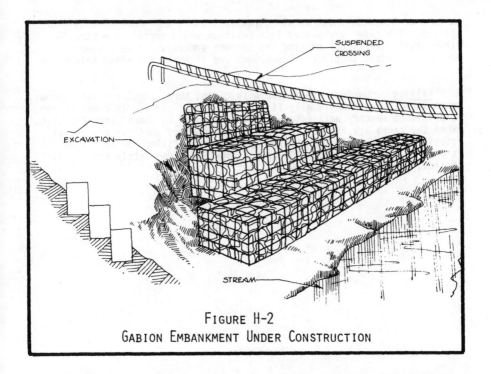

FIGURE H-2
GABION EMBANKMENT UNDER CONSTRUCTION

Materials & Estimates: Gabions to be used in CWS projects are of the same design and materials as those used for trail suspended bridges:

Mesh size: 80 x 100 mm

Mesh wire: 9 SWG   (Ø 3.66 mm)

Selvedge wire: 6 SWG   (Ø 4.88 mm)   All wire of

Binding wire: 11 SWG   (Ø 2.95 mm)   Galvanized iron

Details	Dimensions of gabions (meters)			
	2 x 1 x 1	3 x 1 x 1	2 x 1 x ½	3 x 1 x ½
Volume (m³):	2	3	1	1½
Mesh wire (kgs):	36.00	52.35	24.55	36.00
Selvedge wire (kgs):	3.75	4.85	3.00	3.90
Labor (man-days):	5.53	7.38	4.18	5.43
No. of diaphragms:	1	2	1	2
Dimensions of " :	1 x 1	1 x 1	1 x ½	1 x ½

Assembly: Gabions are assembled by binding them together along the selvedges with 6 SWG binding wire. The cages should be "laced" together

with a continuous length of wire, rather than "tied" together with short
pieces. The cages are placed into position while empty, stretched to
their full dimensions (pegging the corners securely to the ground will
help), and wired together. Diaphragms are inserted and wired into place.

Filling: Gabions are filled with clean, hard, angular rubble stones,
each stone being individually fitted into place, similar to constructing
a dry-stone masonry wall (stones should not just be dumped into the cages).
When the cages are filled, the lids are then wired shut for additional
stability. The gabions should be carefully backfilled for additional
stability. On completion, the gabions should be completely and tightly
filled, square, and true to dimensions.

AMERICAN & METRIC UNITS

Metric Units

Length: 10 millimeters = 1 centimeter
100 centimeters = 1 meter
1000 meters = 1 kilometer

Volume: $1000 cm^3$ = 1 liter = $0.001 m^3$
1000 liters = $1 m^3$

Water: $1 cm^3$ = 1 gram
$1000 cm^3$ = 1 liter = 1 kg
1000 liters = 1000 kg = $1 m^3$

Weight: 1000 grams = 1 kilogram
1000 kgs = 1 metric tonne

mm = millimeters
cm = centimeters
m = meters
km = kilometers
g = gram
kg = kilogram

American Units

Length: 12 inches = 1 foot
3 feet = 1 yard
5280 feet = 1 mile

Volume: 4 quarts = 1 gallon = $231 in^3$ = $0.13 ft^3$
$1 ft^3$ = $1728 in^3$

Water: $1 in^3$ = 0.036 pounds
$1 ft^3$ = 62.4 lbs.
1 gallon = $231 in^3$ = 8.34 lbs

Weight: 16 ounces = 1 pound
2000 lbs = 1 ton

yd = yards
ft = feet (')
in = inches (")
qt = quarts
lb = pounds
oz = ounces
gal = gallons

Conversion Factors

American —— metric

1" = 2.54 cm
1' = 30.48 cm
1 yd = 91.44 cm
1 mile = 1609 m = 1.6 km

1 oz = 28.4 gm
1 lb = 450 gm = 0.45 kg

1 qt = 0.91 liters
1 gal = 3.63 liters

$1 in^3$ = $16.39 cm^3$

$1 ft^3$ = 28.3 liters

Metric —— American

1 cm = 0.39"

1 m = 39" = 3.28'
1 km = 3280' = 0.62 miles

1 gm = 0.035 oz
1 kg = 35 oz = 2.2 lbs

1 liter = 1.1 qt = $0.035 ft^3$
$1 m^3$ = $35.31 ft^3$

Note: In 'English' units, as opposed to 'American' 1 gallon = $277 in^3$ = 10lbs; 2240lb = 1 ton; 1qt = 1.136 litres; and 1 gallon = 4.54 litres.

Reference Table II

INSTALLATION OF UNIONS, FLANGES, & VALVES

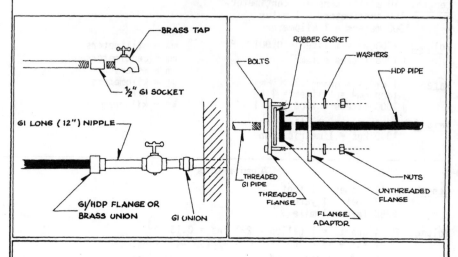

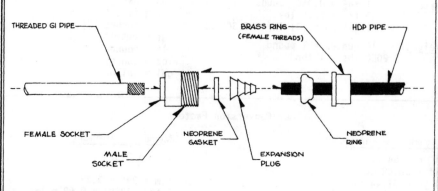

Installing a brass union:

1) Screw the male-half of the union onto the ½" GI pipe;

2) Slip the female brass ring and the neoprene ring onto the 20mm HDP pipe;

3) Over a flame, carefully heat the mouth of the HDP pipe until it is soft. Then hammer in the expansion plug until it is flush with the end of the HDP pipe;

4) Place the neoprene gasket inside the male-half of the union, then put the HDP pipe (expanded end) into it. Slip the brass ring up to the male-half and screw tightly.

Reference Table III

RECOMMENDED TOOL LIST

Item	Size	Remarks	Quantity
Bolts	3/8" x 5"		*
Brush, paint	3"		2
Brush, wire		For GI pipework	1
Bucket, steel	12"	for cement-mixing	½/mason
Crowbar	5'	for excavation	4
File, flat	10"	for GI pipework	2
Hacksaw, frame	12"	for GI & HDP pipework	2
Hacksaw, blades	12"		12
Hammer, claw-headed		for wood-working	1
Hammer, sledge	1-lb	for masons	1/mason
Hammer, sledge	2-lb	for making aggregate	4
Hammer, sledge	10-lb	for breaking rock	4
Heating plate		for HDP pipejoining	1-2
Kerosene		for HDP pipejoining	10 liters
Level, carpenters	24"		1
Nails	1"	for slate/CGS roofing	
Nails	3"	for wood-working	
Oil can	250-ml	for GI pipework	1
Oil		for GI pipe work	1 liter
Paint		for wood & GI pipe	1 liter
Pick & handle		for excavation	4
Pipe threader	½"-1"	for ½" & 1" GI pipe	1
Pipe threader	¼"-2"	for ¼"-2" GI pipe	1
Pipe threader die		according to GI size	2
Pliers, adjustable	10"		1
Rebar (reinforcing)rod	3/8" (8mm)		*
Screening, wire	3mm square	for intakes	1 m^2
Screws, brass	½"	for air-releases	24
Screwdriver	8"		1
Shovel, flat-edged		for cement-mixing	½/mason
Shovel, round-edged		for excavation	4
Stove, kerosene pressure**		for HDP pipejoining	1
String, kite	300m	for caulking GI threads	1 ball
Tape measure, steel	2-m	retractable-type	1
Tape measure, plastic	5'	tailor type	2
Tin cutters		for CGS sheets	1
Trowels, masons		for cement-work	2/mason
Thermochrom crayons		for HDP pipejoining	1 box
Vise, pipe	2"	for up to 2" GI pipe	1
Wrench, pipe	14"	for up to 1" GI pipe	
Wrench, pipe	18"	for up to 2" GI pipe	2 per project
Wrench, pipe	24"	for up to 3" GI pipe	

 * according to design + 10% extra
** more convenient than blowtorches

Reference Table IV

HDP PIPE SPECIFICATIONS

These are the specifications of the HDP pipe as ordered by UNICEF/Nepal. However, due to variations in production methods by the various companies which manufacture the pipe, there are slight differences in dimensions and surface finishes. The HDP frictional headloss table is for HDP pipe of these approximate dimensions.

PIPE SIZE (outer diameter) (mm)	CLASS	WALL THICKNESS (mm) Max	WALL THICKNESS (mm) Min	AVERAGE CROSS-SECT'L AREA (cm²)	VOLUME PER METER (liters)	WEIGHT PER METER (kgs)	LENGTH PER COIL
20mm	IV	2.8	2.3	1.74	0.17	0.13	300
32mm	III	2.8	2.3	5.68	0.57	0.22	200
32mm	IV	4.3	3.6	4.56	0.46	0.33	100
50mm	III	4.2	3.6	13.99	1.40	0.47	100
50mm	IV	6.4	5.6	11.34	1.13	0.80	50
63mm	III	5.2	4.5	22.31	2.23	0.74	50
63mm	IV	8.1	7.1	17.95	1.80	1.26	50
90mm	III	7.3	6.4	54.30	5.43	2.32	25
90mm	IV	-	10.1	38.26	3.82		25

Pressure ratings: Class III = 6 kg/cm² (60m of head)
Class IV =10 kg/cm² (100m of head)

Reference Table V

GI PIPE SPECIFICATIONS

The following specifications are taken from the Indian Standards Institute (ISI) specifications for mild steel tubes (ISI Bulletin IS: 1239 (Part I) 1973) for medium duty pipe. The GI pipe purchased in Nepal is manufactured in India, but there is no guarantee that it is to these ISI standards.

PIPE SIZE (nominal bore)	OUTER DIAMETER (mm) Max	OUTER DIAMETER (mm) Min	WALL THICKNESS (mm)	CROSS-SECT'L AREA (cm²)	VOLUME PER METER (liters)	WEIGHT PER METER (kgs)
½" 15mm	21.8	21.0	2.65	1.77	0.17	1.23
1" 25mm	34.2	33.3	3.25	4.91	0.49	2.46
1½" 40mm	48.8	47.0	3.25	12.57	1.26	3.65
2" 50mm	60.8	59.7	3.65	19.63	1.96	5.17
3" 80mm	89.5	88.0	4.05	50.27	5.03	8.64
4" 100mm	115.0	113.1	4.50	36.59	8.66	12.40

GI pipe typically is provided in 6-meter lengths, with threaded and socketed ends.

Reference Table VI

RESIDUAL HEADS

Tapstands:

Absolute minimum:	7m
Desired minimum:	10m
Ideal:	15m
Desired maximum:	30m
Absolute maximum:	56m

Discharges into tanks:

Absolute minimum:	7m
Ideal:	10m
Absolute maximum:	56m

HGL:

Do not allow the HGL to fall within 10m of the ground profile unless unavoidable; and NEVER allow the HGL to pass underground.

Reference Table VII

GI/HDP SIZES

GI size	HDP size	GI to HDP Fitting
½"	20mm	Brass union
1"	32mm	" "
1½"	50mm	" " or Flange set
2"	63mm	" " " " "
3"	90mm	" " " " "

The GI pipe size refers to the inner diameter (ID) and the HDP pipe size refers to the outer diameter (OD)

MATERIALS & LABOR ESTIMATE TABLE

EXCAVATIONS

Per 1-m^3

a)	Ordinary soil	0.55 man-days
b)	Gravelly soil	0.77 man-days
c)	Boulder mix	1.10 man-days
d)	Medium rock cutting	1.60 man-days
e)	Hard rock cutting	2.50 man-days

WOOD-WORKING

Per 1-m^3 of finished wood

a)	Skilled labor	18 man-days
b)	Unskilled labor	18 man-days

STONE AGGREGATE PRODUCTION

Per 1-m^3 of crushed rock

a)	Unskilled labor	14 man-days

CONCRETE

	Per 1-m^3 of:	1:2:4 mix	1:1 :3 mix
a)	Cement	0.25 m^3	0.33 m^3
b)	Sand	0.50 m^3	0.50 m^3
c)	Aggregate	1.00 m^3	1.00 m^3
d)	Mason labor	1.1 man-days	1.1 man-days
e)	Unskilled labor	4.0 man-days	4.0 man-days

PLASTER*

	Per 1-m^2 of:	Spatterdash (1:4)	1:3 mix	1:2 mix
a)	Cement	0.0025 m^3	0.0030 m^3	0.0050 m^3
b)	Sand	0.01 m^3	0.01 m^3	0.01 m^3
c)	Mason labor	0.14 man-days	0.14 man-days	0.14 man-days
d)	Unskilled labor	0.22 man-days	0.22 man-days	0.22 man-days

*   Each coat of plaster 1 cm thick

BRICK MASONRY @ 1:4 mortar

Per 1-m^3

a)	Bricks	75%
b)	Cement	0.063 m^3
c)	Sand	0.25 m^3
d)	Mason labor	1.4 man-days
e)	Unskilled labor	2.8 man-days

RUBBLE-STONE MASONRY @ 1:4 mortar

Per 1-m^3

a)	Cement	0.089 m^3
b)	Sand	0.35 m^3
c)	Mason labor	1.4 man-days
d)	Unskilled labor	3.2 man-days

DRESSED-STONE MASONRY   @ 1:4 mortar   Per 1-m^3

   a) Cement   0.075 m^3
   b) Sand   0.30 m^3
   c) Mason labor   2.8 man-days
   d) Unskilled labor   5.0 man-days

CGS ROOFING

    Nominal size: 3' x 10'
    Effective size: 70cm x 100cm (with overlap of 1 corrugation)
    Weight: 25 kgs

CEMENT

    Per bag: 50 kgs
    burlap (jute) bag: 32 liters (0.032 m^3)
    paper bag: 34 liters (0.034 m^3)

SPECIFIC WEIGHTS

    Portland cement: 1440 kg/m^3
    brick masonry: 2120 kg/m^3
    stone masonry: 2450 kg/m^3
    concrete: 2409 kg/m^3
    seasoned wood: 650 kg/m^3
    water: 1000 kg/m^3
    dry-stone masonry: 2000 kg/m^3

Reference Table VIII

TRIGONOMETRIC TABLE

Angle	Sine	Cosine	Tangent	Cotan	
0°	0	1	0	1	90°
0°30'	.0087	.99996	.0087	114.6	89°30'
1°	.0175	.99985	.0175	57.29	89°
1°30'	.0262	.99966	.0262	38.19	88°30'
2°	.0349	.99939	.0349	28.64	88°
2°30'	.0436	99905	.0437	22.90	87°30'
3°	.0523	.99863	.0524	19.08	87°
3°30'	.0610	.99813	.0612	16.35	86°30'
4°	.0698	.99756	.0699	14.30	86°
4°30'	.0785	.99692	.0787	12.71	85°30'
5°	.0872	.99619	.0875	11.43	85°
5°30'	.958	.99540	.0963	10.39	84°30'
6°	.1045	.99452	.1051	9.514	84°
6°30'	.1132	.99357	.1139	8.777	83°30'
7°	.1219	.99255	.1228	8.114	83°
7°30'	.1305	.99144	.1317	7.596	82°30'
8°	.1392	.99027	.1405	7.115	82°
8°30'	.1478	.98902	.1495	6.691	81°30'
9°	.1564	.98769	.1584	6.314	81°
9°30'	.1650	.98629	.1673	5.976	80°30'
10°	.1736	.98481	.1763	5.671	80°
10°30'	.1822	.98325	.1853	5.396	79°30'
11°	.1908	.98163	.1944	5.145	79°
11°30	.1994	.97992	.2035	4.915	78°30'
12°	.2079	.97815	.2126	4.705	78°
12°30'	.2164	.97630	.2217	4.511	77°30'
13°	.2250	.97437	.2309	4.331	77°
13°30"	.2334	.97237	.2401	4.165	76°30'
14°	.2419	.97030	.2493	4.011	76°
14°30'	.2504	.96815	.2586	3.867	75°30'
15°	.2588	.96593	.2679	3.732	75°
15°30'	.2672	.96363	.2773	3.606	74°30'
16°	.2756	.96126	.2867	3.487	74°
16°30'	.2840	.95882	.2962	3.376	73°30'
17°	.2924	.95630	.3057	3.271	73°
17°30'	.3007	.95372	.3153	3.172	72°30'
18°	.3090	.95106	.3249	3.078	72°
18°30'	.3173	.94832	.3346	2.989	71°30'
19°	.3256	.94552	.3443	2.904	71°
19°30'	.3338	.94264	.3541	2.824	70°30'
20°	.2420	.93969	.3640	2.747	70°
20°30'	.3502	.93667	.3739	2.675	69°30'
21°	.3584	.93358	.3839	2.605	69°
21°30'	.3665	.93042	.3939	2.539	68°30'
22°	.3746	.92718	.4040	2.475	68°
22°30'	.3827	.92388	.4142	2.414	67°30'
	Cosine	Sine	Cotan	Tangent	Angle

Angle	Sine	Cosine	Tangent	Cotan	
23°	.3907	.92050	.4245	2.356	67°
23°30'	.3987	.91706	.4348	2.300	66°30'
24°	.4067	.91355	.4452	2.246	66°
24°30'	.4147	.90996	.4557	2.194	65°30'
25°	.4226	.90631	.4663	2.145	65°
25°30'	.4305	.90259	.4770	2.097	64°30'
26°	.4384	.89879	.4877	2.050	64°
26°30'	.4462	.89493	.4986	2.006	63°30'
27°	.4540	.89101	.5095	1.963	63°
27°30'	.4617	.88701	.5206	1.921	62°30'
28°	.4695	.88295	.5317	1.881	62°
28°30'	.4772	.87882	.5430	1.842	61°30'
29°	.4848	.87462	.5543	1.804	61°
29°30'	.4942	.87063	.5658	1.767	60°30'
30°	.5000	.86603	.5774	1.732	60°
30°30'	.5075	.86163	.5890	1.698	59°30'
31°	.5150	.85717	.6009	1.664	59°
31°30'	.5225	.85264	.6128	1.632	58°30'
32°	.5299	.84805	.6249	1.600	58°
32°30'	.5373	.84339	.6371	1.570	57°30'
33°	.5446	.83867	.6494	1.540	57°
33°30'	.5519	.83389	.6619	1.511	56°30'
34°	.5592	.82904	.6745	1.483	56°
34°30'	.5664	.82413	.6873	1.455	55°30'
35°	.5736	.81915	.7002	1.428	55°
35°30'	.5807	.81412	.7133	1.402	54°30'
36°	.5878	.80902	.7265	1.376	54°
36°30'	.5948	.80386	.7400	1.351	53°30'
37°	.6018	.79864	.7536	1.327	53°
37°30'	.6088	.79335	.7673	1.303	52°30'
38°	.6157	.78801	.7813	1.280	52°
38°30'	.6225	.78261	.7954	1.257	51°30'
39°	.6293	.77715	.8098	1.235	51°
39°30'	.6361	.77162	.8243	1.213	50°30'
40°	.6428	.76604	.8391	1.192	50°
40°30'	.6494	.76041	.8541	1.171	49°30'
41°	.6561	.75471	.8693	1.150	49°
41°30'	.6626	.74896	.8847	1.130	48°30'
42°	.6691	.74314	.9004	1.111	48°
42°30'	.6756	.73728	.9163	1.091	47°30'
43°	.6820	.73135	.9325	1.072	47°
43°30'	.6884	.72537	.9490	1.054	46°30'
44°	.6947	.71934	.9657	1.036	46°
44°30'	.7009	.71325	.9827	1.018	45°30'
	.7071	.70711	1.	1.000	45°
	Cosine	Sine	Cotan	Tangent	Angle

Reference Table IX

VERTICAL DISTANCE SURVEY TABLE

The table below directly presents the vertical elevation difference between two stations, where the ground distance and vertical angle between the stations is known.

The distance may be either in feet or meters, and direct interpolation between two distances is allowable.

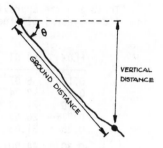

VERTICAL ANGLE θ

GROUND DISTANCE	1°	2°	3°	4°	5°	6°	7°	8°	9°	10°	11°	12°	13°
2	0	0	0	0	0	0	0	½	½	½	½	½	½
4	0	0	0	½	½	½	½	½	½	½	1	1	1
6	0	0	½	½	½	½	½	1	1	1	1	1	1½
8	0	½	½	½	½	1	1	1	1½	1½	1½	1½	2
10	0	½	½	½	1	1	1	1½	1½	1½	2	2	2
12	0	½	½	1	1	1	1½	1½	2	2	2½	2½	2½
14	0	½	½	1	1	1½	1½	2	2	2½	2½	3	3
16	½	½	1	1	1	1½	2	2	2½	3	3	3½	3½
18	½	½	1	1	1½	2	2	2½	3	3	3½	3½	4
20	½	½	1	1½	1½	2	2½	3	3	3½	4	4	4½
22	½	1	1	1½	2	2½	2½	3	3½	4	4	4½	5
24	½	1	1	1½	2	2½	3	3½	3½	4	4½	5	5½
26	½	1	1½	2	2½	2½	3	3½	4	4½	5	5½	6
28	½	1	1½	2	2½	3	3½	4	4½	5	5½	6	6½
30	½	1	1½	2	2½	3	3½	4	4½	5	5½	6	6½

GROUND DISTANCE	14°	15°	16°	17°	18°	19°	20°	21°	22°	23°	24°	25°
2	½	½	½	½	½	½	½	½	½	1	1	1
4	1	1	1	1	1	1½	1½	1½	1½	1½	1½	1½
6	1½	1½	1½	1½	2	2	2	2	2	2½	2½	2½
8	2	2	2	2½	2½	2½	2½	3	3	3	3½	3½
10	2½	2½	2½	3	3	3½	3½	3½	3½	4	4	4
12	3	3	3½	3½	3½	4	4	4½	4½	4½	5	5
14	3½	3½	4	4	4½	4½	5	5	5	5½	5½	6
16	4	4	4½	4½	5	5	5½	5½	6	6½	6½	7
18	4½	4½	5	5½	5½	6	6	6½	6½	7	7½	7½
20	5	5	5½	6	6	6½	7	7	7½	8	8	8½
22	5½	5½	6	6½	7	7	7½	8	8	8½	9	9½
24	6	6	6½	7	7½	8	8	8½	9	9½	10	10
26	6½	6½	7	7½	8	8½	9	9½	9½	10	10½	11
28	7	7	7½	8	8½	9	9½	10	10½	11	11½	12
30	7½	7½	8½	9	9½	10	10½	10½	11	11½	12	12½

GI FRICTIONAL HEADLOSS FACTORS

These are the approximate headloss factors, in m/100m (%), for aged (10-15 years) GI pipe. Flows are in liters/second.

FLOW	½" GI	1" GI	1½" GI	2" GI	3" GI
0.10	5.87	0.38			
0.15	12.24	0.82			
0.20	21.43	1.33	0.20		
0.225	26.53	1.68	0.22		
0.25	31.63	2.04	0.24		
0.30	44.90	2.96	0.40		
0.35	58.16	3.82	0.52		
0.40	74.49	4.79	0.66	0.22	
0.45	91.84	6.02	0.83	0.27	
0.50		7.14	1.02	0.33	
0.55		8.67	1.19	0.39	
0.60		10.20	1.43	0.46	
0.65		11.73	1.63	0.53	
0.675		12.76	1.68	0.55	
0.70		13.27	1.73	0.58	
0.75		15.31	2.14	0.67	
0.80		17.35	2.35	0.77	
0.85		18.88	2.65	0.87	
0.90		21.43	2.86	0.92	
0.95		23.47	3.27	1.02	
1.00		25.51	3.57	1.12	
1.05		29.39	3.83	1.22	
1.10		30.61	4.18	1.33	
1.15		34.69	4.59	1.48	
1.20		35.71	4.92	1.58	
1.30		40.82	5.71	1.84	0.22
1.40		47.96	6.63	2.14	0.26
1.50		54.08	7.55	2.45	0.28
1.60		61.22	8.47	2.65	0.32
1.70		67.35	9.49	3.06	0.35
1.80		76.53	10.51	3.47	0.41
1.90			11.73	3.78	0.43
2.00			12.76	4.08	0.49
2.20			15.31	4.90	0.57
2.40			17.86	5.71	0.66
2.60			20.41	6.63	0.81
2.80			24.49	7.65	0.92
3.00			26.53	8.67	1.02
3.20			29.59	9.69	1.12
3.40			33.67	10.92	1.32

FLOW	½"GI	1" GI	1½" GI	2" GI	3" GI
3.60			37.76	12.24	1.43
3.80			40.82	13.27	1.58
4.00			45.92	14.79	1.73
4.50			56.12	17.86	2.09
5.00				21.43	2.55
5.50				26.53	3.06
6.00				30.61	3.67
6.50				35.71	4.18
7.00				40.82	4.85

HDP FRICTIONAL HEADLOSS FACTORS

These are the approximate headloss factors, in m/100m (%) of HDP pipe manufactured according to UNICEF specifications. Due to the variations in size and quality by different manufacturers, no exact headloss factors will ever be possible.

Headloss factors less than 0.20% are considered negligible. Factors are provided for up to the maximum recommended flow velocity of 3.0 m/sec; factors for flow velocities of less than 0.7 m/sec are flagged by an asterisk (*). Flows are for liters/second.

CLASS III (6 Kg./cm²)

FLOW	32mm	50mm	63mm	90mm
0.10	0.22*			
0.12	0.30*			
0.14	0.38*			
0.16	0.48*			
0.18	0.58*			
0.20	0.72*			
0.225	0.87*			
0.25	1.08*			
0.275	1.27*			
0.30	1.42*			
0.35	1.88*	0.22*		
0.40	2.44	0.28*		
0.45	2.87	0.34*		
0.50	3.70	0.40*		
0.55	4.1	0.47*		
0.60	4.9	0.56*		
0.65	5.6	0.63*		
0.675	5.9	0.67*		
0.70	6.3	0.72*	0.25*	
0.75	7.3	0.81*	0.28*	
0.80	8.2	0.90*	0.31*	
0.90	10.0	1.11*	0.37*	
1.00	11.9	1.34*	0.45*	
1.10	14.1	1.57	0.54*	
1.20	16.5	1.90	0.63*	
1.30	19.0	2.18	0.73*	
1.40	21.6	2.46	0.82*	
1.60	27.4	3.05	1.03*	
1.80	33.6	3.81	1.30	0.24*
2.00		4.6	1.55	0.28*
2.20		5.5	2.46	0.32*
2.50		6.7	2.24	0.40*
2.70		8.3	2.74	0.49*
3.00		9.5	3.08	0.56*
3.20		11.2	3.77	0.67*

FLOW	50mm	63mm	90mm
3.50	12.6	4.1	0.74
3.70	14.4	4.8	0.84
4.00	15.7	5.4	0.96
4.20	18.1	6.0	1.04
4.50	20.1	6.6	1.06
4.70		7.4	1.31
5.00		7.8	1.41
5.50		9.4	1.70
6.00		11.1	2.00
6.50		12.3	2.24
7.00		14.6	2.97

20mm HDP is only available in Class IV series

CLASS IV (10 Kg./cm²)

FLOW	20mm	32mm	50mm	63mm	90mm
0.10	3.1*	0.31*			
0.12	4.5*	0.40*			
0.14	5.6*	0.52*			
0.16	7.3	0.67*			
0.18	9.0	0.81*			
0.20	10.6	0.99*			
0.225	13.4	1.22*			
0.25	15.7	1.43*			
0.275	18.5	1.74*			
0.30	21.8	2.02*	0.25*		
0.35	28.0	2.71*	0.31*		
0.40	36.2	3.36	0.40*		
0.45	45	4.0	0.49*		
0.50	54	4.9	0.59*		
0.55	63	5.7	0.71*		
0.60	73	6.7	0.81*	0.27*	
0.65		7.8	0.94*	0.31*	
0.675		8.4	1.00*	0.34*	
0.70		8.8	1.06*	0.36*	
0.75		10.1	1.23*	0.40*	
0.80		11.2	1.34*	0.45*	
0.90		13.4	1.67*	0.54	
1.00		16.4	2.00*	0.66*	
1.10		19.8	2.37	0.78*	
1.20		22.6	2.77	0.92*	
1.30		26.4	3.19	1.08*	
1.40		30.2	3.61	1.23*	0.22*
1.60		37.5	4.5	1.52	0.28*
1.80			5.6	1.85	0.35*
2.00			6.7	2.24	0.41*
2.20			8.3	2.69	0.49*
2.50			10.1	3.25	0.60*
2.70			12.2	3.92	0.73*
3.00			13.9	4.6	0.84
3.20			17.4	5.5	0.99
3.50			18.9	6.2	1.11
3.70			21.3	6.9	1.29
4.00			23.7	7.7	1.43
4.20				8.7	1.57
4.50				9.5	1.78
4.70				10.8	1.97
5.00				11.8	2.13
5.50				13.4	2.46
6.00				15.9	2.91
6.50					3.36
7.00					3.89

TABLE XII

Flow Nomograph For Plastic & GI Pipe

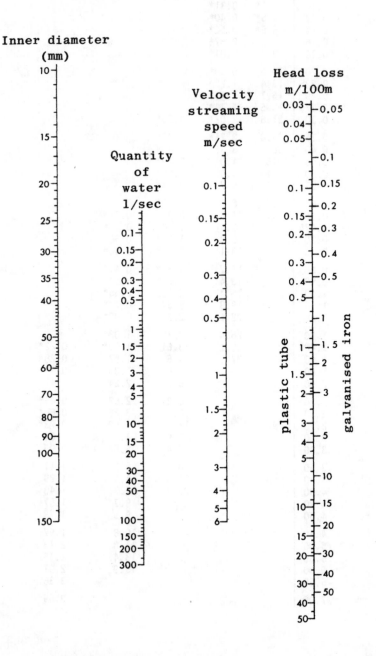